Building a Dream

*A Canadian Guide to Starting
Your Own Business*

*A Canadian Guide to Starting
Your Own Business*

Third Edition

WALTER S. GOOD

McGraw-Hill Ryerson

Toronto Montreal New York Auckland Bogotá
Caracas Lisbon London Madrid Mexico Milan
New Delhi Paris San Juan Singapore Sydney Tokyo

McGraw-Hill
Ryerson Limited

A Subsidiary of The McGraw·Hill Companies

Building a Dream
A Canadian Guide to Starting Your Own Business
Walter S. Good
Third Edition

ISBN: 0-07-552899-1

1 2 3 4 5 6 7 8 9 10   TRI   6 5 4 3 2 1 0 9 8 7

Printed and bound in Canada

Publisher: Joan Homewood
Editor: Erin Moore
Production Editor: Rachel Mansfield
Production Co-ordinator: Nicla Dattolico
Cover Design: Dianna Little
Cover Photo Setup: Jan Scharlach
Page Composition and Design: Lynda Powell
Typefaces: New Caledonia and Helvetica
Printer: Trigraphic

Canadian Cataloguing in Publication Data

Good, Walter S.
    Building a dream: a Canadian guide to starting
your own business

3rd ed.
ISBN 0-07-552899-1

1. New business enterprises.   2. Entrepreneurship.
I. Title.

HD62.5.G66 1997   658.1′1   C96-932446-4

CONTENTS

Preface

Acknowledgements

PREFACE

This self-help guide and workbook is intended to lead prospective small-business people and potential entrepreneurs in a logical and sequential way through the conceptual stages involved in setting up a business of their own.

Many people fantasize about being self-employed and having a business of their own at some stage in their lives. For most, this dream never becomes a reality. They don't really know the risks involved and feel very uncomfortable with the uncertainty associated with taking the initial step. In addition, they don't really understand the tasks required to get a new business venture off the ground successfully.

For about a decade the number of people who have started their own business has increased dramatically across North America. People's level of interest in and awareness of the entrepreneurial option has virtually exploded. This has been fostered and reinforced by governments at all levels, who have come to recognize the positive impact small-business start-ups have on job creation and regional economic development. Business magazines, the popular press, and radio and television have also fuelled this interest with numerous items on the emotional and financial rewards of having a business of your own. They have glamorized the role of entrepreneurs in our society, and established many of them, such as Paul Demerais, Frank Stronach, Steven Jobs, and Victor Kiam, as attractive role models.

Building a Dream has been written for individuals who wish to start a business of their own or want to assess their own potential for such an option. This includes all men and women who dream of some type of self-employment, on either a full-time or a part-time basis. The book contains descriptive information, practical outlines, checklists, screening devices, and various other aids that will enable you to evaluate your own potential for this type of career and guide you through the early stages of launching a successful business of your own.

This book covers a range of topics that will increase your understanding of what it takes to succeed in an entrepreneurial career. From a description of the personality and character traits of the entrepreneur, the text spreads outward to consider how to find and evaluate a possible idea for a business, buy an existing firm, acquire a franchise, carry on your business, and protect your product. It concludes with a detailed framework for conducting a feasibility study and developing a comprehensive and professional business plan.

The book is divided into "Stages," each of which provides a descriptive overview of the topic, some conceptual material indicating the principal areas to be considered or evaluated, and a series of outlines, worksheets, checklists, and other blank forms that can be completed in conducting a comprehensive assessment of that stage in the new venture development process. This provides a practical opportunity for you to realistically assess the potential of your idea and develop a detailed program or plan for your own small business.

STAGE ONE: Assessing Your Potential for an Entrepreneurial Career

This Stage introduces you to the concept of entrepreneurship and gives you some idea of what is required to be successful as an entrepreneur. It provides you with an opportunity to assess your personal attitudes and attributes and to see how they compare with those of "practising" entrepreneurs. It will also enable you to evaluate your managerial and administrative skills and determine your financial capacity for starting a business.

STAGE TWO: Exploring New Business Ideas and Opportunities

This Stage describes a number of sources from which you might obtain ideas for your prospective new venture and identifies a number of areas of opportunity for the future on the basis of dynamic changes now taking place within Canadian society. It also describes the characteristics of the "ideal" or "model" business and presents a framework for assessing the attributes of your product or service ideas in comparison to this ideal. As well, a number of entry strategies are outlined that can help you decide on the best way of proceeding.

STAGE THREE: Starting a New Business or Buying an Existing One

The obvious route to self-employment is to start a business of your own based on a new or distinctive idea. Another route to explore is the possibility of buying an existing firm. This Stage deals with such areas as finding a business to buy and the factors to consider in making the acquisition. It also discusses a number of ways to determine an appropriate price to pay for a business and the pros and cons of buying versus starting one. A comprehensive checklist is provided for considering a number of potential business acquisitions.

STAGE FOUR: Considering a Franchise

For the past several years franchising has been one of the fastest-growing sectors of North American business. More and more people are considering the franchise alternative as a means of getting into business for themselves. This Stage explores the concept of franchising in some detail. It defines franchising so that you know exactly what the concept means. The entire range of available franchises is presented, along with an overview of the legal requirements associated with franchising and the terms of a typical contractual agreement. This Stage also discusses how to find and apply for a franchise, and presents an extensive checklist for evaluating various franchise opportunities.

STAGE FIVE: Organizing Your Business

One of the principal issues to be resolved when starting a new business is the legal form of organization the business should adopt. The most prevalent forms a business might take include individual or sole proprietorship, general or limited partnership, and incorporation. This Stage reviews each of these types and discusses the advantages and disadvantages of each from the standpoint of the prospective entrepreneur. It discusses how to select a name for your business and make sure you are properly registered or incorporated. It also presents an overview of such issues as the types of licences and permits your business might require, your responsibilities for collecting and remitting a variety of employee contributions and taxes, and the impact of employment standards on your business.

STAGE SIX: Protecting Your Idea

Many entrepreneurs are also innovators and inventors, and are faced with the problem of how to protect the idea, invention, concept, system, name, or design that they feel may be the key to their business success. This Stage discusses the various forms of intellectual property such as patents, copyrights, and trademarks, and what is required to protect your interest in their development.

STAGES SEVEN AND EIGHT: Conducting a Feasibility Study — Parts 1 and 2

Stages Seven and Eight provide a step-by-step process for transforming your chosen new venture concept from the idea stage to the marketplace. This is accomplished by means of a feasibility study. A typical feasibility study considers the following areas:

* The concept of your proposed venture
* The technical feasibility of your idea
* An assessment of its market potential
* The supply situation
* Cost/profit analysis
* Your plans for future action

Comprehensive outlines are provided to enable you to assess each of these areas in a preliminary way and put your thoughts and ideas down on paper. Much of this material can be incorporated into your subsequent business plan.

STAGE NINE: Arranging Financing

The principal question relating to any new venture is where the money is going to come from to get the new business off the ground. This Stage examines the major sources of funds for new business start-ups — personal funds, love money, banks, government agencies and programs, venture capital, etc. It also provides a framework for assessing your own ability to secure financing from these sources.

STAGE TEN: Preparing Your Business Plan

This Stage, which serves as a capstone for the book, provides a framework for the development of a comprehensive business plan for your proposed new business venture, whether it is a retail or service firm or a manufacturing company. It explains what a business plan is, and why it is important that you develop such a plan for your proposed venture and actually write it yourself. A sample outline business plan is provided for both a retail or service business and a manufacturing firm. These will serve as comprehensive outlines for you to follow in developing your business plan.

Following the framework outlined in this book will give you hands-on, practical experience with the entire new venture development process and enable you to come up with a comprehensive plan for a proposed venture of your own selection. This plan will not only give you a better understanding of the potential opportunity and success requirements of your new venture idea but also put you in a much stronger position to attract the necessary external resources and support to get your proposed business off the ground. Good luck in successfully building your dream.

ACKNOWLEDGEMENTS

Developing a workbook of this type can only be accomplished with the cooperation and support of a great many people. Much of the material would not have been developed without the dedicated effort of Steve Tax of the University of Victoria, who was largely responsible for many of the ideas that were incorporated into the first edition and have been carried forward to the current one. I am also indebted to David Milstein of David Milstein & Associates of Brisbane, Australia for contributing the material on the "Big Picture" of strategic planning. My appreciation also goes to Carole Babiak whose organizational and word processing skills enabled me to keep the material moving during the revision process.

Thoughtful comments on the revisions were received from Dwight Thomas of Athabasca University, Michael Piczak of McMaster University and Mohawk College, Jonas Sammons of the University of Manitoba, Charlene Hill of Capilano College, Brian Giffen of BCIT, Tom Gallagher of Seneca College, John E. McColl of Humber College. Their remarks were very helpful in organizing and polishing the material and refining the concept for the book. My appreciation must also go to Joan Langevin, Daphne Scriabin, and Margaret Henderson, my editors at McGraw-Hill Ryerson, for expediting the review and production of the material and providing numerous useful comments and suggestions throughout the revision process.

I would also like to thank Moe Levy of the Winnipeg Fur Exchange, and Shannon Coughlan of Industry Canada for their comments on several components of the book and their encouragement during the early stages of the development of the concept behind the workbook. Special thanks go to Chris Spafford for his assistance in putting together the financial templates that accompany the supplement to the college edition of this book. The belief of these individuals in entrepreneurship as a vehicle for successful economic development in Canada and faith in the premise of the self-help concept may finally pay off.

Finally, I would like to thank the college and university students and others who have used the earlier editions of the book over the years and have gone on to start new business ventures of their own. Their insatiable desire to assess their personal capacity for a career in this area and their drive to explore the mysteries of franchising, venture capital, and similar topics associated with the formation of a successful new business has enabled many of them to build their dream. I hope all of us have been able to play a small part in the process.

STAGE
ONE

ASSESSING YOUR POTENTIAL FOR AN ENTREPRENEURIAL CAREER

This book has been developed for aspiring entrepreneurs. Most people give some thought to owning and managing their own business at some point in their lives. And provided you know what it takes to be successful, it can be a very rewarding way of life.

Starting a new business is risky at the best of times, but your chances of succeeding will be better if you spend some time carefully evaluating your personal situation and circumstances and trying to anticipate and work out as many potential problems as you can in advance, before you invest any money.

Stage One will introduce you to the concept of entrepreneurship and give you some idea of what is required. It will provide you with an opportunity to assess your personal attitudes and attributes and see how they compare with "practising" entrepreneurs. It will also enable you to evaluate your managerial and administrative skills and determine your financial capacity. All are key ingredients in determining your readiness for an entrepreneurial career.

WHAT IS ENTREPRENEURSHIP?

Entrepreneurship is difficult to define precisely. Entrepreneurs tend to be identified, not by formal rank or title, but in retrospect — after the successful implementation of an innovation or an idea. The example of Denise Meehan of Lick's Ice Cream & Burger Shops in Exhibit 1.1 may help to illustrate the definition problem for you.

It is difficult to state the precise moment at which Meehan became an entrepreneur. She was raised in an entrepreneurial household as her family owned and operated a resort hotel. Although she had no formal training in business or restaurants, she was comfortable with both, having been raised in a "hotel and hospitality family." What she learned from being raised in that environment was how to approach people, relate to them personally, and a certain comfort with working with the public. Her experiences travelling around North America gave her the confidence to jump into the restaurant business on her own, feeling that she had an excellent opportunity to succeed. Once having established Lick's as a going concern she began thinking about franchising and saw the opportunity to develop her business, first provincially, and then nationally, as she was able to identify potential franchisees who could meet her high personal

1

standards and expectations. Lick's is now embarked on an ambitious expansion program to open four or five new restaurants a year.

Many people have said that entrepreneurship is really a "state of mind." Though you may be extremely innovative and creative, prepared to work hard, and willing to rely on a great deal of luck, these qualities may still be insufficient to guarantee business success. The missing element may be a necessary entrepreneurial mind-set: a single-mindedness and dedication to the achievement of a set of personal goals and objectives; confidence in your intuitive and rational capabilities; a capacity to think and plan in both tactical and strategic terms; and an attitude which reflects a penchant for action, frequently in situations in which information is inadequate.

Entrepreneurship is not the same as management. The principal job of professional managers is to make a business perform well. They take a *given* set of resources — such as employees, money, machines, and materials — and orchestrate and organize them into an efficient production operation. In contrast, the principal job of the entrepreneur is to bring about purposeful change within an organizational context.

EXHIBIT 1.1

Lick's Burger & Ice Cream Shops was founded in 1979 in east-end Toronto. Lick's is known for its fresh food and friendly vibes; a refreshing alternative to more standard hamburger outlets. The young staff is trained to use customers first names and sing out their orders to the beat of 1960s rock-and-roll songs. This is a formula which seems to work as sales of the Lick's chain of company-owned and franchised stores have increased to more than $14 million.

Lick's founder, Denise Meehan, grew up in Sturgeon Falls, Ontario where her parents owned a hotel. A Grade 11 dropout, she travelled across the United States and Canada, sold flowers on the streets of Vancouver, and survived by picking up bartending and waitress jobs. Denise always enjoyed being with the public and after working in so many restaurants thought to herself, "Hey. I can do that."

Upon returning to Toronto in 1979, she did. With $2,000 of her own money and $2,000 from the bank, Ms. Meehan opened a tiny burger outlet on Queen Street East in the Beaches area of Toronto, known for its dense summer crowds.

The first Lick's, now ten times its original size, is still going strong and has been joined by 10 other Ontario locations and one in Florida. Meehan plans to open four or five new restaurants a year, spreading the chain across Canada. But Lick's is in no great hurry to expand. Ms. Meehan has strong ideas about who should run her restaurants. Growth will come only when she feels certain that each new restaurant can be supported and operated properly. Applicants for a

Lick's franchise must not only pass the usual health and financial hurdles but be willing to devote themselves to the franchise full-time and undergo an extensive personal interview that includes formal psychological and other testing.

She says, "I'm looking for owner-operators who are prepared to invest time and energy using motivational skills with employees. Business for me is two-fold — not only making money but feeling good, encouraging growth in the people I've met."

This mix of entrepreneurial enthusiasm and the human potential movement is typical of Ms. Meehan, who spent several years in therapy. The CBC-TV program, Venture, in profiling Lick's several years ago called it "the burger stand where Ayn Rand, Dale Carnegie, and Sigmund Freud converge."

In growing her business Ms. Meehan knew her success depended on attracting people who were prepared to work hard and share her values. "You have to have a burning desire to get ahead, whether you are a man or a woman in any business," Meehan says. "Approach situations with confidence. I think that's what's most important —to have the confidence to move forward."

Adapted from Ellen Roseman, "Trials and Triumphs in a Far-Out Franchise," *The Globe and Mail*, February 7, 1994, p. B6; Sonita Horvitch, "Cone and Burger Chain is Set to Grill Potential Franchisees," *The Financial Post*, April 26, 1991, p. 10; and Tim Talevich, "Striking a Balance," *The PriceCostco Connection Online*.

As agents of change entrepreneurs play, or can play, a number of roles in the economy. They can, for example:

1. Create new product and/or service businesses
2. Encourage better and/or lower-cost production operations
3. Provide employment opportunities and create new jobs
4. Help contribute to regional and national economic growth
5. Encourage greater industrial efficiency/productivity to enhance our international competitiveness

You should keep in mind, however, that other people also play a significant role in determining who will succeed or who will fail in our society. For example, entrepreneurs will succeed only when there are customers for the goods and services they provide. But, in many circumstances, it is the entrepreneurs themselves who play the principal role in determining their success or failure. Many still manage to succeed in spite of poor timing, inferior marketing, or low-quality production by combining a variety of talents, skills, and energies with imagination, good planning, and common sense. The entrepreneurial or self-employed option has many attractions, but along with these come risks and challenges and the chance of failure.

MYTHS AND REALITIES CONCERNING ENTREPRENEURSHIP

According to noted author-lecturer-consultant Peter Drucker, entrepreneurs defy stereotyping. He states, "I have seen people of the most diverse personalities and temperaments perform well in entrepreneurial challenges."[1] This suggests that some entrepreneurs may be true eccentrics while others are rigid conformists; some are short and fat while others are tall and thin; some are real worriers while others are very laid-back and relaxed; some drink and smoke very heavily while others abstain completely; some are people of great wit and charm while others have no more personality than a frozen fish.

By permission of Johnny Hart and Creators Syndicate, Inc.

---

[1] Peter Drucker, *Innovation and Entrepreneurship: Practice and Principles* (New York: Harper and Row, 1985), p. 25.

Despite all that is known about entrepreneurs and entrepreneurship, a good deal of folklore and many stereotypes remain. Part of the problem is that while some generalities may apply to certain types of entrepreneurs and certain situations, most entrepreneurial types tend to defy generalization. The following are examples of long-standing myths about entrepreneurs and entrepreneurship.[2]

- **Myth 1   Entrepreneurs are born, not made.**
- **Reality**   There is increasing evidence that while entrepreneurs are born, they can be made better by a combination of work experience, study, and development of business skills. There is an undeniable core of inborn attributes, which you either have or you don't, but it is apparent that merely possessing them does not necessarily make you an entrepreneur. Other attributes of equal importance can, in fact, be acquired through understanding, hard work, and patience.

- **Myth 2   Anyone can start a business. It's a matter of luck and guts. All you need is a new idea; then go for it.**
- **Reality**   If you want to launch and grow a high-potential new venture you must understand the many things that you have to do to get the odds in your favour. You cannot think and act like a bureaucrat, or even a manager; you must think and act like an entrepreneur.

- **Myth 3   Entrepreneurs are gamblers.**
- **Reality**   Entrepreneurs are not gamblers and they do not take high risks in the usual sense. Successful entrepreneurs take very calculated risks and they get others to share the risk with them, thereby lowering their personal exposure. When they find that they can avoid or minimize risk, they do so.

- **Myth 4   You are better off as an independent, lone entrepreneur, owning the whole show yourself.**
- **Reality**   It is extremely difficult to develop a new venture beyond $1 million in profitable sales by working single-handedly. Higher-potential ventures that succeed usually have multiple founders.

   In choosing a partner it is generally wise for an entrepreneur to avoid persons with personalities similar to his or her own.

- **Myth 5   Being an entrepreneur is the only way you can really be your own boss and completely independent.**
- **Reality**   Higher-potential entrepreneurs are far from independent and have many masters and constituencies to serve and juggle. These can include partners, investors, customers, suppliers, creditors, employees, their spouse, family, and social and community organizations.

- **Myth 6   Entrepreneurs face greater stress and more pressures, and thus pay a higher personal price in their job than do other managers.**
- **Reality**   Being an entrepreneur is undoubtedly stressful and demanding. But there is no evidence it is any more stressful than numerous other highly demanding professional roles, such as being the principal partner in a legal or accounting practice or the head of a large corporation or government agency. Most entrepreneurs enjoy what they do. For them it is fun rather than drudgery, and they thrive on the flexibility and innovative aspects of their jobs.

---

[2]   Adapted from Jeffry A. Timmons, *New Venture Creation: A Guide to Entrepreneurship*, 3rd ed. (Homewood, IL: Richard D. Irwin, 1990), pp. 19–22.

- **Myth 7 Starting your own company is a risky, hazardous proposition that often ends in failure.**
- **Reality** This statement is undoubtedly true in many instances. Statistics indicate that upwards of 80 percent of new businesses fail within their first five years. However, success tends to be more common than failure for the higher-potential ventures, because they tend to be directed by talented and experienced people able to attract the right personnel and the necessary financial and other resources.

    Vince Lombardi, the well-known ex-coach of the Green Bay Packers, is famous for saying, "Winning isn't everything — it's the *only* thing." But a lesser-known quote of his is closer to the true entrepreneur's personal philosophy. Looking back on a season, Lombardi was once heard to remark, "We didn't lose any games last season, we just ran out of time twice."

    Entrepreneuring is a competitive game and an entrepreneur has to be prepared to run out of time occasionally. Walt Disney, Henry Ford, Milton Hershey, and many other well-known entrepreneurs all experienced bankruptcy before achieving success.

- **Myth 8 Money is what makes the difference. If you have enough of it you will succeed.**
- **Reality** Money appears to be by far the least important ingredient in new venture success. If the other pieces and talents are there, the money will follow.

- **Myth 9 Start-ups are for the young and energetic.**
- **Reality** While youth and energy may help, age is no absolute barrier to starting a business of your own. However, many people feel there is some threshold for an individual's perceived capacity for starting a new venture. Over time you gain experience, competence, and self-confidence; these factors increase your capacity and readiness to embark on an entrepreneurial career. At the same time, constraints such as increases in your financial and other obligations grow and negatively affect your free choice. The tradeoffs between individual readiness and these restraints typically result in most new businesses being started by entrepreneurs between the ages of 25 and 40.

- **Myth 10 Entrepreneurs generally have low levels of formal education.**
- **Reality** Contrary to popular belief, most entrepreneurs are not starting their business while their friends are still finishing high school or attending college. The facts are that the most common level of education for entrepreneurs is a bachelor's degree.

- **Myth 11 Entrepreneurs are motivated solely by their quest for the almighty dollar; they want to make money so that they can spend it.**
- **Reality** Growth-minded entrepreneurs are more driven by the challenge of the enterprise and realizing long-term capital gains than by instant gratification through high salaries and perks. Having a sense of personal accomplishment and achievement, feeling in control of their own destiny, and realizing their visions and dreams are also powerful motivators. Money is viewed principally as a tool and as a way of "keeping score."

- **Myth 12 Entrepreneurs seek power and control over others so that they can feel "in charge."**
- **Reality** While many entrepreneurs are driven in this way, most successful, growth-minded entrepreneurs are driven in just the opposite way. They are driven by a quest for responsibility, achievement, and results rather than by the quest for power. They thrive on a sense of accomplishment, achieved by outperforming the competition rather than a personal need for power expressed by dominating and controlling others. They gain control by the results they accomplish.

CHARACTERISTICS OF SUCCESSFUL ENTREPRENEURS

The previous discussion should have served to dispel many of the popular myths concerning entrepreneurship. This section will expand upon the theme of entrepreneurial characteristics by proposing and discussing two important questions which are vital to you if you are interested in an entrepreneurial career:

1. Are there certain common attributes, attitudes, and experiences among entrepreneurs which appear to lead to success?

2. If such attributes, attitudes, and experiences exist, can they be learned or are they inborn and thus available only to those with a "fortunate" heritage?

Research into these questions suggests that the answer to question 1 is yes while the answer to question 2 is both yes and no. These answers, of course, are of little value to you on their own without some further explanation.

Entrepreneurs Are Born and Made Better

In 1980, Tom Wolfe wrote a perceptive bestseller that examined the lives of America's leading test pilots and astronauts. According to Wolfe, becoming a member of this select club meant possessing "The Right Stuff" — i.e., the proper mix of courage, coolness under stressful conditions, a strong need for achievement, technical expertise, creativity, etc. While Wolfe was not talking about entrepreneurs, his viewpoint is similar to the basic thesis held by many members of the "people school" of entrepreneurship: a position which states that a person has to have the "right stuff" to become a successful entrepreneur.

There is considerable evidence, however, that a great deal of the ability and "right stuff" needed to become a successful entrepreneur can be learned (though probably not by everyone).

Entrepreneurial Quiz

While most writers in the field of entrepreneurship agree that there is no single profile, no specific set of characteristics, that defines a successful entrepreneur, there do appear to be some common attributes, abilities, and attitudes. Prior to our discussion of these entrepreneurial characteristics, it is suggested that you take the Entrepreneurial Quiz that appears as Figure 1.1. This will enable you to compare your personal attitudes and attributes with those of "practising" entrepreneurs.

What Attributes are Desirable and Acquirable?

In a study of the 21 inductees into the Babson University Academy of Distinguished Entrepreneurs, including such notables as An Wang (Wang Computers), Ken Olson (DEC), Wally Amos (Famous Amos' Chocolate Chip Cookies), Bill Norris (Control Data), and Soichiro Honda (Honda Motors), only three attributes and behaviours were mentioned by all 21 as the principal reasons for their success, and they were all learnable:

1. Responding positively to all challenges and learning from mistakes

2. Taking personal initiative

3. Having great perseverance[3]

---

[3] Timmons, p. 165.

FIGURE 1.1 ENTREPRENEURIAL QUIZ

Below are a number of questions dealing with your personal background, behavioural characteristics, and lifestyle patterns. Psychologists, venture capitalists, and others believe these to be related to entrepreneurial success. Answer each question by placing an X in the space that best reflects your personal views and attitudes. The most important result of this exercise will be an honest, accurate self-assessment of how you relate to each of these dimensions.

	Rarely or no	Mostly or yes
1. Are you prepared to make sacrifices in your family life and take a cut in pay to succeed in business?	_____	_____
2. Are you the kind of individual that once you decide to do something you'll do it and nothing can stop you?	_____	_____
3. When you begin a task, do you set clear goals and objectives for yourself?	_____	_____
4. When faced with a stalemated situation in a group setting, are you usually the one who breaks the logjam and gets the ball rolling again?	_____	_____
5. Do you commonly seek the advice of people who are older and more experienced than you are?	_____	_____
6. Even though people tell you "It can't be done" do you still have to find out for yourself?	_____	_____
7. When you do a good job, are you satisfied in knowing personally that the job has been well done?	_____	_____
8. Do you often feel, "That's just the way things are and there's nothing I can do about it"?	_____	_____
9. Do you need to know that something has been done successfully before, prior to trying it yourself?	_____	_____
10. Do you intentionally try to avoid situations where you have to converse with strangers?	_____	_____
11. Do you need a clear explanation of a task before proceeding with it?	_____	_____
12. Are you a good loser?	_____	_____
13. After a severe setback in a project, are you able to pick up the pieces and start over again?	_____	_____
14. Do you like the feeling of being in charge of other people?	_____	_____
15. Do you enjoy working on projects which you know will take 5 to 10 years to complete successfully?	_____	_____
16. Do you consider ethics and honesty to be important ingredients for a successful career in business?	_____	_____
17. Have you previously been involved in starting things like service clubs, community organizations, fund-raising projects, etc.?	_____	_____

continued

Entrepreneurial Quiz — continued

		Rarely or no	Mostly or yes
18.	Did your parents or grandparents ever own their own business?	_____	_____
19.	When you think of your future do you ever envision yourself running your own business?	_____	_____
20.	Do you try to do a job better than is expected of you?	_____	_____
21.	Do you make suggestions about how things might be improved on your job?	_____	_____
22.	Are you usually able to come up with more than one way to solve a problem?	_____	_____
23.	Are you between 25 and 40 years of age?	_____	_____
24.	Do you worry about what others think of you?	_____	_____
25.	Do you read books?	_____	_____
26.	Do you take risks for the thrill of it?	_____	_____
27.	Do you find it easy to get others to do something for you?	_____	_____
28.	Has someone in your family shared his or her experience in starting a business with you?	_____	_____
29.	Do you believe in organizing your tasks before getting started?	_____	_____
30.	Do you get sick often?	_____	_____
31.	Do you enjoy doing something just to prove you can?	_____	_____
32.	Have you ever been fired from a job?	_____	_____
33.	Do you find yourself constantly thinking up new ideas?	_____	_____
34.	Do you prefer to let a friend decide on your social activities?	_____	_____
35.	Did you like school?	_____	_____
36.	Were you a very good student?	_____	_____
37.	Did you run with a group in high school?	_____	_____
38.	Did you participate in school activities or sports?	_____	_____
39.	Do you like to take care of details?	_____	_____
40.	Do you believe there should be security in a job?	_____	_____
41.	Will you deliberately seek a direct confrontation to get needed results?	_____	_____
42.	Were you the firstborn child?	_____	_____
43.	Was your father generally present during your early life at home?	_____	_____
44.	Were you expected to do odd jobs at home before 10 years of age?	_____	_____
45.	Do you get bored easily?	_____	_____
46.	Are you sometimes boastful about your accomplishments?	_____	_____

Entrepreneurial Quiz — continued

	Rarely or no	Mostly or yes
47. Can you concentrate on one subject for extended periods of time?	_____	_____
48. Do you, on occasion, need pep talks from others to keep you going?	_____	_____
49. Do you find unexpected energy resources as you tackle things you like?	_____	_____
50. Does personal satisfaction mean more to you than having money to spend on yourself?	_____	_____
51. Do you enjoy socializing regularly?	_____	_____
52. Have you ever deliberately exceeded your authority at work?	_____	_____
53. Do you try to find the benefits in a bad situation?	_____	_____
54. Do you blame others when something goes wrong?	_____	_____
55. Do you enjoy tackling a task without knowing all the potential problems?	_____	_____
56. Do you persist when others tell you it can't be done?	_____	_____
57. Do you take rejection personally?	_____	_____
58. Do you believe you generally have a lot of good luck that explains your successes?	_____	_____
59. Are you likely to work long hours to accomplish a goal?	_____	_____
60. Do you enjoy being able to make your own decisions on the job?	_____	_____
61. Do you wake up happy most of the time?	_____	_____
62. Can you accept failure without admitting defeat?	_____	_____
63. Do you have a savings account and other personal investments?	_____	_____
64. Do you believe that entrepreneurs take a huge risk?	_____	_____
65. Do you feel that successful entrepreneurs must have advanced college degrees?	_____	_____
66. Do you strive to use past mistakes as a learning process?	_____	_____
67. Are you more people-oriented than goal-oriented?	_____	_____
68. Do you find that answers to problems come to you out of nowhere?	_____	_____
69. Do you enjoy finding an answer to a frustrating problem?	_____	_____
70. Do you prefer to be a loner when making a final decision?	_____	_____
71. Do your conversations discuss people more than events or ideas?	_____	_____
72. Do you feel good about yourself in spite of criticism by others?	_____	_____
73. Do you sleep as little as possible?	_____	_____
74. Did you ever have your own paper route?	_____	_____

Adapted from July Balogh et al., *Beyond a Dream: An Instructor's Guide for Small Business Explorations* (Columbus: Ohio State University, 1985), pp. 26–28.

Other research has uncovered different lists of common learnable attributes. These qualities are very desirable, also, in the people with whom entrepreneurs want to surround themselves in building a high-potential business.

Following is a summary of the attitudes and behaviours that can be valuable in turning a business dream into reality. The proposed characteristics represent the conclusions of over 50 separate research studies into the essential nature of the entrepreneur.

COMMITMENT, DETERMINATION, AND PERSEVERANCE

More than any other single factor, a combination of perseverance and total dedication is critical. In many cases these qualities have won out against odds considered impossible to overcome.

Determination and commitment can compensate for other weaknesses you may have. It requires substantial commitment to give up a well-paying job, with its regular paycheques, medical insurance, and pension and profit-sharing plans, and start out on your own.

SUCCESS ORIENTATION

Entrepreneurs are driven by an immense desire to achieve the goals they initially set for themselves and then to aim for even more challenging standards. The competitive needs of growth-minded entrepreneurs are to outperform their own previous best results rather than to just outperform another person. Unlike most people, entrepreneurs do not allow themselves to be concerned with failure. What they think about is not what they are going to do if they don't make it, but what they have to do in order to succeed.

OPPORTUNITY AND GOAL ORIENTATION

Growth-minded entrepreneurs are more focussed on the nature and extent of their opportunity rather than resources, structure, or strategy. They start with the opportunity and let their understanding of it guide these other important issues. Entrepreneurs are able to sense areas of unmet needs and their potential for filling these gaps. Effective entrepreneurs set goals consistent with their interests, values, and talents. These goals are generally challenging but still attainable. Their belief in the "reality" of their goals is a primary factor in their fulfilment of them. Having goals and a clear sense of direction also helps these persons to define priorities and provides them with a measure of how well they are performing.

ACTION ORIENTATION AND PERSONAL RESPONSIBILITY

Successful entrepreneurs are action-oriented people; they want to start producing results immediately. They like to take the initiative and get on with doing it, today. The true entrepreneur is a doer, not a dreamer.

PERSISTENT PROBLEM-SOLVING, NEED TO ACHIEVE

Entrepreneurs are not intimidated by the number or severity of the problems they encounter. In fact, their self-confidence and general optimism seem to translate into a view that the impossible just takes a little longer. They will work with a stubborn tenacity to solve a difficult problem. This is based on their desire to achieve the goals they have established for themselves. However, they are neither aimless nor foolhardy in their relentless attack on a problem or obstacle that can impede their business, but tend to get right to the heart of the issue.

REALITY ORIENTATION

The best entrepreneurs have a keen sense of their own strengths and weaknesses and of the competitive environment in which they operate. In addition, they know when they are in trouble and have the strength to admit when they are wrong. This reality orientation allows them to avoid continuing on an ill-advised course of action.

SEEKING AND USING FEEDBACK

Entrepreneurs have a burning desire to know how they are performing. They understand that to keep score and improve their performance they must get feedback, digest the results, and use the information they receive to do a better job. In that way they can learn from their mistakes and setbacks and respond quickly to unexpected events. For the same reason, most entrepreneurs are found to be good listeners and quick learners.

SELF-RELIANCE

Successful entrepreneurs trust the fate of their ventures to their own abilities. They do not believe that external forces or plain luck determine their success or failure. This attribute is consistent with their achievement and motivational drive and desire to achieve established goals.

In a similar vein, entrepreneurs are not joiners. Studies have shown that the need for affiliation, or a high need for friendship, often acts as a deterrent to entrepreneurial behaviour.

SELF-CONFIDENCE

The self-confidence displayed by entrepreneurs is based on their feeling that they can overcome all the necessary challenges and attain their desired goal. They almost never consider failure a real possibility. While this self-confidence implies a strong ego, it is a different kind of ego — an "I know I'm going to do well" type of attitude.

TOLERANCE OF AMBIGUITY AND UNCERTAINTY

Entrepreneurs tolerate ambiguous situations well and make effective decisions under conditions of uncertainty. They are able to work well despite constant changes in their business that produce considerable ambiguity in every part of their operation.

Entrepreneurs take change and challenge in stride and actually seem to thrive on the fluidity and excitement of such undefined situations. Job security and retirement are generally not of great concern to them.

MODERATE RISK-TAKING AND RISK-SHARING

Despite the myth that suggests entrepreneurs are gamblers, quite the opposite is true. Effective entrepreneurs have been found, in general, to prefer taking moderate, calculated risks, where the chances of losing are neither so small as to be a sure thing nor so large as to be a considerable gamble. Like a parachutist, they are willing to take some measurable and predetermined risk.

The strategy of most entrepreneurs also includes involving other parties in their venture to share the burden of risk: partners put money and reputations on the line; investors do likewise; and creditors and customers who advance payments and suppliers who advance credit all share in the financial risk of the business.

RESPONSE TO FAILURE

Another important attribute of high-performance entrepreneurs is their ability to treat mistakes and failures as temporary setbacks on the way to accomplishing their goals. Unlike most people, the bruises of their defeats heal quickly. This allows them to return to the business world again soon after their failure.

Rather than hide from or dismiss their mistakes entrepreneurs concede their errors and analyze the causes. They have the ability to come to terms with their mistakes, learn from them, correct them, and use them to prevent their recurrence. Successful entrepreneurs know that they have to take personal responsibility for either the success or the failure of their venture and not look for scapegoats when things do not work out. They know how to build on their successes and learn from their failures.

LOW NEED FOR STATUS AND POWER

Entrepreneurs derive great personal satisfaction from the challenge and excitement of creating and building their own business. They are driven by a high need for achievement rather than a desire for status and power. It is important, therefore, to recognize that power and status are a result of their activities and not the need that propels them.

In addition, when a strong need to control, influence, and gain power over other people characterizes the lead entrepreneur, more often than not the venture gets into trouble. A dictatorial and domineering management style makes it very difficult to attract and keep people in the business who are oriented toward achievement, responsibility, and results. Conflicts often erupt over who has the final say, and whose prerogatives are being infringed upon. Reserved parking spaces, the big corner office, and fancy automobiles become symbols of power and status that foster a value system and an organizational culture not usually conducive to growth. In such cases, the business' orientation toward their customers, their market, or their competitors is typically lost.

Successful entrepreneurs appear to have a capacity to exert influence among other people without formal power. They are skilled at "conflict resolution." They know when to use logic and when to persuade, when to make a concession and when to win one. In order to run a successful venture, entrepreneurs must learn to get along with many different constituencies, who often have conflicting aims — customers, suppliers, financial backers, and creditors, as well as partners and others inside the company.

INTEGRITY AND RELIABILITY

Long-term personal and business relationships are built on honesty and reliability. To survive in the long run, an approach of "Do what you say you are going to do!" is essential. With it the possibilities are unlimited. Investors, partners, customers, suppliers, and creditors all place a high value on these attributes. "Success" resulting from dishonest practices is really long-term failure. After all, anyone can lie, cheat, or steal and maybe get away with it once, but that is no way to build a successful entrepreneurial career.

TEAM BUILDER

Entrepreneurs who create and build successful businesses are not isolated, super-independent types of individuals. They do not feel they have to receive all of the credit for their success, nor do they feel they have to prove they did it all by themselves. Just the opposite situation actually tends to be true. Not only do they recognize that it is virtually impossible to build a substantial business by working alone, but they also actively build a team. They have an ability to inspire the people they attract to their venture by giving them responsibility and by sharing the credit for their accomplishments. This hero-making ability has been identified as a key attribute of many successful corporate managers as well.

In addition to these characteristics, other attributes that have been associated with successful entrepreneurs are the following:

1. They are determined to finish a project once it has been undertaken, even under difficult conditions.
2. They are dynamic individuals who do not accept the status quo and refuse to be restricted by habit and environment.
3. They are able to examine themselves and their ideas impartially.
4. They are not self-satisfied or complacent.
5. They are independent in making decisions while willing to listen to suggestions and advice from others.

6. They do not blame others or make excuses for their own errors or failures.

7. They have a rising level of aspirations and expectations.

8. They have a good grasp of general economic concepts.

9. They are mature, self-assured individuals who are able to interact well with people of varying personalities and values.

10. They are able to exercise control over their impulses and feelings.

11. They have the ability to make the very best of the resources at hand.

The consensus among most experts is that all of these personal characteristics can be worked on and improved through concerted practice and refinement. Some require greater effort than others, and much depends on an individual's strength of motivation and conviction to grow. Developing these attributes should not be very different from personal growth and learning in many other areas of your life.

The Not-So-Learnable Characteristics

The attributes listed next are those that many experts consider to be innate, and thus not acquirable to any great degree. Fortunately the list is quite short. It is from these not-so-learnable characteristics that the conclusion that entrepreneurs are "born, not made" is principally derived. However, while possessing all these attributes would be beneficial, there are many examples of successful business pioneers who lacked some of these characteristics or who possessed them to only a modest degree:

1. High energy, good health, and emotional stability

2. Creativity and an innovative nature

3. High intelligence and conceptual ability

4. The ability to see a better future and a capacity to inspire others to see it

It is apparent from this discussion that entrepreneurs work from a different set of assumptions than most "ordinary" people. They also tend to rely more on mental attitudes and philosophies based on these entrepreneurial attributes than on specific skills or organizational concepts.

The following are some of the points that, perhaps, sum up the general philosophy of the entrepreneurial approach to business — an "Entrepreneur's Creed," if you will:

1. Do what gives you energy — have fun.

2. Figure out how to make it work.

3. Anything is possible if you believe you can do it.

4. If you don't know it can't be done, then you'll go ahead and do it.

5. Be dissatisfied with the way things are — and look for ways to improve them.

6. Do things differently.

7. Businesses can fail. Successful entrepreneurs learn from failure — but keep the tuition low.

8. It's easier to beg for forgiveness than to ask for permission in the first place.

9. Make opportunity and results your obsession — not money.

10. Making money is even more fun than spending it.

11. Take pride in your accomplishments — it's contagious.

12. Sweat the details that are critical to success.

13. Make the pie bigger — don't waste time trying to cut smaller pieces.

14. Play for the long haul. It is rarely possible to get rich quickly.

15. Remember: only the lead dog gets a change in view.[4]

Answers to the Entrepreneurial Quiz

The answers provided in Table 1.1 for the Entrepreneurial Quiz represent the responses that best exemplify the spirit, attitudes, and personal views of proven, successful entrepreneurs. Here they are *not* arranged in numerical order (1–74) but by the characteristic that they are measuring (personal background, behaviour patterns, and lifestyle factors).

WHAT DOES YOUR SCORE MEAN?

The Entrepreneurial Quiz is *not* intended to predict or determine your likely success or failure. However, if you have answered and scored the questionnaire honestly, it does provide considerable insight into whether you have the attitudes, lifestyle, and behavioural patterns consistent with successful entrepreneurship.

Indicate the total number of questions for which you gave the most desirable response on the following scale:

NUMBER OF MOST DESIRABLE RESPONSES

0	10	20	30	40	50	60	70

TABLE 1.1 ANSWERS TO ENTREPRENEURIAL QUIZ

PERSONAL BACKGROUND

Most Desirable Response	*Question Number*
Rarely or No	30, 36, 37, 43
Mostly or Yes	17, 18, 23, 28, 32, 35, 28, 42, 44, 74

BEHAVIOUR PATTERNS

Most Desirable Response	*Question Number*
Rarely or No	8, 9, 10, 11, 12, 14, 24, 39, 40, 48, 54, 57, 64, 65
Mostly or Yes	2, 4, 5, 6, 7, 13, 16, 20, 21, 22, 26, 27, 29, 31, 33, 41, 45, 46, 47, 49, 50, 52, 53, 55, 56, 58, 60, 61, 62, 66, 68, 69

LIFESTYLE FACTORS

Most Desirable Response	*Question Number*
Rarely or No	25, 34, 51, 67, 71
Mostly or Yes	1, 3, 15, 19, 59, 63, 70, 72, 73

---

[4] Timmons, pp. 175–176.

The higher your number of most desirable responses — the closer you are to the right-hand side of this continuum — the more your responses agree with those of successful entrepreneurs. High levels of agreement indicate that you *may* have the "right stuff" to succeed in an entrepreneurial career. You should make certain, however, that your responses reflect your real opinions and attitudes.

The word *may* is highlighted above because of the overwhelming importance of one particular set of attributes/characteristics: commitment, determination, and perseverance. Scoring well on the test is not necessarily a guarantee of entrepreneurial success. Anything less than total commitment to your venture, and considerable determination and perseverance, will likely result in failure, regardless of the degree to which you may possess other important attributes. Your total commitment and determination to succeed helps convince others to "come along for the ride." If you are not totally committed, both financially and philosophically, to the venture, it is unlikely that potential partners, your employees, bankers, suppliers, and other creditors will have the confidence in you to provide the level of support your business will require.

Personal Self-Assessment

The purpose of this discussion is to have you evaluate your personal attitudes, behaviour tendencies, and views to determine whether you fit the typical entrepreneurial profile. Figure 1.2, a Self-Assessment Questionnaire, should help you summarize your feelings regarding your potential for self-employment.

EVALUATING YOUR BUSINESS SKILLS

There is a lot more to succeeding as an entrepreneur than just having the proper background, attitudes, and lifestyle. This next section discusses another factor you should consider in assessing your potential for becoming a successful entrepreneur: Do you have the requisite managerial and administrative skills needed to manage and operate a business?

Possessing the necessary managerial skills is an essential ingredient to succeeding in any small venture. It is estimated that the principal reason for the failure of small firms is poor management. Witness the problems of Nick Thompson-Wood (Exhibit 1.2), who, despite the fact he was well suited technically for his business and possessed ample promotional ability, lacked the management skills to successfully grow a business. This deficiency led directly to the demise of Simon the Pieman.

FIGURE 1.2 SELF-ASSESSMENT QUESTIONNAIRE

1. What personal weaknesses did you discover from analyzing your responses to the questionnaire?

_____

_____

_____

_____

continued

Self-Assessment Questionnaire — continued

2. Do you feel you can be an entrepreneur in spite of these weaknesses?

_____

_____

_____

_____

_____

3. What can you do to improve your areas of weakness?

_____

_____

_____

_____

4. What did the questionnaire indicate as your strengths?

_____

_____

_____

_____

_____

5. Do your strengths compensate for your weaknesses?

_____

_____

_____

_____

6. Does your lifestyle appear to be compatible with the demands of an entrepreneurial career?

_____

_____

_____

_____

_____

EXHIBIT 1.2

The genial face and over 'ome accent of "Simon the Pieman" that appeared on CTV's *Canada AM* program in early 1987 tempted many to try the company's wares. For Nick (Simon) Thompson-Wood, founder of Simon the Pieman Inc., the interview kicked off a period of rapid growth. In 1988, he sold almost $450,000 worth of British-style meat pies through two company outlets in suburban Toronto, as well as supplying specialty food shops from Oshawa to Hamilton.

But just as the piemaker's future looked brightest, a series of disastrous decisions plunged the company into bankruptcy. Thompson-Wood was undoubtedly a great cook, and not a bad showman, but he admits to lacking the management skills it takes to grow a business. Ignoring the cardinal rule of retailing, "location, location, location," the 51-year-old entrepreneur literally moved his company out of business.

Thompson-Wood got his start as a piemaker in 1984, after 15 years' catering experience with hotel chains in Britain and Canada. Looking for an unfilled niche in the specialty-food market, he hit on fresh meat pies after a trip to the U.K. A piemaker from his home town in Norfolk, England, furnished recipes for such traditional favourites as pork, steak and kidney, and duck and apricot. With $50,000 in savings and advice from a friend, he established a small but strategic downtown location on Charles St., a stone's throw from Toronto's main drag.

Business boomed, spread roughly 25% retail, 75% wholesale, and within a year Thompson-Wood was supplying 20 Loblaws grocery stores and dozens of specialty and butcher shops. The Charles St. takeout trade was brisk, and he soon introduced British imports such as jam and candies to the Simon line.

In 1987, dazzled by the possibility of increasing his sales to Loblaws, Thompson-Wood took out a $120,000 loan from the Royal Bank of Canada and moved his storefront/kitchen operation 40 km east to a larger, 5,000 sq. ft. premise next to the Pickering commuter train station. Relying on instinct rather than research, Thompson-Wood believed the bedroom community housed the type of upscale citizens who would snap up Simon's wares on the way home from work.

But the move to Pickering created problems on three fronts. Harried commuters didn't stop for pies as often as Thompson-Wood hoped. It was hard to get counter and kitchen staff in the predominantly white-collar community, so he had to pay a premium to attract the people he needed to make and sell pies. Increased distribution costs were the final straw: since the bulk of Simon's retail customers were west of Pickering, the company faced distribution costs that were more than double what they had been at Charles St.

Desperate to increase sales, Thompson-Wood signed a pricey five-year lease at a new mall in the heart of suburban North York — a move he admits was "the right location, but too soon." North York was enjoying a growth spurt, but there wasn't enough traffic at the new mall to support the lease. Overhead soon threatened to swamp the pieman; sales were up slightly, but they couldn't match the carrying costs on two new locations.

Realizing he was in trouble, Thompson-Wood approached the Federal Business Development Bank for assistance in November, 1988. The government agency referred him to a management consultant, who asked him not to make any moves without talking to him first. Thompson-Wood ignored that advice and continued to call the shots.

After that, things went rapidly downhill. With trade sluggish at the mall outlet, he fell behind on the rent. The landlord locked the doors in January — on Friday the 13th, as it happened. The Pickering landlord followed suit two weeks later and the bank stepped in. Debts totalled $318,942, and assets, largely baking equipment and supplies, were $132,000. When trustee Alan Lawson & Partners liquidated the firm in April, it was the end of Thompson-Wood's dream.

For his part, Thompson-Wood looks back on his stint as Simon the Pieman with little nostalgia. Toward the end, he resorted to sleeping pills to stop himself lying awake nights, endlessly re-running his mistakes and imagining ways to rescue the ailing business. In an effort to recoup his losses, he now holds two jobs, neither in the hospitality field. By night, he sorts mail for Canada Post, and during the day he trains sales staff for Encyclopedia Britannica. The hours are as long as when he ran his pie business, but at least he can sleep nights.

Excerpted from Gillian Pritchard, "Death of a pieman," *Small Business Magazine*, December 1989, p. 12. By permission of the author.

What Skills Are Needed by Small-Business Owners?

Businesses, whether large or small, have to perform a number of diverse functions to operate successfully. An entrepreneur, because of the limited amount of resources (human and financial) at his or her disposal, faces a particularly difficult time.

The business skills required by an entrepreneur (or some other member of the organization) can be broken down by function, as shown in Table 1.2.

TABLE 1.2 BREAKDOWN OF ENTREPRENEURIAL BUSINESS SKILLS

1. Managing Money
   a. Borrowing money and arranging financing
   b. Keeping financial records
   c. Managing cash flow
   d. Handling credit
   e. Buying insurance
   f. Reporting and paying taxes
   g. Budgeting

2. Managing people
   a. Hiring employees
   b. Supervising employees
   c. Training employees
   d. Evaluating employees
   e. Motivating people
   f. Scheduling workers

3. Directing business operations
   a. Purchasing supplies and raw materials
   b. Purchasing machinery and equipment
   c. Managing inventory
   d. Filling orders
   e. Managing facilities

4. Directing sales and marketing operations
   a. Identifying different customer needs
   b. Developing new product and service ideas
   c. Deciding appropriate prices
   d. Developing promotional strategies
   e. Contacting customers and making sales
   f. Developing promotional material and media programs

5. Setting up a business
   a. Choosing a location
   b. Obtaining licences and permits
   c. Choosing a form of organization and type of ownership
   d. Arranging initial financing
   e. Determining initial inventory requirements

Where Can You Acquire the Necessary Skills?

It should be apparent from this lengthy list that few people can expect to have a strong grasp of all of these skills prior to considering an entrepreneurial career. The key question then becomes where and how you can acquire these skills. The available means for developing these business skills are outlined below.

JOB EXPERIENCE

Every job you have had should have contributed to the development of some business skills. For example, working as an accountant might teach you:

1. How to prepare financial statements
2. How to make financial projections and manage money
3. How to determine the business's cash requirements, among other things

Working as a sales clerk might teach you:

1. How to sell
2. How to deal with the public
3. How to operate a cash register

Perhaps the best experience, however, is working for another entrepreneur. In that case you will learn to understand the overall process and skills required to operate your own business.

CLUB ACTIVITIES

Many of the functions that service clubs and similar organizations perform in planning and developing programs are similar to those performed by small businesses. Some examples of what can be learned from volunteer activities are:

1. How to organize and conduct fundraising activities
2. How to promote the organization through public service announcements and free advertising
3. How to manage and coordinate the activities of other members of the organization

EDUCATION

Universities, community colleges, and high schools, and government agencies such as local business development organizations and the Business Development Bank of Canada, provide many programs and individual courses in which essential business-related skills can be acquired. Some examples of applicable skills which can be learned from these programs include:

1. Business skills (from particular business classes)
2. Socialization and communication skills (from all school activities)
3. Bookkeeping and record-keeping skills (from accounting classes)

YOUR FRIENDS

Most of us have friends who through their job experience and education can teach us valuable business skills. Some examples of useful information we may acquire from this source are:

1. Possible sources of financing
2. Assistance in selecting an appropriate distribution channel for your products
3. Information on the availability of appropriate sites or locations for your business
4. Sources for finding suitable employees

YOUR FAMILY

Growing up with an entrepreneur in the family is perhaps the best learning experience of all, even though you may not be aware of the value of this experience at the time. Some examples of what you might learn from other members of your family are:

1. How to deal with challenges and problems
2. How to make personal sacrifices and why
3. How to keep your personal life and business life separate
4. How to be responsible with money

HOME EXPERIENCES

Our everyday home experiences help us develop many business skills. Some examples of such skills are:

1. Budgeting income
2. Planning finances
3. Organizing activities and events
4. Buying wisely
5. Managing and dealing with people
6. Selling an idea

It can be hard for a single individual to wear all these "hats" at once. Partnerships or the use of outside technical or general business assistance can be an excellent supplement for any deficiencies in characteristics and skills a small business owner may have. Thus, it often becomes essential to identify an individual, or individuals, who can help you when needed. This outside assistance might come from one of the following sources:

1. A spouse or family member
2. A formal partnership arrangement
3. Hired staff and employees
4. External professional consultants
5. A formal course or training program
6. Regular idea exchange meetings or networking with other entrepreneurs

INVENTORY OF YOUR MANAGERIAL AND ADMINISTRATIVE SKILLS

Now that you understand the range of skills necessary to enable your new business to succeed, the questionnaire in Figure 1.3, adapted from PROFIT magazine, will enable you to rate your business potential in several important areas of business. It will test your ability to think and act in an entrepreneurial fashion in a lighthearted way. For best results, don't try to anticipate the responses the quiz is looking for. Answer all questions candidly and sincerely. There are really no wrong answers; some are just more correct than others.

FIGURE 1.3 DETERMINING YOUR ENTREPRENEURIAL QUOTIENT

YOUR QUALIFICATIONS

1. What is the highest level of schooling you have completed?
   _____ a. High school
   _____ b. Some college or university
   _____ c. Graduate of college or university
   _____ d. Some post-graduate studies
   _____ e. School of hard knocks

2. In school I was most likely found:
   _____ a. In the cafeteria
   _____ b. On the soccer or football team
   _____ c. Working at a job after school
   _____ d. On the student council
   _____ e. Behind the portables

3. Which statement most closely reflects your management experience?
   _____ a. None
   _____ b. Selling pink lemonade
   _____ c. I managed a rock band at school
   _____ d. I've run businesses before
   _____ e. I work for the government

4. My health is:
   _____ a. None of your business
   _____ b. Not what it was
   _____ c. Generally good
   _____ d. Terrific
   _____ e. Going fast

YOUR SUPPORT GROUP

5. What persons close to you are or have been self-employed?
   _____ a. My barber or hairdresser
   _____ b. Close friends
   _____ c. Close family and friends
   _____ d. Parents
   _____ e. Third cousin on my mother's side

6. What would be the reaction of your family if you started your own business?
   _____ a. "Well, if that's what you want."
   _____ b. "We'll stand by whatever decision you make."
   _____ c. "How can we help?"
   _____ d. "How much money do you need?"
   _____ e. "Why couldn't you have been a doctor or a lawyer?"

7. The most important people in an entrepreneur's life are:
   _____ a. Your bank
   _____ b. Your customers
   _____ c. Your customers, staff, and suppliers
   _____ d. Your family, customers, and staff
   _____ e. Yourself

continued

8. How many investors should a growing business have?
_____ a. None
_____ b. Maybe one or two
_____ c. As many as it needs
_____ d. As many as it can get

MANAGEMENT

9. What's the most common single reason offered by PROFIT 100 entrepreneurs for the success of their companies?
_____ a. Government grants
_____ b. Investing in R&D
_____ c. Good product, well timed
_____ d. Their staff
_____ e. Personal brilliance

10. Which statement best sums up your management style?
_____ a. Shoot first and ask questions later
_____ b. Get everything in writing
_____ c. Nothing is impossible to a willing mind
_____ d. Do it, try it, fix it
_____ e. If it ain't broke, don't fix it

11. I believe in holding staff meetings:
_____ a. Whenever anyone leaves the company
_____ b. To discuss major strategic changes
_____ c. Every week, to discuss progress on various initiatives
_____ d. Regularly, to share ideas and information
_____ e. As rarely as possible

12. The day before he's supposed to make a presentation to a potential investor, your financial manager jumps to the competition. What do you do?
_____ a. Cancel the presentation
_____ b. Carry it out in his place
_____ c. Stay up all night to rework the presentation
_____ d. Appoint a new financial officer and then rework the presentation
_____ e. Sue the competitor

13. In a search for a new v-p, you've narrowed the choice down to two candidates: someone on staff and an outsider with an MBA. Who do you choose?
_____ a. It depends. What school granted the MBA?
_____ b. Whichever one will work cheaper
_____ c. Whichever one my management committee prefers
_____ d. The insider, to boost staff morale
_____ e. The outsider, to get new blood into the company

14. In a study, U.S. entrepreneurs rated which of the following characteristics as most important to business success?
_____ a. Being well organized
_____ b. Competitiveness
_____ c. Willingness to take initiative
_____ d. Perseverance
_____ e. A strong desire for financial success

Determining Your Entrepreneurial Quotient — continued

15. In the same study, which characteristic was rated least important?
_____ a. Perseverance
_____ b. Strong desire for money
_____ c. Willingness to tolerate uncertainty
_____ d. Ability to lead effectively
_____ e. A strong need to achieve

16. According to Vancouver real estate dealmaker Peter Thomas, which of the following tactics are most important to smart negotiating?
_____ a. Always reveal your price first
_____ b. Let the other party state their price first
_____ c. Offering more than market value — with conditions — is a good way to get the other side's attention
_____ d. You'll never get what you don't ask for
_____ e. Price is more important than terms

FINANCE

17. Which statement most closely reflects your level of financial knowledge?
_____ a. Two and two makes four
_____ b. I know the difference between equity and debt
_____ c. I understand every word my banker says
_____ d. I'm taking a course to learn more
_____ e. I know pretty much all I have to

18. Okay, prove it. Working capital is calculated as:
_____ a. Retained earnings minus shareholders' equity
_____ b. Assets minus short-term debt
_____ c. An indication of a company's ability to pay its short-term debts
_____ d. Current assets minus current liabilities
_____ e. Taxable income minus interest, dividends, and taxes

19. What is the most common source of startup funds used by entrepreneurs?
_____ a. Bank loans
_____ b. Credit card advances
_____ c. Love money from family and friends
_____ d. Owner's own funds and savings
_____ e. Venture capital

20. Your banker gives you six weeks to pay back a line of credit. You haven't got the money. What would you do?
_____ a. Panic
_____ b. Ask to speak to your banker's superior
_____ c. Call another bank
_____ d. Call five more banks
_____ e. Complain to the media

21. Profit is:
_____ a. What's left over after subtracting expenses from revenues
_____ b. My prize for working hard
_____ c. A reward to be shared with my employees
_____ d. The foundation of my company's future growth
_____ e. The name of a magazine

continued

Determining Your Entrepreneurial Quotient — continued

22. A friend asks you to invest in a business she's starting. Your reaction is:

_____ a. "I don't have any money."

_____ b. "Who else is backing you?"

_____ c. "Let's see your business plan."

_____ d. "Where's your business plan? Who are your partners and customers?"

_____ e. "Sure."

SALES

23. Marketing is …

_____ a. best left to the marketing department

_____ b. a necessary expense

_____ c. an area in which I take a keen interest

_____ d. the responsibility of everyone in the company, especially me

_____ e. overrated

24. You show up for a meeting with a prospect and a secretary says he hasn't time to see you today. What do you do?

_____ a. Gesture obscenely on your way out

_____ b. Leave quietly

_____ c. Refuse to leave until he sees you

_____ d. Leave when you have an iron-clad commitment for another meeting

_____ e. Drop the client. Who needs the aggravation?

25. Your best customer just switched suppliers. What do you do?

_____ a. Throw in the towel

_____ b. Try to get it to change its mind

_____ c. Revamp your products, pricing, and service to win the client back

_____ d. Concentrate on new prospects

_____ e. Call your MP to ask about government assistance

26. Good service in the '90s means:

_____ a. Giving customers what they deserve

_____ b. Surveying customers to ensure their expectations are being met

_____ c. Exceeding customers' expectations

_____ d. Surveying customers to ensure their expectations are consistently being exceeded

_____ e. 30 minutes or the pizza's free

AS YOUR COMPANY GROWS

27. You're falling behind on projects, returning phone calls, and responding to staff requests. This is a sign that:

_____ a. You're in over your head

_____ b. Your company is growing

_____ c. You need to hire a personal assistant

_____ d. You need to start delegating

_____ e. All of the above

28. Opening the books to help employees understand the business better is:

_____ a. As likely as a blizzard in SkyDome

_____ b. A trendy idea that won't work in my business

_____ c. A concept I intend to pursue

_____ d. Working really well

_____ e. Bound to give my competitors an unfair advantage

Determining Your Entrepreneurial Quotient — continued

29. As your firm grows, which of the following initiatives is most important?
_____ a. Giving workers their birthdays off
_____ b. Market research to study and anticipate shifts in customer needs
_____ c. A financing plan to steer the company through its growth phases
_____ d. An organizational plan with trigger points for hiring new managers
_____ e. A wide-area computer network

ADAPTING TO CHANGE

30. Which statement best reflects your ability to work with a computer?
_____ a. How do you turn this thing on?
_____ b. I got 20,000 points in Tetris
_____ c. I can use the spell-checker on my word-processor
_____ d. My notebook has two spreadsheet programs, MS Word, a database manager, and CorelDraw
_____ e. I get along perfectly well with a typewriter and calculator

31. When someone cancels an important meeting on me at the last minute I:
_____ a. Get mad or indignant
_____ b. Shrug and get on with life
_____ c. Continue with what I was doing
_____ d. Use the opportunity to work on projects I can never find time for
_____ e. Think of about 50 ways to get even

32. How do you respond to criticism?
_____ a. I criticize right back
_____ b. It bothers me a little
_____ c. I don't let it bother me
_____ d. I examine whether any of it is valid, then try to learn from it
_____ e. I ignore it. Who has time to dwell on the negative?

33. Your banker says your company is now so big and successful that you're no longer the best person to run it. What's your reaction?
_____ a. Take it under advisement
_____ b. Take a few courses
_____ c. Hire a professional manager to replace you
_____ d. Consult investors and experts on the situation and your qualifications
_____ e. Switch banks

SCORING

Score one point for each "B" answer, two points for a "C", and four points for each "D". Score zero for any "A" or "E".

Rating your score:

120 or more:	You show awesome entrepreneurial flair. Go for it!
80–120:	You show good promise. Shore up your weaknesses.
60–80:	Don't quit your day job.
Less than 60:	Have you considered a career in the civil service?

Seriously, nobody fails this test. Those with low scores should focus on their problem areas a little more closely. Do you have a clear vision of what you wish to do? Do you have sufficient skills to run an organization? Are you persistent enough to overcome all obstacles? Are you constantly looking out for ways to improve your organization? Retake the test in six months and see if you're not better prepared.

ASSESSING YOUR PERSONAL FINANCIAL SITUATION

In addition to your managerial capabilities, your financial capacity will be a very important consideration in your decision as to whether an entrepreneurial career is right for you. It will certainly be a critical factor to those you may approach for a loan to provide investment capital for your venture.

Your Personal Balance Sheet

Your personal balance sheet provides potential lenders with a view of your overall financial situation so they can assess the risk they will be assuming. Generally, if you are in a strong financial position, as indicated by a considerable net worth, you will be considered a desirable prospect. On the other hand, an entrepreneur with a weak financial position and a large number of outstanding debts may not meet the standards of most lenders.

From a personal standpoint you might also want to reconsider becoming a small-business owner if you cannot afford a temporary or perhaps even a prolonged reduction in your personal income.

Your personal balance sheet includes a summary of all your assets — what you own that has some cash value — and your liabilities or debts. Preparing a personal balance sheet is a relatively simple process:

- **Step 1** Estimate the current market value of all your "assets" — the items you own that have cash value — and list them.
- **Step 2** Add up the value of these assets.
- **Step 3** List all your debts, also known as "liabilities."
- **Step 4** Add up your liabilities.
- **Step 5** Deduct your total liabilities from your total assets to find your "net worth."

Figure 1.4 shows a Sample Balance Sheet Form that you can use to help organize your assets and liabilities. The items listed are not exhaustive; the form is provided only as a guide for thinking about your present position. Since every business opportunity has its own unique capital (money) requirements there is no specific dollar value for the personal net worth necessary to start a business. However, you should keep in mind that most private lenders or lending institutions typically expect a new small-business owner to provide at least 40 to 50 percent of the capital required for start-up. In addition, lenders consider the net worth position of a prospective borrower, in order to determine their ability to repay the loan should the new business fail.

In Exhibit 1.3, for example, consider the "Financial Snapshot" provided for Bill Dixon and his family. It illustrates a reasonably good financial position with total assets of $215,000 as opposed to total liabilities of under $93,000. Most of Bill's assets are tied up in their home, his retirements plans (RRSPs), and their cottage. These are typically assets with a solid value but not very liquid from the standpoint of providing the base capital for a business investment. Bill's Balance Sheet, however, does show a net worth of over $122,000, some of which could be used as security to obtain a loan to invest in a new business opportunity.

Developing a Personal Budget

As well as determining your present net worth, you must also consider your personal living expenses when assessing your ability to provide the total financing needed to start a new business. In fact, you should evaluate your personal financial needs while in the process of determining whether an entrepreneurial career is right for you.

FIGURE 1.4 SAMPLE BALANCE SHEET FORM

Name: _____

BALANCE SHEET
as of

_____ _____ 19 _____
(Month)   (Day)   (Year)

ASSETS

Cash & cash equivalents

Cash _____

Chequing/savings _____

Canada Savings Bonds _____

Treasury bills _____

Short-term deposits _____

Money market funds _____

Other _____

Subtotal _____

Business/property

Investment property _____

Business Interests _____

Subtotal _____

Registered assets

RRSPs _____

Employer's pension plan (RPP) _____

RRIFs _____

DPSPs _____

Other _____

Subtotal _____

Personal Property

Home _____

Seasonal home _____

Cars and/or other vehicles _____

Equipment _____

Collectibles (art) _____

Jewelry _____

Household furnishings _____

Subtotal _____

Investments

GICs and term deposits _____

Mutual funds _____

Stocks _____

Bonds _____

Life insurance (cash surrender value) _____

Provincial stock savings plan _____

Subtotal _____

TOTAL _____

continued

Balance Sheet Form — continued

LIABILITIES
Short-term
Credit card debt   _____

Personal line of credit, margin account   _____

Instalment loans (e.g., car, furniture,
    personal loans)   _____

Demand loans   _____

Loans for investment purposes   _____

Tax owing (income and property)   _____

Other   _____

Subtotal   _____

Long-term
Mortgage — home   _____

Mortgage — seasonal home   _____

Mortgage — investment property   _____

Other   _____

Subtotal   _____

TOTAL   _____

NET WORTH ANALYSIS
Liquid assets vs. short-term debt
Total assets   _____

Total liabilities   _____

Assets exceed debt by   + _____

(Debt exceeds assets by)   −(_____)

Debt-equity ratio (liabilities/net worth)   _____

Net worth (assets less total liabilities)   _____

In some situations you will need to take money from the business each month to pay part or all of your personal living expenses. If such is the case, it is crucial that this amount be known and that at least that much be set aside to be paid out to you each month as a salary.

If your new business is starting off on a limited scale, you might wish to continue holding a regular job to cover your basic living expenses and provide some additional capital to your fledgling operation. In some cases, your spouse's income may be sufficient to cover the family's basic living expenses and it may not be necessary to consider your personal financial needs in making a go/no go decision.

The Dixon family's "Financial Snapshot" illustrates their annual expenses in relation to their current annual income of approximately $63,000. Note that their largest expenses are for income tax ($18,200) and the mortgage payments on the family home ($10,840). Food ($6,000) and payments on their auto loan ($3,860) are also significant expense categories. In addition, Bill tries to put some money aside for their children's education ($605), his retirement ($4,520), and family savings ($1,500). Their expenditure pattern probably does provide a reasonable reflection of those of a typical middle-class Canadian family.

EXHIBIT 1.3

"What am I doing wrong?" asks Bill Dixon, sitting back in the immaculate living room of his home on the outskirts of Fredericton. From the outside, the 45-year-old president of the Mechanical Contractors Association of N.B. appears to have it all: a good job, a house in the right neighborhood, two late-model cars in the driveway. But a close look at the Dixon family finances shows that Bill and his wife Bev are struggling to make ends meet.

"I'm certainly in the tax bracket I want to be in," says Bill, a short, round man with a friendly grin who relaxes by playing golf games on an IBM clone he keeps propped on a chair in the couple's newly carpeted basement. (He earns $55,000 a year). "The puzzling thing is, why aren't I more comfortable?"

It's not as if the Dixons are exactly uncomfortable. After nine years of marriage, Bill and Bev figure they're a typical middle-class family, although maybe at the higher end of the scale. They have two daughters (Bev's by a former marriage), Kami, 16, and Krista, 18, who they hope will one day go on to university. Once a year the family makes the annual pilgrimage to the cottage. And occasionally Bill will take a bit of time off during one of his many business trips to make room for a family holiday, like he did last year when he took Bev and the kids to Toronto for a convention. On the way home they stopped off to visit friends in Ottawa and Quebec City. "But it's not as if we're big spenders," says Bev, who earns $8,000 a year as a part-time sales clerk in a local jewelry store. "We don't have the time."

All the same, the money is getting spent — as Bill realizes every time he works out the family finances on his computer. Most of it goes to pay off loans the Dixons have taken out: $900 a month for the mortgage, $322 to pay off Bev's 1992 Dodge Spirit bought in January 1993 for $11,000 (Bill's shiny new Mercury Sable comes with the job). Once a month, Bev puts $50 into a Canadian Scholarship Fund so if her daughters do decide to continue their education there will be something saved up to pay for tuition. Then there are Bill's investments, mainly the $380 a month he puts into RRSPs, which now total just $34,000. What's left after the monthly expenses are paid is just a few hundred

dollars, pocket money as far as Bill is concerned.

Home improvements were the last thing on Bill's mind when he was starting off his career 20 years ago. Back then he wasn't sure if he'd ever own a house. Born in Moncton, he had planned to be a teacher. But after graduating from the University of New Brunswick in 1971 he found teaching jobs were scarce. He tried working in a bank, but it didn't work out. Eventually he found a job in the personnel department of a big mining company, Heath Steele Mines Ltd., in northern New Brunswick, and this time he landed on his feet. "I was making good money," he says of the 12 years he spent there climbing the corporate ladder. "I always had a new car." He also acquired a small cottage for $20,000 — the only material remnant of his bachelor days which, he concedes with a grin, did not involve much saving.

Those days came to an end when he married Bev in 1984. They had met two years earlier, at a curling match in the town of Newcastle where Bill was working and Bev, who had a job as a store clerk, had been raised.

A year later Bill accepted a job in personnel and benefits administration with a new mining company, Dennison-Potacan Potash Co., near Saint John in the southern part of the province. It meant moving away from Bev's family, which she describes as a culture shock, but Bill figured it was a step up the career ladder. Unfortunately, it didn't work out that way. "I was there for four years. It seemed like an eternity," he says.

When he saw his current job advertised in the paper, Bill jumped at the opportunity. It was a chance to put his experience to work and to run his own show. Bill's office is small — just himself and a secretary. Which is fine by him, because it means he gets to make most of the decisions. "I guess I've always been a bit of an entrepreneur at heart," he says. He spends a lot of time traveling.

Often he's on the road most of the week, especially during the summer when construction is in full swing. Sometimes he and his wife, who works evenings, pass each other on the highway. "We just wave," says Bev with a sigh.

When Bill does get home, likely as not he'll head downstairs to his computer to play golf games or track his finances for three or four hours. "I find it relaxing," he says. He can figure out anything. How much he owes. How much he has in the bank. He has even figured out the daily values of 10 or so mutual funds he owns.

"What I'd like to see," says Bill, "is about three months salary sitting in the bank. So when we need something, we can go out and get it." There are plenty of things the Dixons would like to get.

But right now they just don't have the money. It's going toward bills for other things they had to have. "We are smart shoppers, you have to give us that," says Bill. He and his wife spent six months comparing prices before they bought the car that Bev now uses to get to work.

Bill and Bev both figure the house was a good deal, too — although it's costing them a lot. They bought it for $89,000 five years ago and still owe $82,200 on the mortgage. "We didn't have much equity in our last house," explains Bill sheepishly, adding that it was really a problem of the housing market being off when they sold.

Finding a less expensive place to live was not a question. When the Dixons first saw this four-bedroom side-split, they both fell in love with it, recalls Bev. There was plenty of space, the neighborhood was great and it was close to the mall where Bev worked and to Bill's office. Plus, it was a lot cheaper buying on the outskirts rather than in Fredericton itself, where prices were a lot higher.

Of course, the house still required a lot of work. The big lot needed landscaping and the basement was unfinished. Today, the Dixon home sits in the middle of a lush green lawn, there's new carpeting and a big deck out back where the family enjoys summer barbecues. "I figure we've added at least $10,000 to the value of the place," says Bill. "The money we spent hasn't disappeared."

Source: Excerpted from "Where Does All the Money Go?" John Greenwood, *The Financial Post Magazine*, July-August, 1994, pp. 42–44.

FINANCIAL SNAPSHOT

Income

Bill's salary	54,600
Bev's salary	8,000
Investment income	320
Total	**$62,920**

Expenses

Mortgage	10,840
Mortgage insurance	420
Property taxes (home)	830
Property taxes (cottage)	310
Auto Loan	3,860
Auto maintenance, gas, etc.	1,260
Deductions	2,450
Income tax	18,200
Household expenses	4,790
Life insurance	640
Food	6,000
Entertainment	600
Clothing	2,000
Savings	1,325
RRSPs	4,520
RESPs	605
Vacations	500
Charitable donations	1,400
Miscellaneous	3,700
Total Expenses	**$64,250**

Assets

Home	115,000
Cottage	21,000
Furniture, contents	11,750
Personal effects, clothing	10,000
RRSPs	35,400
RESPs	5,600
GIC	6,000
Savings	1,500
Car	9,000
Total Assets	**$215,250**

Liabilities

Mortgage	82,000
Auto loan	9,000
Credit cards	1,825
Total Liabilities	**$92,825**

Net Worth	**$122,425**

The Personal Living Expenses Worksheet shown in Figure 1.5 is an effective means of estimating your present cost of living. From the totals on the worksheet, you can calculate the minimum amount of money you and your family will require on a regular monthly basis and determine from what sources this regular income will be obtained.

ARE YOU READY FOR AN ENTREPRENEURIAL CAREER?

External Role Demands

It is not enough simply to possess a large number and high level of the characteristics previously discussed as prerequisites for a successful entrepreneurial career. There are also certain external conditions, pressures, and demands inherent in the small-business ownership role itself.

While successful entrepreneurs may share several characteristics with successful people in other careers, entrepreneurs' preference for and tolerance of the combination of requirements unique to their role is a major distinguishing feature.

Many of these requirements have been alluded to earlier. What follows is a discussion of a few of the most relevant issues you should consider concerning your degree of readiness and preparedness for such a career.

Need for Total Commitment

As an entrepreneur you must live with the challenge of trying first to survive in the business world, then to stay alive, and always to grow and withstand the competitive pressures of the marketplace. Almost any venture worth considering requires top priority on your time, emotions, and loyalty. As an entrepreneur you must be prepared to give "all you've got" to the building of your business, particularly during the initial stages of its development. Anything less than total commitment will likely result in failure.

Management of Stress

Stress, the emotional and physiological reaction to external events or circumstances, is an inevitable result of pursuing an entrepreneurial career option. Depending on how it is handled, stress can be either good or bad for an entrepreneur. The better you understand how you react to stressful situations, the better you will be able to maximize the positive aspects of these situations and minimize the negative aspects, such as exhaustion and frustration, before they lead to a serious problem.

Stress, in the short term, can produce excellent results, because of its relationship to the type of behaviour associated with entrepreneurial activities, especially during the start-up stage of a new business. There is some evidence that once individuals become accustomed to producing under stressful conditions, they seem to continue to respond in a positive manner; entrepreneurs tend to create new challenges to replace the ones they have already met, and to continue to respond to those challenges with a high level of effectiveness.

Economic and Personal Values

Entrepreneurs engaged in "for-profit" as opposed to social or "not-for-profit" organizations must share the basic values of the free enterprise system: private ownership, profits, capital gains, and growth. These dominant economic values need not exclude social or other values. However, the nature of the competitive market economy requires belief in, or at least respect for, these values.

FIGURE 1.5   PERSONAL LIVING EXPENSES WORKSHEET — DETAILED BUDGET*

1. REGULAR MONTHLY PAYMENTS

Rent or house payments (including taxes) $ _____
Car payments (including insurance)   _____
Appliances/TV payments   _____
Home improvement loan payments   _____
Personal loan payments   _____
Health plan payments   _____
Life insurance premiums   _____
Other insurance premiums   _____
Miscellaneous payments   _____
    Total $ _____

2. FOOD EXPENSE

Food at home $ _____
Food away from home   _____
    Total $ _____

3. PERSONAL EXPENSES

Clothing, cleaning, laundry, shoe repair $ _____
Drugs   _____
Doctors and dentists   _____
Education   _____
Union or professional dues   _____
Gifts and charitable contributions   _____
Travel   _____
Newspapers, magazines, books   _____
Auto upkeep, gas, and parking   _____
Spending money, allowances   _____

4. HOUSEHOLD OPERATING EXPENSES

Telephone $ _____
Gas and electricity   _____
Water   _____
Other household expenses, repairs, maintenance   _____
    Total $ _____

GRAND TOTAL

1. Regular monthly payments $ _____
2. Food expense   _____
3. Personal expenses   _____
4. Household operating expenses   _____
    Total Monthly Expenses $ _____

---

* This budget should be based on an estimate of your financial requirements for an *average* month based on a recent 3- to 6-month period, and should not include purchases of any new items except emergency replacements.

A Final Analysis

The Entrepreneurial Assessment Questionnaire in Figure 1.6 is designed to help you recap your thinking concerning what you need to become a successful entrepreneur. The questions involve considerations at various stages of a business' development, and some may not be applicable to the stage you have currently reached in your business planning. However, you should answer all applicable questions.

If you have answered all the questions carefully, you've done some hard work and serious thinking. That's a positive step. If your answer to most of the questions was yes, you are on the right track. If you answered no to some questions you have more work to do; these questions indicate areas where you need to know more or that you need to do something about. Do what you can for yourself, but don't hesitate to ask for help from other sources.

This assessment of your entrepreneurial potential is based on a series of self-evaluations, and for it to reveal anything meaningful an absolute requirement is for you to be completely honest with yourself. This, however, is only the first step. The road to entrepreneurship is strewn with hazards and pitfalls and many who start on it fall by the wayside for one reason or another. However, those who persevere and reach the end by building a successful venture may realize considerable financial and psychological rewards as well as a lot of personal satisfaction.

The remainder of this book can help you evaluate other important parts of this process and improve your chances for success. It will help you decide what else you need to consider and enable you to go after it. Good luck!

FIGURE 1.6 ENTREPRENEURIAL ASSESSMENT QUESTIONNAIRE

	Yes	No
WHAT ABOUT YOU?		
1. Are you the kind of person who can get a business started and run it successfully?	____	____
2. Think about why you want to own your own business. Do you want it badly enough to work long hours without knowing how much money you'll end up with?	____	____
3. Does your family go along with your plan to start a business of your own?	____	____
4. Have you ever worked in a business similar to the one you want to start?	____	____
5. Have you ever worked for someone else as a supervisor or manager?	____	____
6. Have you had any business training in school?	____	____
WHAT ABOUT THE MONEY?		
7. Have you saved any money?	____	____
8. Do you know how much money you will need to get your business started?	____	____
9. Have you figured out whether you could make more money working for someone else?	____	____
10. Have you determined how much of your own money you can put into the business?	____	____
11. Do you know how much credit you can get from your suppliers — the people from whom you will buy?	____	____

continued

Entrepreneurial Assessment Questionnaire — continued

	Yes	No

12. Do you know where you can borrow the rest of the money needed to start your business? _____ _____

13. Have you figured out your expected net income per year from the business? (Include your salary and a return on the money you have invested in the business.) _____ _____

14. Can you live on less than this so that you can use some of it to help your business grow? _____ _____

15. Have you talked to a banker about your plans? _____ _____

YOUR BUSINESS AND THE LAW

16. Do you know what licences and permits you need? _____ _____

17. Do you know what business laws you have to obey? _____ _____

18. Have you talked to a lawyer about your proposed business? _____ _____

HOW ABOUT A PARTNER?

19. If you need a partner who has money or know-how, do you know someone who will fit — someone with whom you can get along? _____ _____

20. Do you know the good and bad points about going it alone, having a partner, and incorporating your business? _____ _____

WHAT ABOUT YOUR CUSTOMERS?

21. Do most businesses in your community seem to be doing well? _____ _____

22. Have you tried to find out how well businesses similar to the one you want to open are doing in your community and in the rest of the country? _____ _____

23. Do you know what kind of people will want to buy what you plan to sell? _____ _____

24. Do such people live in the area where you want to open your business? _____ _____

25. Do you feel they need a business like yours? _____ _____

26. If not, have you thought about opening a different kind of business or going to another neighbourhood? _____ _____

STAGE
TWO

EXPLORING NEW BUSINESS IDEAS AND OPPORTUNITIES

In Stage One you had an opportunity to evaluate your own potential for an entrepreneurial career from the standpoint of your personal fit with the requirements for success, the business skills required to start and run a business of your own, and the adequacy of your financial resources. Assuming that you feel you have the "right stuff" to continue to explore this career option, you will need an idea — the seed that will germinate and, hopefully, grow and develop into a profitable enterprise. This is the topic of Stage Two. Ideas that succeed are difficult to find and evaluate, but they are critical to the entire process. It is rare for extraordinary amounts of money or effort to overcome the problems associated with what is fundamentally a bad idea.

In some instances what was felt to be a good idea was the key element stimulating an individual to think of going into business. In others it was the lack of an acceptable concept that was the principal factor holding back an aspiring entrepreneur. Perhaps you fall into this category. If so, it is important not to be impatient. It may take several years to fully develop and evaluate an idea which is suited to your particular circumstances and which you feel represents a real opportunity. Don't try to force the issue. Actively pursue a range of possible options, but wait until the right situation presents itself before investing your time and money.

There is no shortage of good ideas. For example, the finalists in the 1994 Canadian Woman Entrepreneur of the Year Award were involved in a wide range of activities including processing underutilized food products, the management of a health spa, importing pharmaceutical products, managing a private training school, and franchised home care services:

- **Grace White, Dartmouth, Nova Scotia**, operates a food export business that specializes in underutilized food products such as chicken backs and leg quarters, beef livers, kidneys, hearts, suet, tripe, feet and tails, ewe mutton, pork feet and pickled pork tails, turkey necks, pickled and frozen mackerel, frozen herring, frozen shark fins, frozen and dried squid, and salt pollock. She finds customers for these products overseas, obtains them from suppliers in Canada and other countries, then arranges delivery.

- **Juanita Corbett, 100 Mile House, British Columbia**, is vice president of a successful international health spa and resort located over 300 miles north of Vancouver.

- **Sylvia Vogel, Montreal, Quebec** imports and sells a line of pharmaceuticals including psoralens, medication for genital warts, an exfoliant, and a range of dermatological products to consumers in Quebec and British Columbia, with plans to expand into Ontario soon.

- **Kay Lemessurier, St. John's, Newfoundland**, runs a number of private training schools in the Atlantic Provinces providing training to students in data entry and accounting functions.

- **Bev McMaster, Brandon, Manitoba**, operates a chain of franchised, privately owned home health care operations from B.C. east to Ontario.[1]

In Stage Two we will describe a number of sources from which you might obtain ideas for a prospective new venture, and present a variety of techniques you can use to evaluate the conceptual, technical, and financial aspects of your idea.

LONG-TERM EXPECTATIONS FOR YOUR BUSINESS

Whether your plans are to own and operate a business for a number of years or sell it shortly after it becomes operational, you will want to consider the long-term prospects of your venture. If you plan to keep the business, you are bound to have an interest in how it is expected to prosper; if you plan to sell the business, the prospective buyer will consider the long-term viability of the business in his or her purchase offer. So, either way, the long-term performance — the kind of firm your business may become — is important in evaluating alternatives. Opportunities with higher growth potential generally offer greater economic payoffs. However, those are not the only kind of payoffs that are important. Some small but stable ventures provide very enjoyable situations and lucrative benefits to their owners.

For purposes of assessing the expected long-term prospects of your venture, three types of possibilities should be considered:

1. Lifestyle ventures
2. Small, profitable ventures
3. High-growth ventures

Lifestyle Ventures

These include most "one-man shows," mom-and-pop stores, and other lifestyle businesses such as gas stations, restaurants, drycleaning shops, and small independent retail stores. Typically, their owners make modest investments in fixed assets and inventory, put in long hours, and earn considerably less income than the average unskilled auto worker or union craftsperson. The profit in reselling these businesses tends to be quite low.

The operator of a lifestyle business often risks his or her savings to capitalize the enterprise, and works longer hours with less job security than the average employee. Most lifestyle businesses have a high risk of failure. Unless you are willing to put up with these inherent conditions, such types of businesses should probably be avoided in favour of staying with your job until a more attractive opportunity can be identified.

---

[1] From "Women Entrepreneurs: Canada's New Competitive Advantage," *The Financial Post*, Joint Venture Supplement, October 8, 1994, pp. S11–S18.

Small, Profitable Ventures

Small manufacturing firms, larger restaurants and retail firms, small chains of gas stations, and other multi-establishment enterprises commonly fall into this category. Usually they involve a substantial capital investment — $100,000 or more. Some owners put in long hours, others do not. Once established, many owners enjoy a comfortable living. The profit in reselling the business can be high to a buyer who sees both an attractive job and a profitable investment.

You might be surprised at how many small, virtually unnoticed businesses around your city or town have managed to provide a very comfortable living for their founders. Almost always there is a very particular reason that they are able to do so: a contract the entrepreneur was able to land at favourable terms, or a market that was unknown to others or too small to attract competitors which therefore permitted a high profit margin, or special skills or knowledge on the part of the proprietor which enabled him or her to charge high rates for his or her time. The business' advantage may be its location, perhaps purchased for a low price many years earlier, or a patented process others are not able to copy. It may even be simply a brand that is protected by trademark and which has become well known by the passage of time or through successful advertising.

High-Growth Ventures

Much rarer than lifestyle ventures or small, profitable ventures, but typically more highly publicized, are small firms that have the capability of becoming large ones. They include many high-technology companies formed around new products with large potential markets, and also some of the small, profitable firms which, due to such factors as having amassed substantial capital or having hit upon a successful formula for operating, can be expanded many times. Ventures of this type are often bought up and absorbed by larger companies. The potential for significant capital gain on resale of the business can be substantial.

A key factor in starting a high-growth venture is choosing the right industry to enter. The rate of growth of the industry as a whole often plays a large role in determining the growth patterns of start-ups within it. In addition, however, there has to be some property of the business that can readily be multiplied by that company but cannot easily be duplicated by others for there to be significant growth potential. In franchising, for example, it can be a format for doing business which has proven exceptionally effective and can be taught. In high-technology firms, it is specialized know-how in creating something at a hard-to-reach frontier of engineering for which there is a demand. If a technology is common knowledge and not too capital-intensive, then companies providing it generally do not grow very rapidly.

SOURCES OF IDEAS FOR A NEW BUSINESS

In Stage One it was suggested that your previous jobs, hobbies, personal experiences, and the like could provide you with some of the requisite business and technical skills needed to operate your own business. Similarly, your past work experience, hobbies, and acquaintances can provide a starting point for developing a list of business ventures you might wish to consider for further investigation. The following is a brief description of some of the sources most often used by entrepreneurs in search of new business opportunities.

Your Job

Prior work experience is the most common source of new business ideas. It has been estimated that as many as 85 percent of the new businesses started are based on product ideas similar to those of prior employers of the founders. When you think about it the attractions of starting a business in a field in which you have experience and expertise are obvious. You are already familiar with the products and services you will provide, you understand the competitive environment, you have some knowledge and understanding of customer requirements, you may already know several prospective clients, and so on.

Ideas from your previous employment can take several forms. For example, you might set yourself up as a consultant in some technical area using the background and experience you acquired in a previous job. You might develop a product or service for which your prior employer might be a prospective customer, as illustrated by the case of Dusanka Filipovic in Exhibit 2.1. You might even be interested in providing a product or service similar or related to that provided by your previous employer. In this last case you should check with a lawyer to ensure your plans do not violate the legal rights of that employer. You must be certain your actions do not infringe on any patent, trademark, or other proprietary rights, break any non-competition clause of other agreements you may have signed, involve the direct solicitation of your former employer's customers, or raise similar legal or ethical problems.

Your Hobbies

Some people are deeply involved with their hobbies, often devoting more time to them than to their regular job. There are many instances of such secondary interests leading to new business ventures. For example, serious athletes may open sporting goods stores, amateur photographers open portrait studios, hunters offer guiding services and run hunting lodges and game farms, pilots start fly-in fishing camps, philatelists open coin and stamp stores, and so forth.

Witness the case of Gary Stanley described in Exhibit 2.2, an avid gardener and orchid grower, who came up with the idea of an entirely new concept providing gardeners with an inexpensive new orchid plant, turning more people on to the hobby of orchid growing and giving a financial boost to his recently established business.

Many such ventures do very well, but there can be considerable conflict. Hobbies are typically activities that you and others are prepared to do at your own expense. This can exert downward pressure on the likely profitability of your business. As a result, margins are quite low

EXHIBIT 2.1

Dusanka Filipovic of Mississauga, Ontario is turning ozone-layer protection into a multi-million-dollar business in tough economic times.

The 40-year-old chemical engineer is commercializing a device she co-invented while working at Union Carbide. The "blue bottle" collects ozone-depleting chlorofluorocarbons (CFCs).

Her company, Halozone Recycling, will create 30 jobs in this Toronto suburb when it opens a $10-million CFC recycling plant in March.

"The technology is unique," says Filipovic, who moved to Canada from the former Yugoslavia in 1974. "It allows the country to take the lead in solving new global problems such as ozone depletion."

Filipovic's product is a metal cylinder — equipped with a honeycomb filter she compares to "intelligent sand" — that captures CFCs in products ranging from common refrigerators to huge office-tower air-conditioning systems.

Once contained, the CFCs are recycled instead of escaping into the atmosphere, where they gnaw at the ozone blanket that shields the Earth from the sun's ultraviolet rays.

Filipovic and a business partner started the company two years ago.

From *Vancouver Sun*, February 28, 1994, p. D11.

EXHIBIT 2.2

Winnipeg entrepreneur Gary Stanley has come up with a new product which he thinks will help warm the hearts of winter-weary, recession-battered Canadians.

The product is called Orchids in a Mini-Greenhouse. As the name suggests, it's basically a small orchid plant enclosed in a reusable mini-greenhouse.

Stanley, an avid gardener and orchid grower, ... tried to turn more Manitobans on to the hobby of orchid-growing by renting some retail space at two local garden centres and trying to sell mature orchid plants.

"People would walk by and say 'nice plant,'" Stanley said. But as soon as they saw the $40 price tag and found out the plant was an orchid, their interest would quickly evaporate.

Stanley attributed that to a couple of things — the recession and the fact that orchids have a reputation of being hard plants to grow. ...

So last December he set out to design a product that would provide new gardeners with an inexpensive new orchid plant. And maybe along the way it would also help debunk the myth that orchids are hard to grow and give his fledgling business — Village Orchids — a healthy shot in the arm.

Now, five months, countless 14-hour days and several thousand dollars later, Stanley has a product that he thinks will fit the bill nicely — an easy-to-grow orchid that comes in a reusable mini-greenhouse package and sells for less than $10.

Stanley said about 80 flower shops and garden centres across Canada ... have already agreed to carry his new product. And he's hoping that by Mother's Day that number will have grown to about 100.

Excerpted from Murray McNeill, "Orchid hothouse fits in your hand," *Winnipeg Free Press*, April 7, 1992 (Tuesday), p. B20. By permission.

in such areas as the production of arts and crafts, small-scale farming, trading in stamps, coins, and other collectibles, antique automobile restorations, and similar hobby-based operations.

Personal Observation

For many people personal observation is the most practical way of identifying a business idea. Personal observations may arise from either casual observation or deliberate search.

Casual Observation

Often, ideas for a new product or service result from chance observation of daily living situations. This commonly occurs when people travel and observe product or service concepts being provided that are not yet available in the United States, Canada, or, perhaps, the person's local market area.

Restaurant themes and concepts, such as Thai, Mexican, health food, and salads, typically are only established in most cities after they have proven to be successful somewhere else. Sporting trends, such as sailboarding and rollerblading, and fashion colours and styles are also usually imported from outside the country.

For this type of observation to yield results, you have to recognize the need for a new type of product or service offering and then work out some kind of solution. This was the approach followed by Guy Bouvier and Robert Carrière, Noreen Kapp, and Nikki Yokokura whose cases are described in Exhibits 2.3, 2.4, and 2.5.

The observation may emerge from your own experience in the marketplace, be expressed by someone else who has recognized some opportunity or problem, or be the result of observing the behaviour of other people. Regardless of its source, this type of simple observation can be the source of numerous excellent new business ideas.

EXHIBIT 2.3

Manitoba brothers-in-law Guy Bouvier and Robert Carrière logged countless hours with their kids on local skating rinks. But fun turned to frustration as they saw children hurt themselves using chairs and pylons while learning to skate. That concern led them to develop E-Z Skater, a $36.95 prop that gives 2- to 10-year-olds the stability they need to develop proper balance and skating skills.

Railway-worker Bouvier and Carrière, a cabinetmaker, built their prototype at home in Otterburne, 50 km south of Winnipeg, in 1990. Made from tubular steel, the E-Z Skater works much like a walker. A horizontal crossbar steadies the skater while twin runners glide along the ice. Investing $45,000 to form Carvier Innovations Inc., the pair unveiled E-Z Skater at a sporting goods show in 1991.

Carvier has now sold 1,000 E-Z Skaters in sports stores across Canada, and Boston distributor Bosmosco Inc. is selling the device in Russia. Last year Bouvier and Carrière introduced an E-Z Skater for adults, and now they're branching out into new products for summer sports.

Reprinted by permission of Daniel Kucharsky, a Montreal-based freelance journalist.

Deliberate Search

While deliberate search may seem to be the most rational way of finding viable business ideas, in fact most new ventures do not start in this manner. The majority of business start-ups arise almost incidentally from events relating to work or everyday life. However, this approach should not be completely ignored, as it can be fruitful if you are committed to investigating the possibilities of starting a new business but lack the seed of any real, likely idea. A deliberate search process can be initiated by consulting the following sources:

PUBLICATIONS

Reading business publications and other printed sources such as newspapers, specialty magazines, newsletters, and trade publications can provide ideas that might stimulate your entrepreneurial thinking. Some of the more important of these sources are listed below.

EXHIBIT 2.4

Don't Wake The Baby

Every parent knows it's sacrilege to wake a sleeping baby, especially one with colic. So when Lacombe, Alta., real estate agent Noreen Kapp couldn't find a snowsuit that let her undress her sleeping baby without waking him, she designed her own. Her solution is an armless, cocoon-like snowsuit that uses a unique drawstring system to adjust to fit growing babies from newborns to 18 months.

Kapp made 30 prototypes before she was satisfied. "It had to be warm, durable, good quality, and easy and fast to get on and off." The drawstrings inside the fabric allow the poly-cotton suit to be custom-fit. She figures she beat a one million-to-one longshot by successfully patenting Cocooni in Canada and the U.S.

A second Cocooni, with arms, was introduced in 1990 for children sized 12 months to 3X. Kapp Fashion Ltd. has now sold more than 1,000 suits through Alberta clothing stores.

Kapp says it has taken more than $50,000 to bring Cocooni to market, and now she's looking for investors to help boost production and distribution. In the meantime she's designing other innovative children's accessories, including a portable bed, a hip-hugger infant carrier, and others she won't discuss. Clearly, designing for kids is no child's play.

Reprinted by permission of *Diane Luckow.*

EXHIBIT 2.5

Two businessmen bow, exchange pleasantries, and trade cards. It's a common occurrence in Japan, but the ritual has a cultural subtext lost on most outsiders. Now whether you're traveling for business or pleasure, there's a way to familiarize yourself with details about everything from Japanese geography to cultural protocol before you land. But it's not a guidebook you'll be reading.

Japanese language instructor Nikki Yokokura has turned computers into classrooms with her Compact-Disc Read-Only Memory (CD-ROM) software program, Exotic Japan. Part cultural debriefing, part language tutor, the program pushes integrated media technology to the limit by combining visuals, text and audio as never before.

Yokokura spent 3,500 hours crafting the program on her Macintosh computer. Users can watch animated Japanese figures perform various acts, such as greetings, while reading pop-up text explaining who should bow first and what phrases to use for the occasion. "Tourists and business people should be able to get a good grounding in Japanese culture from this," says Yokokura. The language component features audio in both male and female voices — since Japanese words differ slightly for men and women — and a recording function lets users play back their own pronunciations.

Yokokura began dabbling in software to computerize lessons for her students. Exotic Japan, the first program from her Toronto company, Pixonics Inc., was a natural extension of her hobby and profession. To get the program to market, Yokokura turned to California software publisher Voyager Co. in 1990. It was Voyager that suggested she produce the program on CD-ROM, the compact disk storage system whose high capacity allowed her to offer a depth of information and flexibility that's hard to match in conventional software.

Since its launch in August, 1991, about 2,000 copies of Exotic Japan have been sold at US$99, in Canada, the U.S., France, Australia and even Japan. A PC-Windows version appears later this year. Meanwhile, Yokokura is hoping to link up with other software developers: "I've got other educational software projects in mind that I'd like to do."

Reprinted by permission of Jennifer Low.

Newspapers and Magazines *The Wall Street Journal, The Globe and Mail, The Financial Post,* and *The Financial Times* offer business and classified sections which provide a listing or make other reference to available small-business opportunities. A number of Canadian magazines such as *Canadian Business, PROFIT: The Magazine for Canadian Entrepreneurs,* and *The Financial Post Magazine,* and U.S. publications such as *Inc., Success, Entrepreneur,* and *Fortune* provide further descriptions of a range of business possibilities.

Newsletters Thousands of newsletters are available covering almost every conceivable subject. The information they contain is current and specialized, and can provide invaluable access to opportunities in any field. For further information, contact the reference librarian at your public library, and ask for the *National Directory of Newsletters and Reporting Services* (Gale Research Company, Book Tower, Detroit, MI 48226). It lists every major publication.

Trade Publications A list of available trade publications can be obtained from *Standard Rate and Data Service* (3004 Glenview Road, Womet, IL 60091), *Canadian Advertising Rates and Data* (481 University Avenue, Toronto, Ont. M5W 1A7), or similar publications available in most libraries. Trade magazines are usually the first to publicize a new product. In many cases the manufacturer is looking for help in distributing a new line. The ads will also provide information about potential competitors and their products. These trade publications are some of the best sources of data about a specific industry, and frequently print market surveys, forecasts, and articles on needs the industry may have. All this information can serve as a stimulating source of ideas.

INVENTORS' SHOWS, TRADE SHOWS, AND CONVENTIONS

Inventors' Shows These shows provide inventors and manufacturers with a place to meet to discuss potential products for the marketplace. There are major inventors' shows held annually in the larger cities throughout Canada and the U.S. Information on upcoming shows may be available from the Chamber of Commerce in these cities or from the Office of Inventions and Innovations, National Bureau of Standards, Washington, D.C. 20234, who can provide a list of the major shows held in the U.S.

Trade Shows Shows covering the industry you want to enter can also be an excellent way to examine the products and services of many of your potential competitors. It can also be a way for you to meet distributors and sales representatives, learn of product and market trends, and identify potential products or services for your venture. Trade shows usually take place several times a year, in various locations. You will find trade show information in the trade magazines servicing your particular field or industry, or you may refer to the following sources:

- *Exhibits Schedule: Directory of Trade and Industrial Shows*, Bill Communications, Inc., 633 Third Avenue, New York, NY 10017
- *Trade Show & Convention Guide*, Amusement Business Division, Billboard Publications Inc., Affiliated Publications Inc., Nashville, TN 37202
- *Trade Shows and Professional Exhibits Directory*, Gale Research Company, Book Tower, Detroit, MI 48226

Conventions Fairs or conventions are also an excellent place to stimulate your creative thinking. At a convention you are exposed to panels, speakers, films, and exhibitions. You also have an opportunity to exchange ideas with other people attending. Information on conventions and meetings scheduled to take place around the world can be obtained from:

- *Directory of Conventions, Successful Meetings Magazine*, Bill Communications, Inc., 633 Third Avenue, New York, NY 10017
- *World Meetings: U.S. and Canada*, World Meeting Information Center, Macmillan Information Corp., 866 Third Avenue, New York, NY 10022

PATENT BROKERS AND PRODUCT LICENSING INFORMATION SERVICES

An excellent way to obtain information about the vast number of new product ideas available from inventors, corporations, or universities is to subscribe to a service that periodically publishes data on products offered for licensing. Licensing means renting the right to manufacture or distribute a product within agreed rules or guidelines. For example, you might purchase the right to manufacture T-shirts and sweaters with the logo of Casper the Ghost, Garfield, or other popular fictional characters, or use the trademark of a popular product such as Labatt's or Coca-Cola on similar apparel. The owner of the licence retains ownership and receives a royalty or fixed fee from you as the licensee. Here are some of the information services you can contact to locate product or service licensing opportunities:

Licensing Opportunities Section
Business Services Centre
Industry Canada
C. D. Howe Building
235 Queen Street
Ottawa, Ontario
K1A 0H5

Government Inventions Available for Licensing
National Technical Information Service (NTIS)
P.O. Box 1533
Springfield, VA 22151

Technology Mart
Thomas Publishing Company
250 West 34th Street
New York, NY 10001

Also:

Dr. Dvorkovitz and Associates
P.O. Box 1748
Ormond Beach, FL 32074

or their Canadian representatives:

Canadian Industrial Innovation Centre
156 Columbia Street West
Waterloo, Ontario
N2L 3L3

The Intellectual Property Directorate of Consumer and Corporate Affairs Canada also administers the Patent Information Exploitation (PIE) Program. The PIE Program is designed to make technological information contained in the Canadian patent system more readily available to the public. Technical information searches provided by the Program can assist you in identifying new products you might wish to market, license, or distribute. For more information, contact:

Enquiries Group
Intellectual Property Directorate
Consumer and Corporate Affairs Canada
Hull, Quebec
K1A 0C9

FRIENDS, ACQUAINTANCES, AND OTHER SOCIAL CONTACTS

Discussions with those you know should not be overlooked as a source of insight into needs that might be fulfilled by a new venture. Comments such "wouldn't it be nice if someone came up with something to do away with ..." or "what this place needs is ..." and other complaints and observations can provide a number of potential ideas.

FEDERAL AND PROVINCIAL GOVERNMENT AGENCIES AND DEPARTMENTS

Industry Canada, the provincial departments of economic development; the Business Development Bank (BDB); university entrepreneurship centres; small-business development centres; community colleges and various other federal and provincial government agencies are all in the business of helping entrepreneurs by means of business management seminars and courses, advice, information, and other assistance. You can also get feedback on the viability of your business idea, or even suggestions. The cost in most cases is nominal.

Numerous other government agencies, such as the Canada Business Services Centres of Industry Canada also have publications and resources available to stimulate ideas for new business opportunities. Your public library can provide you with further information on all the government departments relevant to your area of interest. It is possible to get your name on mailing lists for free material, or even a government source list so that others can find out about goods or services that you may want to provide.

The range of sources discussed here is certainly not exhaustive. Through careful observation, enthusiastic inquiry, and systematic searching, it is possible to uncover a number of areas of opportunity.

As you go about this kind of search it is important to write down your ideas as they come to mind. If you don't, a thought that might have changed your life may be lost forever.

AREAS OF FUTURE OPPORTUNITY

In searching for a unique business idea the best thing to keep in mind is the dynamic changes taking place within our society, our economy, and our everyday way of doing things. These changes are usually difficult to get a handle on, and it is hard to understand their implications for new business possibilities, but they represent the principal areas of opportunity available today. If you think about it for a minute, most of the major growth areas in business today — such as computers and information technology; cable television systems; fast food; a wide range of personal services; and direct selling by mail, telephone, and television — did not even exist just a few short years ago. But now they are so commonplace we take them for granted. Getting information on emerging trends and assessing their implications for various business situations can be a major road to significant business success.

What can we expect in the future? No one has a crystal ball that can predict these changes with 100 percent accuracy, but many books and business publications provide projections of future trends and changes that can be useful to the insightful observer. For instance, John Naisbitt and Patricia Aburdene, in a recent bestseller, identified a number of major transformations they foresaw occurring in North American society that could have dramatic implications for an enterprising individual.[2] These included:

- A period of unprecedented economic prosperity with the world becoming a single, integrated global economy
- A resurrection of the visual and performing arts as society's primary leisure activity
- The dismantling of the traditional political structures in eastern Europe and the emergence of "free-market socialism"
- The evolution of new, universal, international lifestyles in food, music, fashion, and other areas
- The emergence of Asia and cities around the Pacific Rim as the principal centres of world trade
- A shift from the models and metaphors of physics symbolizing the mechanistic industrial age to the era of biotechnology

As we have seen within the past four to five years, many of these changes foreseen by Naisbitt and Aburdene have, in fact, materialized as they had projected. These kinds of global social changes define the future orientation of our society and all can spell potential opportunity for an aggressive entrepreneur.

In a similar vein, Jo Marney has identified a number of trends in Canadian consumer markets that could modify the face of contemporary business and represent significant opportunity for observant business people. Among the more significant are:

- **"Cocooning"** This was a term originally coined by futurist Faith Popcorn and was viewed as a retreat by consumers to the home environment to escape the stress and congestion of the outside world. This was reflected in a surge in demand for home renovation and hardware products, garden supplies, home security devices, fine furniture, saunas and spas, and a broad range of other home-oriented products and services. Recent social changes have given

[2] John Naisbitt and Patricia Aburdene, *Megatrends 2000* (New York: Avon Books, 1990).

the term an expanded meaning. Older people "cashing out," or retiring early, more businesses being started in the home or people working at home, and similar social changes have contributed to perpetuating this notion. In addition, technology has helped make the establishment of the "home retreat" possible complete with its cellular telephone, personal computer, fax machine, modem, home video, and interactive television.

- **Self Gratification** People who have deprived themselves during the recession of the early 1990s want to play catch-up now and treat themselves. This may be reflected in increased purchases of pricey, upscale products by some consumers; the special treat by others who have built the demand for a broad range of relatively expensive but high quality products such as Häagen Daz ice cream and President's Choice private label products.

- **Staying Alive** The fitness rage of the late 1980s and early 1990s fuelled by the desire to "look good" is over. In the new age the focus will be on long-term health and fitness — moderation, nutrition, fitness, holistic medicine, meditation, and stress management. The baby boomers will strive to remain active, alert, and independent in spite of their advancing years. Such products as New Age remedies, organic foods, and herbal medicines along with services and programs such as yoga, tai chi, and longevity centres combining wellness activities along with entertainment and social interaction are likely to do well.

- **"Wildering"** People are looking for a touch of the outdoors in their lifestyles. This is evidenced by the current popularity of such products as the Jeep, knapsacks, and hiking boots.

- **Save Our Society** This trend shows up in the renewed interest in ethics, education, and the environment. Buying environmentally-friendly products will become more and more mainstream as the young generation of "green" consumers hits the marketplace.

- **Globalnomics** The world is getting smaller and trade treaties will open new markets and alter consumer tastes. These treaties like NAFTA will bring a flood of lower-cost products into Canadian markets but will also provide tremendous opportunity for Canadian businesses to venture abroad.

- **Moving Targets** It is predicted that marketers will need to try some new targeting practice. As more and more men struggle with contemporary societal views and women experiment more with hedonism, products that have traditionally not been marketed to women, such as beer and cars, and to men, such as food, cosmetics, and household products, will be in the future. Gender-specific advertising will diminish or at least change its character.

  It is also predicted that the generation Xers and the baby boomers will merge to form a super market segment that will dictate the social, political, and marketing themes of the next several decades.

- **One-on-One Marketing** There has been a lot of discussion about "customized" marketing and it is now really beginning to happen. Consumers seem to be becoming more concerned with distinctiveness and individuality rather than following the crowd. The relative ease of developing and maintaining a computer data base has now given many companies that capability in a broad range of products such as jeans and other clothing items, cars, homes, vacations, and even perfume.[3]

Any one of these trends would represent an area of significant opportunity for the observant individual. Keeping on top of these shifts can provide the inspiration for many significant new business opportunities. As John Naisbitt has said, "Trends, like horses, are easier to ride in the direction they are going."

---

[3] This list is adapted from Jo Marney, "Towards the Next Millennium," *Marketing*, July 24, 1995, p. 17.

Some Specific Ideas and Concepts for the new Millennium

In view of all these evident trends a number of specific business ideas are expected to do well in the marketplace of the future. The list that follows is by no means complete, but it will give you a few things to think about:

1. The privatization of government services. Due to tight budget pressures, governments at all levels will be looking to shift more and more of their traditional activities to the private sector particularly in the areas of pollution control, technology transfer, and facilities management of such institutions as hospitals, correctional facilities and similar institutions.

2. Children's products and services. Young people, including teens and preteens, have become a significant market in their own right, with considerable exposure to conventional media and billions of dollars of discretionary income of their own. In addition, parents and grandparents increasingly want their children and grandchildren to have "everything" and are prepared to pay for the "best."

3. The aging population will create growth opportunities for many products and services specifically meeting the need of older Canadians. In addition, this group has the highest discretionary income of any age group and, not being burdened by the same financial responsibilities as other market segments, are more likely to spend on themselves. Their diverse needs will create opportunities for business ranging from private nursing homes; large-print book stores; specialized housing developments with health care, recreational, and similar facilities already built in; travel agencies and tour packages specifically developed for the needs of this group; food products, processes and package sizes developed with the requirements of seniors in mind; and a broad range of similar services.

4. Consumer demand for the various types of fast foods seems to be virtually insatiable. While hamburgers, and other beef products, pizza, and Mexican food appear to have stabilized, the market for other food types continues to expand. Low-fat foods such as low-fat shakes and "veggie" burgers, salads, diet menus, and other types of "healthy" food will be hot possibilities.

5. Programs for continuing education and personal self-development will expand. Consumers are looking to renew and improve themselves, and seminars and other educational programs designed to facilitate this personal growth are likely to do well.

6. The automotive after-market is growing and is expected to continue to remain strong. The high price of new automobiles, which is causing consumers to hang onto their cars longer, and the growth of self-service stations without repair facilities are factors that contribute to this situation. Specialized repair shops focussing on such areas as mufflers, brakes, transmissions, cleaning and detailing, painting, and cooling systems are all likely growth businesses.

7. Leisure and recreational activities will continue to grow. Jogging, squash, cross-country skiing, and similar activities appear to be on the wane, but walking, golf, snowboarding, downhill skiing, surfing, and the like are expanding everywhere.

    Specialized sports products and clothing are also increasing in popularity, not only among participants but also among those who merely wish to achieve that "look." In fact, most surf wear, ski jackets, and similar products are sold to non-surfers and non-skiers.

8. Products and services that claim minimal or no impact on the environment or encourage recycling are likely to increase in popularity. Environmentally friendly soaps, cleaners, shampoos, packaging materials, and similar items will probably find a growing market. Similarly, products that can be recycled and systems that provide a means for recycling these items will be successful.

9. Energy management and products that provide for the more efficient use of scarce energy resources will also do well.

10. Increasing consumer affluence and more leisure time will provide endless opportunities for new products and services. Tennis and recreational clubs, full-service campgrounds, exotic travel ideas and tour packages, social clubs and organizations, do-it-yourself concepts, and services that enable people to experience unique activities — from skydiving to bungee jumping — are all likely to do well.

11. Franchising is one of the fast-growth areas of the Canadian economy, and shows very few signs of slowing down. While the concept has principally been associated with the fast food business, the majority of this future growth is likely to occur in other sectors, such as: (1) professional practices in dental care, legal services, optical services, and taxation and financial services; (2) non-food retailing of postal and packaging services, home renovation and repair, temporary health services, printing and copying centres, weight control centres, and hair and beauty salons; (3) convenience services and stores providing home furnishings and accessories, picture framing, rental of home videos, computers and home electronics, and "fill-in" items of various sorts that consumers require between their regular visits to conventional supermarkets and department stores.

EVALUATING YOUR IDEAS

Since it is quite likely you may identify a number of ideas worthy of further investigation, it is helpful to arrange them into related groups. Table 2.1 represents just one way of classifying and grouping your opportunities, but it is structured around a basic logic that you should find helpful. You can use it to classify each of the general ideas you may be considering. For example, how would you categorize each of these ideas on the classification system? (Mark their location in red). Do they tend to fall into a small number of categories or are they all over the place? In what areas of the classification system have you had some previous background or experience? (Mark them in blue or black). Is there much overlap between the categories into which most of your ideas fit and those where you have had significant experience?

Discovering ideas is only part of the process involved in starting a business. The ideas must be screened and evaluated, and a selection made of those that warrant further investigation. It is essential that you subject your ideas to this analysis to find the "fatal flaws," if any exist (and they often do). Otherwise, the marketplace will find them when it is too late and you have spent a great deal of time and money.

Reprinted by permission of United Feature Syndicate, Inc.

TABLE 2.1 A CLASSIFICATION OF BUSINESS OPPORTUNITIES

RETAIL TRADE

1. Food
   a. General grocery
   b. Fast food
   c. Convenience
   d. Snack bar or restaurant
   e. Bar or lounge
   f. Specialty food store
2. General merchandise
3. Apparel and clothing
4. Furniture and appliances
5. Hardware and building materials
6. Specialty stores (flowers, computers, etc.)
7. Door-to-door sales
8. Party plan or home parties
9. Mail order
10. Rental business
11. Craft shows and fairs
12. Swap meets and flea markets

EXTRACTION INDUSTRIES

1. Agriculture
   a. Ranching
   b. Mixed farming
   c. Livestock farming
   d. Horticulture
2. Commercial trapping and fishing
3. Mining
   a. Minerals
   b. Sand and gravel
   c. Petroleum
4. Forestry
   a. Logging
   b. Tree farming
   c. Sawmilling

MANUFACTURING AND PROCESSING

1. Metalworking
   a. Sheet metal
   b. Machine shop
      i. General
      ii. Special
   c. Foundry or mill
2. Plastic
   a. Formulation
   b. Extrusion
   c. Application
3. Food processing
   a. Meat
   b. Vegetables
   c. Prepared and frozen foods
   d. Baked goods
   e. Specialty products

CONSTRUCTION

1. General contracting
2. Subcontracting
   a. Carpentry
   b. Masonry
   c. Plumbing and heating
   d. Electrical
   e. Floor-covering installation
   f. Painting and wallpaper
   g. Roofing and siding
   h. Cabinetry
   i. Drywall
3. Land development
   a. Residential
   b. Commercial
   c. Industrial
4. Repair and renovation
5. Interior decoration

TRANSPORTATION

1. Trucking
2. Rental or charter services
3. Bus, taxi, and limousine services
4. Commercial aviation
   a. Charter service
   b. Crop spraying
   c. Emergency transport

COMMUNICATIONS

1. Broadcast or print media
   a. Commercial printing communications
   b. Newsletters
   c. Audiovisual production
2. Photography
3. Commercial or industrial communications

SERVICES

1. Professional services
   a. Doctor
   b. Lawyer
   c. Dentist
   d. Architect
   e. Chiropractor
   f. Health care
   g. Psychologists
   h. Music and other teachers
2. Financial services
   a. Mutual funds
   b. Financial planning
   c. Brokerage and real estate
   d. Public accounting
   e. Insurance agency
3. Business services
   a. Advertising and promotion
   b. Janitorial
   c. Security
   d. Equipment rental
   e. Temporary help
   f. Training and education
   g. Employment services
   h. Travel services
   i. Equipment maintenance and repair
   j. Management consulting
   k. Research and development
4. Personal services
   a. Barber and beauty shops
   b. Funeral homes
   c. Floor covering and upholstery
   d. Jewelry repair
   e. Shoe and watch repair
   f. Drycleaning and laundry
   g. Appliance repair
   h. Automobile service and repair
   i. Temporary help
   j. Referral services
   k. Training and education programs
   l. Catering
5. Recreational and leisure services
   a. Accommodation
   b. Equipment rental
   c. Theatres and shows
   d. Bowling alleys
   e. Skating rinks
   f. Swimming pools and spas
   g. Ski resort
   h. Golf course
   i. Tennis club
   j. Private lakes and parks
   k. Marinas
   l. Camp grounds
   m. Horse ranches
   n. Gymnasiums
   o. Recreation clubs
   p. Health clubs
   q. Weight control clinics
   r. Dance classes

DISTRIBUTIVE TRADES

1. Manufacturer's agent
2. Jobber
3. Broker
4. Merchant wholesaler

Of course, no matter how exhaustive your evaluation, there is no guarantee of success. The challenge is to make an effort toward conducting a complete evaluation, knowing that at some point you will have to make a decision with incomplete information and less than scientific accuracy.

Richard Buskirk of the University of Southern California has designed a framework you can use to evaluate the pros and cons of your potential business ideas.[4] It is built around what he calls the "Ideal" or "Model" business. The framework contains 19 distinct factors that affect the chances of success for any new business. Very few ideas will conform precisely to the specifications of the model, but the more a business idea deviates from the "ideal," the more difficulties and greater risks you will encounter with that venture. Testing your concepts against the model will also help identify the areas in which you might expect to have difficulties with your business.

The model is presented in Table 2.2. Let us briefly discuss each of the factors listed.

TABLE 2.2 CHARACTERISTICS OF THE "IDEAL" BUSINESS

- Requires no investment
- Has a recognized, measurable market
- A perceived need for the product or service
- A dependable source of supply for required inputs
- No government regulation
- Requires no labour force
- Provides 100 percent gross margin
- Buyers purchase frequently
- Receives favourable tax treatment
- Has a receptive, established distribution system
- Has great publicity value
- Customers pay in advance
- No risk of product liability
- No technical obsolescence
- No competition
- No fashion obsolescence
- No physical perishability
- Impervious to weather conditions
- Possesses some proprietary rights

Requires No Investment If you don't have to put any money into your business, then you can't lose any if it fails. You only lose the time you have invested. The more money that must be committed to the venture, the larger the risk and the less attractive the business becomes. Some new businesses, such as fancy theme restaurants, may require so much initial capital there is really no way they can be financially profitable. Smart business people tend to avoid businesses that require a large investment of their own money.

Has a Recognized, Measurable Market The ideal situation is to sell a product or service to a clearly recognized market that can be relied on to buy it. This may require doing a preliminary investigation of the market acceptance of your idea or concept. Look for some market confirmation of what you propose to offer before proceeding any further.

A Perceived Need for the Product or Service Ideally, your intended customers should already perceive a need for what you intend to sell them. They should know they need your

---

[4] Richard Buskirk, *The Entrepreneur's Handbook* (Los Angeles: Robert Brian, Inc., 1985), pp. 41–45.

product or service now, thus simplifying your marketing efforts. If they don't recognize their need, you have to first persuade them they need the product and then convince them to buy it from you. Try to avoid products or services that require you to educate the market before you can make a sale.

A Dependable Source of Supply for Required Inputs Make certain you can make or provide what it is you plan to sell. Many businesses have failed because they were unable to obtain essential raw materials or components under the terms they had originally planned. Sudden changes in price or availability of these key inputs can threaten the viability of your entire venture. Large corporations commonly try to directly control or negotiate long-term contracts to assure reliable and consistent supplies. You have to be just as concerned if there are only one or two sources for the materials you require.

No Government Regulation The ideal business would not be impacted at all by government regulation. This is impossible in today's world but some industries are more subject to government involvement than others. Food, drugs, financial services, transportation, communications, etc. are all examples of businesses that require extensive government approval. If your business falls into this category, make sure you understand how government regulations will affect you in terms of time and money.

Requires No Labour Force The ideal business would require no labour force. This is possible in one-person operations — the "one-man show." Once you hire an employee you have a lot of government paperwork to deal with relating to unemployment insurance, Canada Pension, and other legal requirements. You are also subject to a broad range of regulations concerning such things as occupational health and safety, human rights, and pay equity. Few small-business people enjoy dealing with these requirements, and they can be quite time-consuming. If your business demands the hiring of additional employees you must be prepared to take on the responsibility for managing these people effectively.

Provides 100 Percent Gross Margin While virtually no businesses provide a 100 percent gross margin, the idea is that the larger the gross margin, the better the business. Gross margin is what you have left after paying the *direct* material and labour costs for whatever it is you are selling. For example, say you are running an appliance repair business. A typical service call takes one hour, for which you charge the customer $50. However, this call costs you $15 in direct labour and $5 in parts and materials; therefore, your gross margin is $30, or 60 percent. Service industries like this generally have larger gross margins than manufacturing businesses.

In businesses with low gross margins, small errors in estimating costs or sales can quickly lead to losses. These businesses also tend to have a high breakeven point, making it very difficult to make a lot of money. High-margin businesses, on the other hand, can break even with very small sales volumes and generate profits very quickly once this volume of business is exceeded.

Buyers Purchase Frequently The ideal business would provide a product or service that customers purchase very frequently. This gives you more opportunities to sell to them. Frequent purchasing also reduces their risk in case your offering doesn't live up to their expectations. You are much more likely to try a new fast food restaurant that has opened in town than you are to purchase a new brand or type of washing machine, fax machine, stereo system, or other such item.

Receives Favourable Tax Treatment Firms in certain industries may receive tax incentives such as accelerated depreciation on capital assets, differential capital cost allowances, investment tax credits, or various other tax breaks. The ideal business will receive some sort of favourable or differential tax treatment. This sort of advantage can make your business more profitable and attractive to other investors should you require outside capital.

Has a Receptive, Established Distribution System Ideally, your business would sell to established middlemen and distributors who are eager to handle it. If you have to develop a new method of distribution or are unable to obtain access to the existing one, getting your product to market can be a long and costly process. If traditional wholesalers and retailers are not prepared to carry your line, achieving any reasonable level of market coverage can be extremely difficult.

Has Great Publicity Value Publicity in magazines, in newspapers, and on television has great promotional value, and what's more, it's free. If your offering is sufficiently exciting and newsworthy to grab people's attention, the resulting publicity may be sufficient to ensure a successful launch for your business. The publicity given to the Chip and Pepper Wetwear, the radio and television coverage of a business to clean up the "doggie doo" in one's backyard, and favourable reviews of local restaurants by newspaper food critics are all examples of tremendously helpful public notice of new products.

Customers Pay in Advance A major problem facing most new businesses is that of maintaining an adequate cash flow. Typically, small firms are chronically short of cash, the lifeblood they require to pay their employees, their suppliers, and the government on an ongoing basis. The ideal business would have customers who pay in advance. This is in fact the case for many small retail service firms, the direct mail industry, and manufacturers of some custom-made products. Businesses where customers pay in advance are usually easier to start, have smaller start-up capital requirements, and don't suffer the losses due to bad debts incurred on credit sales.

No Risk of Product Liability Some products and services are automatically subject to high risk from product liability. Anything ingested by the customer, amusement facilities such as go-cart tracks and water slides, and many manufactured products which possibly could cause injury to the user — all are loaded with potential liability. Liability can occur in unexpected situations, such as the serious injury recently sustained by a golfer whose golf club shattered and impaled him in the chest.

Try to avoid such high-risk businesses, or take every precaution to reduce risk, and carry lots of insurance.

No Technical Obsolescence The ideal product or service would not suffer from technical obsolescence. The shorter the product's expected technical life expectancy, the less desirable it is as an investment. Products like popcorn, shampoo, garden tools, and electric drills seem to have been with us for as long as most of us can remember. On the other hand, the CD player, videocassette recorder, and personal computer are of recent origin and are undergoing rapid technological transformation. Businesses built around these products are extremely risky for smaller firms with a very high probability of failure.

No Competition Too much competition can be a problem, since aggressive price competitors can make it very difficult for you to turn a profit. Not having any competition can certainly make life much easier for a new small business. But if you should ever find yourself in this happy situation, you should ask yourself why. True, your offering may be so new to the marketplace that no other firms have had a chance to get established. But maybe it is just that other firms have already determined there really is no market for what you are planning to provide.

No Fashion Obsolescence Fashion products usually have extremely short life cycles. You must be sure you can make your money before the cycle ends, or be prepared to offer an ongoing series of acceptable products season after season, if you hope to build your business into a sizeable enterprise. Fashion cycles exist not only for clothing and similar products but also for items like toys — witness what happened with the hula hoop, Wacky Wall Walker, Rubik's Cube, and Cabbage Patch dolls.

No Physical Perishability Products with a short physical life have only a limited window available for their disposition. This applies not only to most food items but also to a wide variety of other goods such as photographic film. If your product is perishable, your business concept must include some method of selling your inventory quickly or a contingency plan to dispose of aged merchandise before it spoils.

Impervious to Weather Conditions Some businesses are, by their very nature, at the mercy of the weather. If the weather is right for them, they prosper; if not, they may go broke. Pity the ski resort owner without any snow, the water slide operator with a year of unseasonably cold weather, the beach concession during a summer of constant rain, the market gardener in the midst of an unexpected drought. The ideal business would not be impacted by these unpredictable changes in the weather.

Possesses Some Proprietary Rights The ideal business would possess significant proprietary rights that give it some unique characteristic and protection against competition. These rights can be in the form of registered patents, trademarks, copyrighted material, even protected trade secrets, licensing agreements that provide some sort of exclusive manufacturing arrangements, or perhaps rights for exclusive distribution of certain products in particular markets. Gendis Corporation, for example, was largely built on the rights to distribute first Papermate pens and then Sony products in Canada on an exclusive basis.

To summarize the characteristics of your business in terms of how well it fits with our "Model" business you might wish to complete Figure 2.1.

FIGURE 2.1 COMPARING YOUR IDEA TO THE "IDEAL" BUSINESS

1. Begin by indicating the extent to which your planned new venture possesses or does not possess each of the indicated factors. If your score is Average or Poor, can you think of any way to overcome the situation or other solutions to the problem?

FIT WITH MODEL BUSINESS

	Very Good	Average	Poor
No investment			
Recognized market			
Perceived need			
Dependable supply			
No government regulation			
No labour force			
100% gross margin			
Frequent purchase			
Favourable tax treatment			
Established distribution			
Great publicity value			
Payment in advance			
No liability risk			
No technical obsolescence			
No competition			
No fashion obsolescence			
No physical perishability			
Impervious to weather			
Proprietary rights			

2. Does it still make sense to proceed with your business idea? Can you explain why?

For a more formal evaluation of your invention or innovation, the Canadian Industrial Innovation Centre through the Waterloo Inventor's Assistance program will conduct a comprehensive Critical Factor Assessment to assist you in the product management decisions you must make regarding your idea. The fee for this service ranges for $245 to $595 depending on whether you are a small individual inventor or a large corporation. For more information, contact Canadian Industrial Innovation Centre/Waterloo, 156 Columbia Street West, Waterloo, Ontario, N2L 3L3, Phone 1-800-265-4559 or (519) 885-5870.

DECIDING HOW TO PROCEED

Once satisfied you have identified an idea that represents a significant business opportunity, you must determine the best way to proceed. There are all sorts of *entry strategies* — ways people start new enterprises. Figure 2.2 describes a number of the more common approaches. Pick the one you think most appropriate in your circumstances.

Reflecting on these alternatives and judging how they fit with your specific idea and your particular abilities and circumstances will enable you to turn them into real opportunities. No general rules have been developed to guarantee success, or even to indicate which concepts and strategies will work best in different situations; but being aware of the possibilities will give you a clearer picture of the job you need to do in order to succeed.

FIGURE 2.2 CHOOSING AN ENTRY STRATEGY

Yes **No**

1. One possibility is to find a business presently operating in your area of interest, buy it, and take over its operations. You may want to buy the business either because it is already quite successful but the current owners want to get out for some reason, or because the business is not doing very well under the current owners and you feel you can turn it around.

   This can be a good entry strategy. A good deal of time and effort are involved in the startup phase of any business. This stage can be bypassed when you buy a going concern. You also acquire a location, customers, established trade relationships, and a number of other positive elements.

   These advantages don't come for free, however. Buying an existing business may cost you more than getting into a similar business on your own. The current owner may expect to receive "goodwill" for certain assets already acquired or the effort devoted to the business so far. You may also inherit some problem, such as obsolete equipment, the bad image and reputation of the previous owners, or labour difficulties.

   For a more complete discussion of this entry strategy refer to Stage Three of this book. _____ _____

2. Another alternative is to buy the rights to operate a business that has been designed and developed by someone else, i.e., to acquire a *franchise*. Under a franchise agreement, an established company, the *franchisor*, with one or more successful businesses operating in other locations provides assistance to a new firm in breaking into the marketplace. In return, the new owner, or *franchisee*, pays a fee for the assistance, invests money to set up and operate the business, pays a percentage of sales as a royalty to the franchisor, and agrees to operate the business within the terms and conditions laid out in the franchise agreement. The assistance provided by the franchisor can take many forms, such as:
   • The right to use the franchisor's brand names and registered trademarks
   • The right to sell products and services developed by the franchisor

Yes　No

- The right to use operating systems and procedures developed by the franchisor
- Training in how to run the business
- Plans for the layout of the business facilities and the provision of specialized equipment
- A regional or national advertising program
- Centralized purchasing and volume discounts
- Research and development support

While the failure rate of franchised businesses is reported to be lower than that for independently established firms, there are a number of disadvantages associated with the concept.

For more detailed information refer to Stage Four of this book.　_____　_____

3. The third and probably most common means of getting into business for yourself is to start a business of your own from scratch. This is the route most frequently travelled by the true entrepreneur who wants a business that is really his or her own creation. Starting your own business can take many forms and involve a variety of entry strategies. While we are unable to discuss all the possibilities here in any detail, a few alternatives will be mentioned to get you thinking about their fit with your particular situation. Some of the possibilities available for you are:

   a. Develop an entirely new product or service, one unlike anything else available in the market.　_____　_____

   b. Acquire the rights to manufacture or sell someone else's product under licence. These rights could be exclusive to a geographic area or a specific market.　_____　_____

   c. Recondition or rebuild products that have come to the end of their primary useful life.　_____　_____

   d. Supply raw materials or build components or parts for other firms to incorporate into their market offerings.　_____　_____

   e. Add incremental value to products and services already available in the market. This may involve putting the product through an additional production process, combining it with other products, or providing it as one element in a larger package.　_____　_____

   f. Improve an existing product or service by making it more convenient or inexpensive; safer, slower, cleaner, or faster; easier to package, store, or transport; easier to use; lighter, stronger, adjustable, thinner, or more compact; and so on.　_____　_____

   g. Find a product or service that is doing well in the market and copy it.　_____　_____

   h. Look for products that may have previously failed due to poor management or faulty marketing and develop a new strategy for them.　_____　_____

   i. Look for patents that may have commercial value but which have never been marketed. Arrangements can be made to buy them or license them.　_____　_____

   j. Become an agent or distributor for products or services produced by someone else. These may be domestically produced or imported from other countries.　_____　_____

   k. Open a trading house or become a selling agent for Canadian firms who may be interested in selling their products or services abroad.　_____　_____

continued

Choosing an Entry Strategy — continued

	Yes	No

l. Develop a consulting service or provide information to other people in a subject area you know very well.

m. Find uses for byproducts of other production processes, leftover and surplus material, or imperfect or substandard production of other firms.

n. Improve on existing products by finding lighter, cheaper, or stronger materials from which to make them.

o. Become a supplier to another producer or large institutional customer. Large organizations require an extensive range of raw materials, supplies, and components to run their business. A small portion of their requirements may represent a significant volume of sales for you.

p. Identify an opportunity to replace a product being imported into the country with one produced domestically or vice versa.

q. Identify a situation where another firm has dropped what may still be profitable products or product lines. They may have abandoned customer groups or market segments that are uneconomic for them to serve effectively but which may still be quite lucrative for a smaller company.

r. Combine two or more different products or services into a single offering which may be unique or quite distinct. This could involve combining the sale of a product with an installation program or in conjunction with an extensive service package, for example.

s. Employ the talents and skills of unemployed or underemployed people in the community to your advantage. For example, professionals and trades-people often moonlight on weekends and in the evening. They could provide you with a source of competitive advantage.

t. Borrow an idea from one industry and transfer it to another. A product or service that has been well accepted in one industry situation may well represent a substantial opportunity in other circumstances.

u. Look for products that have been developed by other people but which need more effective distribution or marketing to succeed.

v. Find a product or service that is quite successful in your local market and identify new areas of opportunity, perhaps in another geographic location.

w. Organize and promote conferences, conventions, trade shows, festivals, and other types of meetings and special events.

x. Look for opportunities to capitalize on unusual occurrences or special circumstances or events. You may be able to "piggyback" your business on these situations.

STAGE
THREE

STARTING A NEW BUSINESS OR BUYING AN EXISITNG ONE

Stages One and Two of this book have provided you with a means of evaluating your personal potential for an entrepreneurial career and a procedure for generating and evaluating the basic technical and financial feasibility of an idea upon which to base your own business. The obvious route to self-employment is to start a business of your own based on this idea. Another route which should be explored is that of buying an existing firm. For many people this may even be their preferred course of action. How do you decide which route to take?

Stage Three discusses the various aspects that should be evaluated in considering whether you should start a new business or buy an existing one.

HOW TO FIND THE RIGHT BUSINESS TO BUY

Just finding a business to buy is easy. Dozens are listed every day in the "Business Opportunities" classified section of your local newspaper as well as the major business newspapers. However, what tends to be found in these classified sections are mostly hotel, motel, restaurant, and franchise propositions, which are largely high-risk, low-profit ventures generally unattractive to investors. Many of these are failing businesses that their current owners are trying to unload.

Seeking out a business acquisition to match your desires and experiences can be a very time-consuming and difficult process. Hundreds of businesses change hands every year, so it should be possible to find one that appeals to you if you are sufficiently determined and persistent. However, rather than being sold as a result of an advertisement in some newspaper, most businesses are sold to people who had some active business relationship with the company when it became available. It is usually not sufficient for an individual determined to acquire a business to sit and wait for the right opportunity to come along. One must go looking.

There are basically five different sources through which you may obtain information regarding attractive companies to buy:

1. The first is contact through your present business activity. Acquisition candidates may include present or potential competitors of your current employer; suppliers; customers; and perhaps even your present employer. These situations probably provide the best match

between your experience and strengths and the unique requirements of the business. Doug Morley, for example, was able to acquire the training arm of the company he was working for to run as an independent business (Exhibit 3.1).

2. A second source of leads results from direct independent contact. This may involve making "cold calls" on firms that look good or in which you have an interest; such firms may be identified from Chamber of Commerce directories and trade association membership lists. Another way is to place "Acquisition Wanted" advertisements in several major newspapers. In addition, despite what has been said earlier, you may wish to follow up on some advertisements in the "Business Opportunities" section of the major financial papers as mentioned previously. Every now and then an advertisement may appear in these sections which would warrant your consideration, as evidenced by the case of David Pitt in Exhibit 3.2.

3. A third source of leads is middlemen such as business brokers and commercial real estate agents, professionals who work at bringing buyers and sellers together for a commission.

EXHIBIT 3.1

A "company man" for almost 25 years, Doug Morley left the giant Honeywell Bull organization in 1990 when he saw middle-management jobs being squeezed by the recession.

An entrepreneur at heart, if not in practice, he bought the computer arm of Honeywell Bull, called the Institute for Computer Studies, a division he helped establish in the early 1980s to educate computer programmers and systems analysts.

In the past five years, the 53-year-old businessman has seen the institute grow from an organization that employed four trainers, taught 100 students a year and had revenue under $1 million, to one that has eight full-time instructors (plus 14 on contract), 350 students, a corporate education division, and annual revenue of about $7 million.

When he made the move, Morley remembers, some friends and colleagues questioned his decision. Under Honeywell Bull, the institute was basically a break-even operation, he says. "It did one thing: computer programming and systems analysis."

He was convinced there was room for growth in this fast-changing field. He also believed he could expand the business in a privately owned organization in ways he could not inside a large corporation.

First, Morley became the self-described chief cook and bottlewasher. "When we started I was the bookkeeper, janitor, I fixed the computers, … I did everything." That helped chop about $100,000 off the overhead.

Hard work and quality training account for the rest of the institute's success, says Morley.

The Institute offers two courses: the career college geared at individuals who want to enhance their computer skills, and the other at corporations that want employees brought up to speed with advanced technology training.

Individuals pay about $8,800 for an intensive five-month program for which the institute is licensed by the Ontario Ministry of Education and Training to issue diplomas. Corporate education costs about $375 a day (usually for three- to five-day stints) in classes of eight people. (That compares with 30 students a class in the five-month course).

Clients include Bell Canada, Ontario Hydro, and Bank of Montreal.

Morley says that, since opening the doors of his own business, he has not looked back. The timing, he adds, was just right.

"Large companies have changed in the past five years. When I left they were downsizing and everybody was scrambling.

"I just didn't want to be in that environment. So I decided to create an environment of my own, where I can do what I like in an organization with people I like."

Source: Excerpted from Gayle MacDonald, "Taking an Educated Gamble on Learning," *The Financial Post*, May 13, 1995, p. 34.

EXHIBIT 3.2

David Pitt had no idea his life was about to change four years ago when he opened the newspaper and glanced through the classified ads.

He had just wanted another job — life on the road as a medical publications salesman was taking him away from his young family too often.

And then he spotted an interesting ad — Worm Farm For Sale.

Pitt plunked down $7,500 and the business was his. From medical texts to worms in one easy leap.

Sure-Sprout Environmental Products is now a thriving business. And Pitt has spent the past four years delving deeply into the world of vermiculture — the care and feeding of worms.

"There's more to a worm than we realize," he said poking a purplish African crawler to frantic life in the palm of his hand.

Pitt operated the business from his basement at first, but when he tripled the stock in three months he moved into a store. He ran out of space again last year and landed in a spacious old workshop in September.

"The demand for worms is incredible," Pitt said.

Pitt also scoured the libraries for "wormlore" and recruited his father Ernie and wife Darlene to help out. …

Pitt's worm farm is actually several businesses.

First, there's the worms, and Pitt has two kinds: African crawlers and Redworms.

Redworms are bred for the vermi-composting business. They turn kitchen scraps into high-quality nutrient-enriched soil conditioner, and come in a bright red plastic composter for about $60. Redworms are sold by weight, about $11.25 per kilogram.

African crawlers, which sell $60 for 1,000, are a tropical worm which, unlike Canadian nightcrawlers, need no refrigeration. They're "frisky" on the end of a hook and prized by anglers.

Pitt estimates gross sales will approach $150,000 this year. His biggest cost is serving dinner to the troops, who consume their own weight in feed every 24 hours.

Excerpted from "Tired of travelling, salesman wriggles into new job — worm farming," *Winnipeg Free Press*, May 10, 1992, p. A3. Courtesy of Press News Limited.

The commission, typically payable by the seller, varies with the size of the deal but may be as high as 10 percent of the negotiated purchase price.

4. A fourth source is confidential advisors such as the loans officer at your bank, securities brokers, professional accountants, and lawyers. These advisors are often aware of what businesses are or may soon be available for sale. These sources may be difficult to use, however, because their information is shared mostly with other clients with whom they have developed some relationship over time. In many cases it may be necessary for you to have gained the confidence of the source over an extended period.

5. A fifth category includes a variety of different sources, such as venture capital firms, personal friends and acquaintances, and insurance brokers and agents. Essentially you should consider all individuals within your personal network of business contacts who may have access to information on attractive businesses for sale. This requires letting many of these people know about your search and the kind of business for which you are looking. You will need to keep reminding them about your interest, so that when the information comes along there is a good probability that it will make its way back to you.

Which of these lead sources you should utilize depends on many factors, such as the time you have available, whom you know within the business community, and the kind of company you are looking for. You should experiment with each of these sources and decide on the one or two that work best for you.

IMPORTANT FACTORS TO CONSIDER

An essential requirement for the successful purchase of an existing firm is knowing how to assess and evaluate the operation. This is a complicated process, so you are well advised to have professionals such as an accountant, lawyer, or business evaluator assist you in negotiations when considering buying a business. As a potential buyer, you should also have a good understanding of the nature of the target business and the industry in which it competes to be able to assess its future performance, strengths, weaknesses, unexploited market opportunities, and other factors. Learning about a business after the fact can be a sure recipe for failure. A number of basic factors must be considered in determining the value of the business to you. Some of these are more complex and involved than others, but each one must be carefully investigated and studied. The most important of these concerns are discussed below.

Why Is the Business for Sale?

You should have this question in mind at all times during the evaluation of a possible acquisition. When the owner of a business decides to dispose of it, the reason presented to the public may be somewhat different from the facts of the situation. Owners may be quite willing to express some reasons for wanting to sell their businesses. They wish to retire, or they want to move to another city, or illness is pressuring the owner to leave the business. But there are a number of others that the current owner may not be quite so likely to volunteer. For example, they may be experiencing family pressures or marital problems, or perhaps they see a better business opportunity somewhere else. None of these reasons is cause for concern. But what if the company needs more financing than the owner can raise, or the current market for the firms' products is depressed? What if competitors are moving in with more effective products or methods, or the current plant and equipment is worn out or obsolete, and the firm is no longer able to compete successfully? And what if the firm is having to contend with new government regulations that are creating some difficulties, or certain key employees are leaving the firm to set up a business of their own?

As you can see, there are many possible explanations of why a business may be up for sale. It is important that you retain a sceptical attitude, because behind each of the offered explanations may be a number of hidden ones. A sceptical attitude forces you to examine the situation from all angles and not necessarily accept everything you are told at face value. When the real reasons for selling are factors that may lead to the eventual collapse of the company, the present owner may be hard pressed to justify your purchase of the enterprise.

This is not to say that all businesses for sale are bad buys. Many companies are sold for very plausible and honest reasons. However, to keep from losing your shirt as well as your savings, a detailed evaluation should be conducted in order to determine the true character of the business.

Financial Factors

An analysis of the financial statements of the firm being sold, preferably with the help of a professional accountant, can help you assess its current health. You should not fall into the trap, however, of accepting these statements as the absolute truth. Though the statements may have been audited, many accounting techniques allow business owners to present a less than accurate picture of the financial situation of their company. You must be careful to ensure that the statements have not been biased in favour of the seller.

The most important financial factors are: (1) the trend in profits, (2) ratio analysis, (3) the value of the business' tangible assets, (4) the value of the business' intangible assets, and (5) cash flow. Let us discuss each in turn.

The Trend in Profits

A study of the records of the business will indicate whether sales volume and profits have been increasing or decreasing. If they have been going up, it is useful to know which departments within the business, or products within the firm's product line, have accounted for this increased sales and/or profitability.

If sales and profits are declining, the question may arise as to whether this is due to a failure by the firm to keep up with the competition, to its inability to adjust to changing circumstances, or perhaps to a lack of selling effort. Some experience with this type of business situation, plus a few questions directed to appropriate sources, may elicit an explanation.

Ratio Analysis

For every size and type of business there are certain financial ratios that have become generally accepted as reasonable for that kind of operation. Some information on these ratios is collected and published by trade organizations and associations such as the National Retail Hardware Association or the National Association of Retail Grocers. Ratios have been developed by various manufacturers for use by retailers that handle their product lines. Ratios for firms in a wide variety of retail, service, and manufacturing sectors are published by Dun & Bradstreet, Robert Morris and Associates, and other companies. A study of the ratios of any business offered for sale, compared with standard ratios for that industry and size of company, will quickly indicate any discrepancies. These discrepancies may be due to mismanagement, neglect, carelessness, or perhaps even the lack of appropriate financing. The most frequently considered ratios are:

1. **Current ratio** The current ratio is defined as current assets divided by current liabilities. It is a measure of short-term solvency. Current assets normally include cash, marketable securities, accounts receivable, and inventories. Current liabilities consist of accounts payable, short-term notes payable, income taxes payable, and accrued expenses. A general rule of thumb is that a current ratio of 2:1 could be considered satisfactory for a typical manufacturing business. Service firms typically have a lower ratio, since they tend to have less inventory. However, as with any rule of thumb, extreme care should be exercised in evaluating this ratio. A cash-poor firm may be unable to pay its bills even though its ratio appears to be acceptable. On the other hand, many businesses with a current ratio less than the rule of thumb are quite solvent.

   Too high a ratio can indicate the business is not utilizing its cash and other liquid assets very efficiently; too low a ratio may raise questions about the firm's ability to meet its short-term obligations. In practice, however, what is more important than the absolute level of the current ratio is how the ratio is changing over time. An improving current ratio would tend to indicate improved short-term financial solvency unless the business is building up excessive or obsolete inventories.

   $$\text{Current Ratio} = \frac{\text{Current Assets}}{\text{Current Liabilities}}$$

2. **Quick ratio** The quick ratio is obtained by dividing current liabilities into current assets minus inventories. The quick ratio can be used to estimate the ability of a firm to pay off its short-term obligations without having to sell its inventory. Inventories tend to lose their value faster than other assets if disposed of in a hurry. The quick ratio is probably a more valid test of the firm's ability to meet its current liabilities and pay its bills than the current ratio.

   $$\text{Quick Ratio} = \frac{\text{Current Assets} - \text{Inventories}}{\text{Current Liabilities}}$$

3. **Debt to net worth** The debt-to-net-worth ratio indicates the firm's obligations to its creditors relative to the owner's level of investment in the business. Debt includes current liabilities, long-term loans, bonds, and deferred payments; the owner's net worth includes the value of common stock, preferred stock, any capital surplus, and retained earnings. Any outstanding shareholder's loans to the business should be considered part of the owner's net worth rather than as part of the business' present debt. This ratio is commonly used by creditors to assess the risk involved in lending to the firm. For example, if the debt-to-net-worth ratio is too high, say about 2:1 or 3:1, you may find it difficult to borrow additional funds for the business. Too low a ratio, on the other hand, may indicate the business is not being operated very efficiently and some profits are being sacrificed.

$$\text{Debt-to-Net-Worth Ratio} = \frac{\text{Total Outstanding Current and Long-Term Debt}}{\text{Net Worth}}$$

4. **Gross profit to sales** This ratio is determined by dividing gross profit or gross margin by net sales. Gross profit is determined by deducting costs of goods sold from net sales. No general guidelines exist for this ratio, or even among companies within an industry, as it can vary substantially.

$$\text{Gross-Profit-to-Sales Ratio} = \frac{\text{Gross Profit}}{\text{Net Sales}}$$

5. **Net profit to sales** This ratio is calculated by dividing net profit by net sales. You may use net profit either before or after taxes. As with the previous ratio, no general guidelines exist because of the variability among companies and industries. This figure can be as low as 1 percent or less for retail food stores and supermarkets, and as high as 8 or 9 percent in some service sectors.

However, you might evaluate how these ratios compare with those of other, similar companies or how they have been changing over time. If the ratio has recently been declining, why? This may indicate that the firm's costs have been increasing without a commensurate increase in prices, or perhaps competition may have increased and the company is forced to keep its prices low in order to compete.

$$\text{Net-Profit-to-Sales Ratio} = \frac{\text{Net Profit (Before or After Taxes)}}{\text{Net Sales}}$$

6. **Return on assets** This ratio is determined by dividing net profit (before or after taxes) by total assets. It is an excellent indicator of whether all the firm's assets are contributing to its profits and how effectively the assets are being employed — the real test of economic success or failure. Unfortunately, this is not an easy ratio to apply, because it is a measure of the movement of assets in relation to sales and profits during a particular period of time. The methods used by accountants to determine the level of total assets in the business can have a great effect on this ratio, and there are no real general or convenient rules of thumb for finding out whether the current return on assets is acceptable.

$$\text{Return on Assets} = \frac{\text{Net Profit (Before or After Taxes)}}{\text{Total Assets}}$$

7. **Sales to Inventory** This ratio is determined by dividing annual net sales by the average value of inventories. This does not indicate actual physical turnover since inventories are usually valued at cost while sales are based on selling prices, including markups, but this

ratio does provide a reasonable yardstick for comparing stock-to-sales ratios of one business with another or with the average values for the industry.

$$\text{Sales to Inventory Ratio} = \frac{\text{Net Sales}}{(\text{Beginning Inventory} + \text{Ending Inventory})/2}$$

8. **Collection Period** To determine the average collection period for the business' outstanding accounts receivable, annual net sales are divided by 365 days to determine the business' average daily credit sales. These average daily credit sales are then divided into accounts receivable to obtain the average collection period. This ratio is helpful in assessing the collectability of any outstanding receivables.

$$\text{Average Collection Period} = \frac{\text{Accounts Receivable}}{\text{Net Sales} / 365}$$

All these ratios are calculated from information on the firm's income statement or balance sheet. Figures 3.1 and 3.2 illustrate simplified financial statements for a hypothetical firm called The Appleton Co. The value of each of these ratios for that company would be as follows:

1. Current ratio $= \dfrac{\$158,000}{\$95,000} = 1.66$

2. Quick ratio $= \dfrac{\$78,000}{\$95,000} = 0.82$

3. Debt to net worth $= \dfrac{\$135,000}{\$50,000} = 2.70$

4. Gross profit to sales $= \dfrac{\$133,000}{\$425,000} = 0.31$ or 31%

5. Net profit to sales $= \dfrac{\$13,500}{\$425,000} = 0.03$ or 3%

6. Return on assets $= \dfrac{\$13,500}{\$185,000} = 0.07$ or 7%

7. Sales to Inventory Ratio $= \dfrac{\$425,000}{(\$75,000 + 80,000)/2} = 5.48$

8. Average Collection Period $= \dfrac{\$53,000}{\$425,000/365} = 45$ days

It would appear from these ratios that The Appleton Co. is in reasonably sound shape financially. Its debt-to-net-worth ratio is within acceptable limits, and the business is quite solvent as indicated by the current and quick ratios. The other ratios are more difficult to evaluate, but they would be quite acceptable for firms in many lines of business.

FIGURE 3.1   EXAMPLE OF SIMPLIFIED BALANCE SHEET

THE APPLETON CO.
BALANCE SHEET
AS OF DECEMBER 31, 19Y0

ASSETS		(000s)	
Current Assets			
Cash		$ 25	
Accounts receivable		53	
Inventory		80	
Total current assets			$ 158 **(A)**
Fixed Assets			
Machinery	$ 40		
Less: Accumulated depreciation	25	15	
Equipment and fixtures	30		
Less: Accumulated depreciation	18	12	
Total fixed assets			27 **(B)**
Total Assets (C = A + B)			$ 185 **(C)**
LIABILITIES AND OWNER'S EQUITY			
Current Liabilities*			
Accounts payable	$ 60		
Notes payable	35		
Total current liabilities		95	
Long-Term Liabilities			
Notes payable†	$ 40		
Total long-term liabilities		40	
Total liabilities			$ 135 **(D)**
OWNER'S EQUITY			
Capital investment		20	
Retained earnings		30	
Total owner's equity			50 **(E)**
Total Liabilities and Owner's Equity (F = D + E)			$ 185 **(F)**

* Debt is due within 12 months.
† Debt is due after 1 year.

To illustrate the range of possible values for each of these ratios, some typical examples for Canadian companies in a number of industries are shown in Table 3.1. Notice that there can be considerable variation in the value of each ratio within economic sectors as well as between sectors. Within a sector these ratios represent an average for each industry code and, therefore, may be somewhat misleading. These figures include a range of firms, some of which may be doing extremely well and others that may be on the verge of bankruptcy. The variations from sector to sector are largely due to structural differences that impact the financial profile of firms in each line of business in quite different ways.

Keep in mind that financial ratios are open to wide interpretation and should only be relied on to get a general perspective on the relative financial health of the business, to measure the financial progress of the business from one time period to another, or to flag major deviations from an industry or sector norm.

Value of Tangible Assets

In assessing the balance sheet of the prospective acquisition, you must determine the actual or real value of the tangible assets. A physical count of the inventory must be taken to determine if the actual level corresponds to the level stated on the balance sheet. This inventory must also be appraised in terms of its age, quality, saleability, style, condition, balance, freshness, etc. Most large inventories will have some obsolescence. You must determine whether the present inventory is consistent with current market conditions. Also, take care that the seller does not sell this inventory after you have checked it. Any consignment goods in inventory should be clearly identified as well. This evaluation is best performed by someone with considerable experience in the industry involved. Perhaps you can hire the services of the owner of a similar but non-competing firm to assist you in this appraisal.

You must also check the age of any outstanding accounts receivable. Some businesses continue to carry accounts receivable on their books that should have been charged off to bad debts, resulting in an overstatement of the firm's profit and value. Generally, the older the receivables, the lower their value. Old outstanding accounts may reveal a slack credit policy by the present owner. These old accounts will have to be discounted in determining the present value of the business.

FIGURE 3.2 EXAMPLE OF SIMPLIFIED INCOME STATEMENT

THE APPLETON CO.
INCOME STATEMENT
FOR YEAR ENDING DECEMBER 31, 19Y0

		(000s)	
Gross sales	$428		
Less: Returns	3		
Net Sales		**$425**	**(A)**
Cost of goods sold:			
Beginning inventory	$ 75		
Plus: Net purchases	297		
Cost of goods available	372		
Less: Ending inventory	80		
Cost of Goods Sold		292	**(B)**
Gross Profit (C = A − B)		$133	**(C)**
Selling expenses		$ 29	**(D)**
Administrative expenses:			
Office salaries	$ 60		
Interest	9		
Depreciation	10		
Other administrative expenses	7		
Total Administrative Expenses		86	**(E)**
Profit Before Income Tax (F = C − D − E)		$ 18	**(F)**
Income Tax (G = 25% of F)		4.5	**(G)**
Net Profit (G = F − G)		$ 13.5	**(H)**

The fixed assets of the business must also be scrutinized. You should determine if the furniture, fixtures, equipment, and building are stated at their market or depreciated value. Some questions you should ask include: How modern are these assets? Are they in operating condition? How much will it cost to keep these assets in operation? Are the assets all paid for? You must be aware of any liens or chattel mortgages which may have been placed against these assets. This pledging of assets to secure a debt is a normal business practice; however, you should know about any such mortgages. Other liabilities such as unpaid bills, back taxes, back pay to employees, and so on, may be hidden; you must be aware of the possibility of their existence, and contract with the seller that all claims not shown on the balance sheet will be assumed by him or her.

TABLE 3.1 KEY BUSINESS RATIOS IN CANADA — CORPORATIONS

Line of Business	I Current Ratio (Times)	III Debt/ Net Worth (Times)	IV Gross Profit/ Sales (%)	V Net Profit/ Sales (%)	VI Return on Assets (%)	VII Sales to Inventory (Times)	VIII Collection Period (Days)
ALL COMPANIES	1.0	2.23	33.1	7.1	11.3	7.6	—
RETAIL TRADE	1.4	2.17	25.7	2.5	20.9	6.4	—
Books & stationery stores	1.3	3.05	37.4	2.3	22.0	5.0	—
Women's clothing	1.5	2.06	43.0	3.5	12.8	5.6	—
Florists	1.2	2.71	53.6	2.6	24.0	10.6	—
Furniture and appliances	1.5	2.00	30.7	1.9	13.0	4.7	—
Shoe stores	1.5	1.40	42.9	1.8	8.1	3.5	—
Variety stores	1.6	1.58	28.1	1.8	12.1	4.9	—
WHOLESALE TRADE	1.3	2.19	18.2	1.9	14.0	7.4	39
Food	1.3	1.84	12.7	1.9	21.4	16.6	20
Metal products	1.3	2.54	15.6	2.5	19.4	6.3	53
Petroleum products	1.1	1.32	10.6	1.7	8.7	28.5	30
MANUFACTURERS	1.5	1.20	22.7	4.5	12.4	7.2	42
Bakery products	1.2	.89	30.0	5.3	17.8	28.0	20
Women's clothing	1.6	1.71	22.6	2.8	16.8	5.7	58
Fruit and vegetable canners	1.5	1.31	28.2	4.8	20.0	5.0	27
Heating equipment	1.9	2.13	23.2	4.0	17.8	3.8	67
Metal fabricating	1.5	1.45	23.5	5.9	20.2	6.4	60
Sawmills and planing mills	1.6	1.38	20.5	7.3	21.2	6.5	30
CONSTRUCTION	1.3	2.75	24.5	3.2	23.3	10.5	60
Building contractors	1.3	4.00	14.5	2.7	25.3	6.3	56
SERVICES	1.0	2.45	79.6	7.0	23.5	—	—
Funeral directors	1.5	1.70	81.3	11.1	20.5	—	—
Hotels	0.7	3.65	52.2	2.9	15.5	—	—
Recreational services	1.0	3.85	92.8	21.0	145.9	—	—
TRANSPORTATION, STORAGE, AND UTILITIES	0.8	2.51	78.0	6.6	9.9	—	46
Radio and TV	0.9	1.84	99.5	4.7	6.6	—	51
Taxicabs	1.1	2.23	96.4	6.4	24.1	—	37
Truck transport	0.9	2.64	99.0	2.7	16.4	—	45

Adapted from *Key Business Ratios*, 1990, Dun & Bradstreet International.

Value of Intangible Assets

In addition to the more obvious physical goods and equipment, certain intangible assets may also have a real value to a prospective purchaser. Among the most important of these are goodwill, franchise and licensing rights, and patents, trademarks, and copyrights.

You must be very realistic in determining what you can afford or are prepared to pay for goodwill. Is the public's present attitude toward the business a valuable asset that is worth money, or is it a liability? Typically, few businesses that are for sale have much goodwill value. Is any goodwill associated with the business personal to the owner or largely commercial due to the location, reputation, and other characteristics of the business? If largely personal, this goodwill may not be transferable to a new owner so you should not pay very much for it. Many business owners, however, often have very unrealistic and inflated ideas of the goodwill associated with their business because they have built it up over the years with their own "sweat equity" and, therefore, are not very objective. So you should be careful, and talk to customers, suppliers, neighbours, employees, and perhaps even competitors, to determine if this level of goodwill in fact exists.

If franchise, licensing, or other rights are involved in the business, you should make certain that you understand the terms and conditions associated with such rights, and that these rights will be in fact transferred to you upon acquisition of the company. An effort should also be made to determine the market value of any patents, trademarks, or copyrights the company may hold, and make sure these are part of the sale — i.e., do not remain with the current owner upon completion of the transaction.

Cash Flow

You must also observe the cash flows generated by the operation. A business can be very profitable, but chronically low in cash due to overly generous credit terms, excessive inventory levels, or heavy fixed interest payments. You must assure yourself that upon your entry into the business you would have sufficient inflows of cash to meet your cash outflow requirements. Constant cash problems can indicate that the business is possibly being run by ineffective management or that the firm's resources have generally been badly allocated. You must ask yourself if you have the know-how to overcome this misallocation of resources. If the firm's cash flow is very low, and the long-term debt is quite high, the business may be eating up its capital to pay the debt, or possibly defaulting on its debt. If you are to contend with such issues, you may have to increase the firm's debt or be prepared to invest more capital in the business in order to ease the cash flow problem.

Marketing Considerations

The previous section deals with the internal aspects of the firm's profitability; there has been no discussion of the external determinants of these conditions. But you must be concerned with analyzing markets, customers, competition, and various other aspects of the company's operating environment.

You must carefully examine the company's current market situation. Each market segment served by the firm must be analyzed and understood. Studying maps, customer lists, traffic patterns, and other factors can help you to determine the normal market size for the business. Once the market and its various segments are understood, the composition of these segments should be determined in order to identify the approximate number of customers in the total market. As a buyer, you should be concerned with:

1. The company's trading area
2. Population demographics
3. The trend and size of the market

4. Recent changes in the market

5. Future market patterns

All these factors help in determining whether the firm's market area is changing, or there is a declining relevant population, or technological or other changes may be creating an obsolete operation.

This kind of information can assist you in assessing trends in the level of the business' market penetration. For example, if its market share has been increasing, then perhaps you should anticipate further growth. But if the business' market penetration has been declining or static, you should be aware that something could be wrong with the operation. It may be that the business is nearing the end of its life cycle. A shrewd seller, aware that the operation is approaching a natural decline, may be bailing out.

Competition facing the business must also be evaluated and understood. First and foremost, you should make sure that the present owner will not remain in competition with you. Very often an owner will dispose of a business only to open up a similar operation. If the business is largely based on the personality and contacts of the owner, you may be hard pressed to maintain the necessary rapport with customers, suppliers, and financial sources. A legal agreement may help ensure that the vendor will not go on to compete with you.

Another aspect of assessing competition is to look at that presently faced by the firm. You should be aware of the business' major competitors and what trends can be foreseen in the nature of their activity. Most of this information can be obtained either from direct observation or by talking with other people in the business.

Other aspects of the environment also should not be overlooked. You must be tuned in to developments in the economy, changes in technology, government policy and regulations, and trends in society at large that can affect your business situation. Your banker or other professionals may be able to tell you what the experts are saying about such variables. Both national and regional economic factors must be studied in order to develop accurate projections as to the size of the market opportunity available to the business.

Human Factors

When a business is being purchased, manpower must be considered equal in importance to financial and marketing factors, for usually it is desirable to retain certain key people to provide some continuity. As a prospective buyer, you should assess the value of the company's personnel and try to become acquainted with the attitudes of the present employees. For example, will key employees continue to work for the firm under your management? If these key people are likely to leave, you must anticipate the consequences.

Both the quality and the quantity of trained personnel must be evaluated. The skill level of the employees has some bearing on the sale value of the business. Highly trained staff, for example, can increase the seller's bargaining power. On the other hand, inefficient and poorly trained staff may permit you to negotiate a lower purchase price because of the long-term expense involved in retraining or hiring additional employees.

Other Concerns

In assessing a business to buy, you will also have to take into account a number of other factors. These include various legal considerations as well as past company policies. The legal aspects of doing business are becoming increasingly more complex and the use of a lawyer is practically a fact of business life. A lawyer can help you in such areas as deciding on an appropriate form of legal organization; identifying real estate documents such as zoning restrictions and covenants that may put you at a disadvantage; labour laws and union regulations; complying with all licensing and permit requirements; the transferability of intangible assets such as copyrights, patents, dealerships, and franchises; and whether buying the shares or the assets of the firm is the most advantageous way of purchasing the company.

You should also have some understanding of the historical practices of the firm relating to employees, customers, and suppliers if future policies are to enhance your opportunities for business growth. An evaluation of these practices and policies will determine if you should continue with past practices or make modifications. If you fail to do so, you may eventually find yourself in a situation where you have to continue policies that are ill-advised in the long run. For example, it may be necessary to tighten credit policies or make a change in labour practices, even though this may cause a short-term loss of customers or employees.

HOW TO DETERMINE AN APPROPRIATE PRICE TO PAY FOR A BUSINESS

Buying a business is a serious matter involving a substantial financial and personal investment. A business bought at the wrong price, or at the wrong time, can cost you and your family much more than just the dollars you have invested and lost. After you have thoroughly investigated a business opportunity according to the factors in the previous section, weighed the wealth of information you have gathered, and decided that your expectations have been suitably fulfilled, a price must be agreed upon with the seller.

Determining an appropriate price to pay for a business is a complex and technical process. If you are making this determination on your own, you should either have a sound knowledge of general accounting principles and evaluation techniques or use the services of a professional accountant.

Setting the purchase price for a going concern typically involves two separate kinds of evaluations:

1. **Balance sheet methods** — evaluation of the firm's tangible net assets
2. **Earnings-based methods** — evaluation of the firm's expected future earnings

The balance sheet methods are generally less reliant on estimates and forecasts than the earnings-based methods; however, it should be remembered that they totally ignore the future earnings capability of the business.

Balance Sheet Methods

If the company has a balance sheet, the quickest means of determining a valuation figure is to look at its net worth as indicated there. You simply take the total assets as shown in the financial statement and subtract total liabilities to get the *net book value*. The advantage of this method is that for most firms the numbers are readily available.

Its drawbacks, however, are numerous. The company's accounting practices will have a big impact on its book value. Similarly, book value does not necessarily reflect the fair market value of the assets or the liabilities. For example, buildings and equipment shown on the balance sheet may be depreciated below their actual market value, or land may have appreciated above its original cost. These differences will not be reflected on the company's balance sheet. Despite these drawbacks, however, net book value may be useful in establishing a reference point when considering the asset valuation of a business. This approach is illustrated in Section I of Figure 3.3 on the basis of the balance sheet for The Appleton Company presented in Figure 3.1.

FIGURE 3.3   APPLICATION OF BALANCE SHEET METHODS

BUSINESS VALUATION — THE APPLETON CO.
BALANCE SHEET METHODS

	(000s)
I. NET BOOK VALUE	
Total stockholder's equity*	$ 50
Net Book Value	**$ 50**
II. MODIFIED BOOK VALUE	
Net book value	$ 50
Plus:	
Excess of appraised market value of building and equipment over book value	25
Value of patent not on books	10
Modified Book Value	**$ 85**
III. LIQUIDATION VALUE	
Net book value	$ 50
Plus:	
Excess of appraised liquidation value of fixed assets over book value	9
Less:	
Deficit of appraised liquidation value of inventory over book value	(5)
Deficit due to liquidation of accounts receivable	(3)
Costs of liquidation and taxes due upon liquidation	(8)
Liquidation Value	**$ 43**

* Item E from Figure 3.1.

To correct for differences from the real situation, you may wish to make some modifications to create a *modified book value*. This is simply the book value adjusted for major differences between the stated book value and the fair market value of the company's fixed assets and liabilities. This refinement of the plain book value approach still has a number of drawbacks, but it does, however, give a more accurate representation of the value of the company's assets at current market value than book value does. The application of this method is illustrated in Section II of Figure 3.3.

A third approach is to go beyond the books of the company to get a more detailed evaluation of specific assets. Generally this involves determining the *liquidation value* of the assets or how much the seller could get for the business or any part of it if it were suddenly thrown onto the market. This approach is ordinarily a highly conservative evaluation and, as such, is frequently useful in determining the lowest valuation in a range of values to be considered. The liquidation value approach is presented in Section III of Figure 3.3.

Earnings Methods

In most cases a going concern is much more than just the sum of its physical assets. While the cost of reproducing or liquidating these assets can be closely determined, the cost of duplicating the firm's experience, management, technical know-how, and reputation is not so easily determined. These intangible factors will be reflected in the firm's past and expected future earnings.

To study past earnings trends, it is important to select a time period that is true and representative. A period of five years is generally considered to be an appropriate length of time to observe an earnings trend; however, economic cycles and other factors must be taken into consideration.

Once earnings have been determined, various approaches can be used in order to determine an appropriate price. The most popular approach is a simple *capitalization of an average of past profits* or *capitalization of earnings*. In this method, the profits for a selected period of years are adjusted for unusual items and an appropriate capitalization rate is applied to the average profit level derived. (See Figure 3.4, and Section I of Figure 3.6.)

A variation on this method is to weight the earnings of prior years to give greater emphasis to more recent profit levels (for example, the most recent year is given a weight of 5, the previous year 4, the next previous year 3, and so on).

The major advantage of this approach is that it is easy to use. However, the selection of an appropriate capitalization rate or multiple to apply to past or expected future earnings is not a simple, straightforward process. For illustrative purposes we have selected a desired rate of return of 16 percent, or approximately six times earnings in Figure 3.6.

The rate that can be earned on secure investments usually serves as the "base" rate or minimum capitalization rate that would be used. The chosen capitalization rate is really an assessment of the risk you perceive to be related to the business in comparison to the risk related to obtaining the "base" rate. It is an indication of the rate of return you are prepared to accept for assuming that risk in relation to the rates of return you could earn from other, more secure investments such as bonds, guaranteed income certificates, etc.

The selection of a capitalization rate can have a large impact on your evaluation of a business. If, for example, your desired rate of return is increased from 16 percent to 20 percent in Figure 3.6, the estimated value of The Appleton Co. based on capitalization of their past earnings would be reduced from $60,000 to $48,000. The estimated values using discounted future earnings and discounted cash flow would be similarly reduced if we were to use a 20 percent rather than a 16 percent expected rate of return.

FIGURE 3.4 EXAMPLE OF SUMMARY OF EARNINGS SHEET

THE APPLETON CO.
SUMMARY OF EARNINGS FOR PAST FOUR YEARS

Year	Earnings After Taxes (000s)
0	$13.5
−1	12.1
−2	10.8
−3	7.2
−4	4.6

FIGURE 3.5 EXAMPLE OF PROJECTED INCOME SHEET

THE APPLETON CO.
PROJECTED FIVE-YEAR EARNINGS AND CASH FLOW

Year	Projected Earnings After Taxes (000s)	Projected Cash Flow (000s)
+1	$14.0	$16.9
+2	16.8	21.1
+3	20.2	26.4
+4	24.2	33.0
+5	29.0	41.2

Assumptions:
1. Earnings are expected to grow at a rate of 20% per year.
2. Cash flow is expected to grow at a rate of 25% per year.

FIGURE 3.6 APPLICATION OF EARNINGS METHODS

BUSINESS VALUATION — THE APPLETON CO.
EARNINGS METHODS

I. CAPITALIZATION OF EARNINGS

	Average Earnings Over Past Five Years (Figures 3.2 and 3.4) (000s)
19X6	$ 4.6
19X7	7.2
19X8	10.8
19X9	12.1
19Y0	13.5
Total	$48.2 in the previous 5 years

Average Earnings = $9.6

Divided By: Investor's desired rate of return = 16%*

Value of Company Based on Capitalization of Past Earnings = 9.6 x 100/16 = $60.0

II. DISCOUNTED FUTURE EARNINGS

	Projected After-Tax Earnings (Figure 3.5) (000s)	x	Present Value Factor Assuming 16% Return	=	Present Value of After-Tax Earnings (000s)
+1	$ 14.0		0.862		$12.1
+2	16.8		0.743		12.5
+3	20.2		0.641		13.0
+4	24.2		0.552		13.4
+5	29.0		0.476		13.8
Total	$104.2			**Total**	$64.8

Value of Company Based on Discounted Future Earnings = $64.8

III. DISCOUNTED CASH FLOW

	Projected Cash Flow (Figure 3.5) (000s)	x	Present Value Factor Assuming 16% Return	=	Present Value of Cash Flow (000s)
+1	$ 16.9		0.862		$14.6
+2	21.1		0.743		15.7
+3	26.4		0.641		16.9
+4	33.0		0.552		18.2
+5	41.2		0.476		19.6
Total	$138.6				$85.0

Value of Company Based on Discounted Cash Flow = $85.0

* The actual rate of return to use depends upon your cost of capital, as well as the perceived risk inherent in the investment.

The *discounted future earnings* approach requires estimating after-tax earnings for a number of years in the future as well as determining an appropriate rate of return for the investor. Each future year's earnings are then discounted by the desired rate of return. A higher discount rate might be considered in this case since the estimates are based on projections of future earnings rather than historical results and may be very subjective in nature. In addition, since net earnings, after tax, are used as the basis for the projection, the discount rate used should be net of tax as well. The sum of these discounted values is the estimated present value of the company (Figure 3.5 and Section II of Figure 3.6).

The advantage of this approach is that future earnings potential becomes the principal investment criterion, taking into account the time value of money. The principal disadvantage is that in many situations, future earnings cannot be projected with any real accuracy because of the uncertainties of the operating environment and the marketplace.

The *discounted cash flow* approach is essentially the same as the discounted future earnings one, except that future anticipated cash flows rather than earnings are used in the computation, as can be seen in Section III of Figure 3.6. The difference between earnings and cash flow is that earnings will include provision for depreciation, amortization, deferred taxes, and similar "non-cash" expenses. Like the discounted future earnings approach, this method of valuation also depends upon highly uncertain estimates and assumptions. Many people feel, however, that this method and the discounted future earnings method typically provide the most reasonable estimates of a company's value.

Each of these evaluation methods is illustrated for the case of Appleton. The following assumptions are reflected in these calculations:

1. Future earnings are estimated with new management in place.

2. Earnings are expected to grow at a rate of 20 percent per year.

3. The income tax rate, including federal and state or provincial income taxes, is 20 percent.

4. Your desired return on investment is 16 percent.

As illustrated in Figure 3.7, the values of The Appleton Company vary widely according to the valuation method used. The actual value of the company will depend upon which method is most appropriate for the circumstances. For example, the seller will argue that the valuation method yielding the highest value — modified book value or discounted cash flow — is the most appropriate one. However, you would argue that the one reflecting the lowest value for the business — liquidation value — is probably the most appropriate. The price actually agreed upon will result from extensive negotiation between you and the prospective seller, and will involve considering not only these formal evaluation methods but a host of other business and personal considerations as well.

FIGURE 3.7 APPLETON VALUATIONS ACCORDING TO DIFFERENT METHODS

Method	Estimated Value (000s)
Net book value (Figure 3.3, I)	$50.0
Modified book value (Figure 3.3, II)	85.0
Liquidation value (Figure 3.3, III)	43.0
Capitalization of earnings (Figure 3.6, I)	60.0
Discounted future earnings (Figure 3.6, II)	64.8
Discounted cash flow (Figure 3.6, III)	85.0

Rule-of-Thumb Approaches

In some situations, especially the purchase of service industries, certain rules of thumb have been developed to serve as useful guides for the valuation of a business. They typically rely on the idea of a "price multiplier." One common rule of thumb in firms where there are substantial assets is to add up the fair market value of the company's fixed assets, plus the owner's cost of current inventory, plus approximately 90 percent of what appear to be good accounts receivable, plus a percentage of the company's net income before taxes as goodwill. In companies where there are relatively few tangible assets, another rule of thumb is to calculate the selling price as a percentage of the net or gross annual receipts of the business. This method is illustrated in Table 3.2 for various types of businesses. In this table, other important conditions to consider, and key things to watch out for, are listed as well.

Using one of these rules of thumb does not mean that the balance sheet and the income statement for the business can be ignored. These rules are merely a starting point for business valuation and must be reviewed in the context of the other business factors discussed earlier in this section.

WHAT TO BUY — ASSETS OR SHARES?

The acquisition of a business may be structured under one of two basic formats:

1. You can purchase the seller's stock or shares in the business.
2. You can purchase part or all of the business' assets.

Although these alternatives are treated somewhat the same for financial reporting purposes, the tax consequences can differ significantly. A major consideration in the purchase or sale of a business may be the effect on the tax liability of both the buyer and the seller. The "best" form of a particular transaction will depend on the facts and circumstances of each case. Since the tax implications of acquiring or disposing of a business can be very complex, and a poorly structured transaction can be disastrous for both parties, it is suggested that you seek competent tax advice from your accountant or lawyer regarding this matter. Another factor to consider in deciding whether to buy assets or shares are "contingent liabilities." If assets are acquired, in most instances the buyer takes no responsibility for any contingencies that may arise subsequent to the sale such as lawsuits, environmental liabilities, or tax reassessments.

In some cases there may not be any choice. If the company is a sole proprietorship, for example, there are no shares, only assets and liabilities accumulated in the course of doing business which belong to the proprietor personally. So when acquiring the company, you and the owner must decide which of these assets and liabilities are to be transferred and which are to stay with the present owner. You may feel that some of the assets are not really essential to carry on the business and the seller may desire to keep something — often the real estate, which you may be able to lease rather than buy from him. This may be one way of reducing the cost of the business to you. These are matters which would have to be discussed in detail between you and the prospective seller.

ADVANTAGES AND DISADVANTAGES OF BUYING AN EXISTING BUSINESS

The case for buying an existing firm, as against setting up a new one of your own, is not clear-cut either way. Each situation must be decided on its merits. There are distinct advantages and disadvantages to each course of action. You must consider how well your personal preferences fit into each of these options.

TABLE 3.2 VALUING A SMALL BUSINESS BY RULE OF THUMB

Business	Price Multiplier	Important Conditions	Watch For:
Apparel stores	0.75 to 1.5 times net plus equipment and inventory	Location, competition, reputation, specialization	Unfavourable shopping patterns, inadequate parking, outdated inventory
Beauty salons	0.25 to 0.75 times gross plus equipment and inventory	Location, reputation, boutique image	Excessive staff turnover
Car dealerships	1.25 to 2 times net plus equipment	Type of dealership, location, reputation of company	Brand new manufacturers, factory allocation policy
Employment agencies	0.75 to 1 times gross, equipment included	Reputation, specialization, client relations	Excessive staff turnover
Fast food stores	1 to 1.25 times net	Location, competition, neatness of premises, lease terms	Inadequate street traffic, inadequate servicing space or seating area
Gas stations	$1.25 to $2 per gallon pumped per month, equipment included	Gallons/month, lease terms, location, competition, other services	Poor traffic pattern, short lease
Grocery stores	0.25 to 0.33 times gross, equipment included	Location, lease terms, presence of liquor, condition of facilities	Nearby supermarkets or convenience stores
Insurance agencies	1 to 2 times annual renewal commissions	Client demographics and transferability, carrier characteristics	Agent turnover, account mix
Newspapers	0.75 to 1.25 times gross, equipment included	Location, demographics, economic conditions, competition, lease terms	Stagnant or declining area
Real estate offices	0.75 to 1.5 times gross, equipment included	Tenure of salespeople, franchised office, reputation	Intensity of competition
Restaurants	0.25 to 0.5 times gross, equipment included	Competition, location, reputation	Predecessor failures
Travel agencies	0.04 to 0.1 times gross, equipment included	Revenue mix, location, reputation, lease terms	Negative climate for international travel
Video shops	1 to 2 times net plus equipment	Location, competition, inventory	Obsolescence of tapes, match of tapes to customers

Excerpted from S. M. Pollan and M. Levine, *Playing to Win: The Small Business Guide to Survival & Growth,* advertising supplement to *U.S. News & World Report* and *The Atlantic,* 1988. Used by permission.

Reasons for Buying an Established Business

Here are some reasons why one *should* consider buying an established business:

1. Buying an existing business can reduce the risk. The existing business is already a proven entity. And it is often easier to obtain financing for an established operation than for a new one.
2. Acquiring a "going concern" with a good past history increases the likelihood of a successful operation for the new owner.
3. The established business has a proven location for successful operation.
4. The established firm already has a product or service that is presently being produced, distributed, and sold.
5. A clientele has already been developed for the product or service of the existing company.
6. Financial relationships have already been established with banks, trade creditors, and other sources of financial support.
7. The equipment needed for production is already available and its limitations and capabilities are known in advance.
8. An existing firm can often be acquired at a good price. The owner may be forced to sell the operation at a low price relative to the value of the assets in the business.

Disadvantages of Buying an Established Business

Here are some reasons why one may decide *not* to buy an existing business:

1. The physical facilities (the building and equipment) and product line may be old and obsolete.
2. Union/management relationships may be poor.
3. Present personnel may be unproductive and have a poor track record.
4. The inventory may contain a large amount of "dead" stock.
5. A high percentage of the assets may be in poor-quality accounts receivable.
6. The location of the business may be bad.
7. The financial condition of the business, and its relationships with financial institutions, may be poor.
8. As a buyer, you inherit any ill will that may exist toward the established firm among customers or suppliers.
9. As an entrepreneur, you have more freedom of choice in defining the nature of the business if you start one of your own than if you purchase an existing firm.

As you can see, there are both pluses and minuses in choosing to acquire an established business. You should view this option in terms of whether it will enable you to achieve your personal objectives. How do these advantages/disadvantages compare with those of starting a new business of your own? In buying an existing business do you see a reasonable opportunity to succeed? No one else can really advise you what to do. Instead, you must "do your own thing" and match the alternatives with your abilities and interests.

CHECKLIST FOR A BUSINESS ACQUISITION

Should you start a new business or buy an existing one? At this point in your deliberations, this is the critical question. The material in the Business Acquisition Questionnaire, Figure 3.8, will aid you in making this choice.

If, after answering the questions in Part A, you decide to enter an established business rather than to start one of your own, then you should proceed to the questions in Part B. You may want to reproduce these pages and answer the same questions for several businesses you have in mind. Go through the questionnaire and answer the questions concerning each business as conscientiously as you can.

FIGURE 3.8 BUSINESS ACQUISITION QUESTIONNAIRE

PART A

Before deciding whether you will purchase an established business, you need to give consideration to the positive and negative features of this alternative. You should rate each point in the questionnaire as you perceive its significance and importance to you.

1. How would you define the nature of the business in which you are interested?

_____

_____

_____

2. How important are each of the following factors to you in electing to buy an established business? Indicate the importance of each factor to you on a scale ranging from 0 (not important at all) to 10 (extremely important):

a. Having a business with a proven performance record in sales, reliability, service, and profits _____

b. Avoiding the problems associated with assembling the composite resources — including location, building, equipment, material, and people _____

c. Avoiding the necessity of selecting and training a new workforce _____

d. Having an established product line _____

e. Avoiding production problems typically associated with the start-up of a new business _____

f. Having an established channel of distribution to market your product _____

g. Having a basic accounting and control system already in place _____

h. Avoiding the difficulty of having to work out the "bugs" that commonly develop in the initial operation of a new business _____

i. Having established relationships with suppliers and financial institutions _____

j. Being able to acquire the assets of the business for less than their replacement value _____

Total _____

3. In checking back over the points covered in question 2, the closer your total score on all items is to 100, the more purchasing an established business is likely to be of interest to you as a means of going into business for yourself.

PART B

The following is a set of considerations to be assessed in evaluating an established business. Your responses, information from the present owner, and other information concerning the status of the business should guide you to a comfortable decision as to whether this business is for you.

1. Why is the Business for Sale?

_____

_____

_____

_____

continued

Business Aquisition Questionnaire — continued

2. Financial Factors

a. Recent sales trend:

_____ Increasing substantially

_____ Increasing marginally

_____ Relatively stable

_____ Decreasing marginally

_____ Decreasing substantially

b. Recent trend in net profit:

_____ Increasing substantially

_____ Increasing marginally

_____ Relatively stable

_____ Decreasing marginally

_____ Decreasing substantially

c. Are the financial statements audited?

Yes _____ No _____

d. Apparent validity of financial statements:

Accurate _____ Overstated _____ Understated _____

Check the following:

• Relationship of book value of fixed assets to market price or replacement cost

• Average age of accounts receivable and percentage over 90 days

• Bad debts written off in the past 6 months, 12 months

e. Ratio analysis:

	This Company			
	Industry Standard	*Year To Date*	*Last Year*	*Two Years Ago*
Current ratio	_____	_____	_____	_____
Quick ratio	_____	_____	_____	_____
Debt-to-net-worth ratio	_____	_____	_____	_____
Gross-profit-to-sales ratio	_____	_____	_____	_____
Net-income-to-sales ratio	_____	_____	_____	_____
Return on assets	_____	_____	_____	_____

3. Tangible Assets

a. Are the land and buildings adequate for the business?

Yes _____ No _____

b. Is the location acceptable?

Yes _____ No _____

c. Is the machinery and equipment worn and out of date?

Yes _____ No _____

d. How does it compare with the latest available?

_____

_____

_____

Business Aquisition Questionnaire — continued

   e. What is the maintenance status of the plant and equipment?

     Excellent _____ Good _____ Fair _____ Poor _____

   f. Is the plant of sufficient size and design to meet your current and projected requirements?

     Yes _____ No _____

   g. Does the plant appear to be well laid out for the efficient use of people, machines, and material?

     Yes _____ No _____

   h. What is the approximate value of the company's inventory?

Raw material	$_____
Work-in-process	$_____
Finished goods	$_____
Total	$_____

   i. Does the inventory contain a high proportion of obsolete or "dead" stock?

     Yes _____ No _____

4. Intangible Assets

   a. Does the company name or any of its trade names have any value?

     Yes _____ No _____

   b. What kind of reputation does the business have with its customers?

     Positive _____ Neutral _____ Negative _____

   c. What kind of reputation does the business have with its suppliers?

     Positive _____ Neutral _____ Negative _____

   d. Are any franchise, licensing, or other rights part of the business?

     Yes _____ No _____

     Are they included in the deal?

     Yes _____ No _____

   e. Are any patents, copyrights, or trademarks part of the business?

     Yes _____ No _____

     Are they included in the deal?

     Yes _____ No _____

5. Marketing Factors

   a. Is the market for the firm's product/service:

     _____ Increasing?

     _____ Stable?

     _____ Declining? If *declining*, this is principally attributable to:

           _____ i. Decreasing demand due to lower popularity

           _____ ii. A changing neighbourhood

           _____ iii. A declining target population

           _____ iv. Technological change

           _____ v. Lack of effort by present owner

           _____ vi. Other factors

6. Human Factors

   a. Is the present owner in good health?

     Yes _____ No _____

continued

b. Does the present owner plan to establish a new business or acquire another business that would compete with yours?

Yes _____ No _____ Uncertain _____

What are the intentions of the present owner?

_____

_____

_____

c. How efficient are current personnel?

i. What is the rate of labour turnover? _____ %

ii. What is the rate of absenteeism? _____ %

iii. What proportion of production is completed without rejects? _____ %

iv. Can you accurately determine the cost of producing an individual unit of the product or service? Yes _____ No _____

v. How has this changed in the past year?

Increased _____ Stayed the same _____ Decreased _____

d. Has a union recently won an election to serve as a bargaining agent for the company's employees?

Yes _____ No _____

e. Will most of the key employees continue to work for the firm under your management?

Yes _____ No _____

f. Will you have to incur considerable costs in retraining or hiring additional employees?

Yes _____ No _____

7. Other Considerations

a. Are there any zoning restrictions or caveats on the property that may put you at a competitive disadvantage?

Yes _____ No _____

b. Can you satisfy all the federal and provincial licensing and permit requirements?

Yes _____ No _____

c. Have you considered what would be the most advantageous way of purchasing the company?

Buy shares _____ Buy assets _____ Don't know _____

d. Have you had a lawyer and an accountant review the material you received from the vendor and any other information you may have regarding the business?

Lawyer   Yes _____ No _____

Accountant Yes _____ No _____

8. Your Evaluation of the Business

What have you determined to be the approximate value of the business based on the following valuation approaches?

a. Net book value $ _____

b. Modified book value $ _____

c. Liquidation value $ _____

d. Capitalization of past earnings $ _____

e. Discounted future earnings $ _____

f. Discounted cash flow $ _____

The areas covered by this checklist are not meant to be exhaustive; they are presented merely to guide and stimulate your own thinking about buying an existing business. The more information you can compile to assist you in making this decision the better.

STAGE
FOUR

CONSIDERING A FRANCHISE

In addition to exploring the possibilities of starting your own business or buying an existing one, you may want to investigate the opportunities presented by *franchising*. Franchising allows you to go into business for yourself, and at the same time be part of a larger organization. This reduces your chances of failure, because of the support that the established company can provide. If this appears to be an attractive situation, then a franchise may be the answer for you. Let's look at what this means in the context of starting a business of your own.

AN INTRODUCTION TO FRANCHISING

Franchising has often been referred to as an industry or a business. However, it is neither. It can best be described as *a method of doing business* — a means of marketing a product and/or service which has been adopted and used by a wide variety of industries and businesses.

What Is Franchising?

There is no single, simple definition of franchising. For example, Statistics Canada defines it as "A system of distribution in which one enterprise (the franchisor) grants to another (the franchisee) the right or privilege to merchandise a product or service." The International Franchise Association, the major trade association in the field, defines it as "A continuing relationship in which the franchisor provides a licensed privilege to do business, plus assistance in organizing, training, merchandising, and management in return for consideration from the franchisee." These are just two of the many definitions that have been offered.

Regardless of the formal definition, however, it is best to think of franchising as a legal and commercial relationship between the owner of a trademark, trade name, or advertising symbol and an individual or group of people seeking the right to use that identification in a business. A franchisee generally sells goods and services supplied by the franchisor or that meet the franchisor's quality standards. Franchising is based on mutual trust and a legal relationship between the two parties. The franchisor provides business expertise such as a proven product or service offering, an operating system, a marketing plan, site location, training, and financial controls that otherwise would not be available to the franchisee. The franchisee brings to the franchise operation the motivation, entrepreneurial spirit, and often the money, to make the franchise a success.

Virtually all franchise arrangements contain the following elements:

1. A continuing relationship between two parties
2. A legal contract which describes the responsibilities and obligations of each party
3. Tangible and intangible assets (such as services, trademarks, and expertise) provided by the franchisor for a fee
4. The operation of the business by the franchisee under the franchisor's trade name and managerial guidance

Franchise arrangements can be subdivided into two broad classes:

1. **Product distribution arrangements**, in which the dealer is to some degree, but not entirely, identified with the manufacturer/supplier
2. **Entire-business-format franchising**, in which there is complete identification of the dealer with the supplier

In a *product distribution arrangement*, the franchised dealer concentrates on one company's product line, and to some extent identifies his or her business with that company. Typical of this type of franchise are automobile and truck dealers, gasoline service stations, and soft drink bottlers.

Entire-business-format franchising is characterized by an ongoing business relationship between franchisor and franchisee that includes not only the product, service, and trademark, but the entire business format — a marketing strategy and plan, operating manuals and standards, quality control, and continuing two-way communications. Restaurants, personal and business services, rental services, real estate services, and many other businesses fall into this category.

Entire-business-format franchising has been primarily responsible for most of the growth of franchising since 1950. Most of our comments will relate to this form of franchising.

Advantages of Franchising

As has been pointed out, franchising is one means for you (the *franchisee*) to go into business for yourself, but yet at the same time also be part of a chain, with the support of an established company (the *franchisor*) behind you. This can enable you to compete with other chains through the use of a well-known trademark or trade name. In addition, the franchisor may provide you with assistance in such areas as site selection, equipment purchasing, national advertising, bookkeeping, the acquisition of supplies and materials, business counselling, and employee training.

As a franchisee you will have the opportunity to buy into an established concept with reduced risk of failure. Statistics show that a typical franchisee has an 80 percent chance of success. Several factors may explain this result. First, your risk is reduced because you are supposedly buying a successful concept. This package includes proven and profitable product or service lines, professionally developed advertising, a known and generally recognized brand name, the standardized design or construction of a typical outlet, and a proven and market-tested operating system. Second, you are often provided with training for your new job and continuing management support. You have the ongoing assistance of a franchisor, who can afford to hire specialists in such areas as cost accounting, marketing and sales, and research and development. These are important assets usually not available to the small, independent businessperson.

As a franchisee you may also be able to take advantage of the lower cost of large-scale, centralized buying. You may be able to purchase supplies at reduced cost, since the franchisor can purchase in bulk and pass the savings along. You may also have access to financing and credit arrangements that would not otherwise be available to an independent business. Banks and other lending institutions are usually more willing to lend money to a franchisee who has the backing of a large, successful franchisor than they are to a completely independent business.

A franchisee has the opportunity to acquire a proven system which has already been developed, tested and refined, with all of the bugs already worked out. This allows you to avoid a lot of the start-up problems typically associated with starting an independent business.

Disadvantages of Franchising

While franchising has a considerable number of advantages, there are also several disadvantages of which you should be aware. One of the principal complaints is the degree of control which franchisors exert over their franchisees. While you will be an independent businessperson, in effect you do not have complete autonomy and must operate within the operating system as defined by the franchisor. You are usually in a subordinate position to the franchisor and must abide by the often extremely rigid terms and conditions of the franchise agreement. All franchise contracts give the franchisor either an open right to terminate the contract or the right to terminate upon breach of the agreement. As a result, you may find yourself in a weak bargaining position.

Franchisees also have certain reporting obligations to the franchisor and may be subject to frequent inspection and constant supervision. To fit comfortably into such an arrangement, you must accept the necessity of such controls. These restrictions, however, may be unacceptable to some individuals. You must seriously assess your personal suitability for the role of a franchisee.

Another disadvantage of franchising is that the cost of the services provided to you by the franchisor is based on your total sales revenue. These costs can amount to 10 percent or more of your total revenue or an even larger share of your profits. A related complaint is that the markup which the franchisor may add to the products you must buy from them can increase your operating costs, particularly if equally good products could be purchased elsewhere at lower prices. While you might initially feel that your operating costs are likely to be lower as a result of the franchisor's central purchasing program, it may not become apparent until later that you are actually paying a huge markup on the material, equipment, and supplies you acquire.

Acquiring a franchise is not necessarily a licence to print money. Besides an initial franchise fee, you will probably also have to make periodic royalty payments and advertising contributions based on a percentage of your gross revenues. Even with these expenditures, you still run the risk of not achieving the expected sales, and thus the profit, which the franchisor stated was possible.

It should also be remembered that, as a matter of fact, the benefits available through franchising have not always materialized. Franchisors have not always supplied the services they promised or truthfully disclosed the amount of time and effort the franchisee would have to commit to the franchise. Termination policies of many franchisors have given franchisees little or no security in many cases.

TYPES OF FRANCHISES

Franchise Formats

There are three major ways a franchise can be formatted:

- **Single-unit franchise** This is the most popular and simplest format. In it, the franchisor grants you the right to establish and operate a business at a single location. This has been the most popular means of franchise expansion and the method by which many independent entrepreneurs have become involved in franchise distribution.

- **Area franchise** This format involves a franchisor's granting you the right to establish more than one outlet within a specified territory. This territory can be as large as an entire state, a province, or even a country, or it can be as small as part of a city. To assure that this territory is adequately serviced, the franchisor will usually require the construction and operation of a specific number of outlets within a period of time. Area franchising may be a means of achieving certain economies of scale, and perhaps a lower average franchise cost. On the other hand, it requires a larger total capital outlay for plant and equipment. Area franchisees with a large number of outlets can sometimes acquire greater financial strength than their franchisors. This has happened in a number of instances in the fast food industry.

- **Master franchise** In this format, a franchisor grants you (the *master franchisee*) the right, not only to operate an outlet in a specific territory, but also to sell subfranchises to others within that same territory. Granting master franchises is the fastest way for a franchisor to expand, but it is also very complex and results in a division of fees and royalties between the franchisor and subfranchisor. A master franchisee may not need as much initial capital as an area franchisee, but he or she must learn not only how to open and operate a franchise business but also how to sell franchises.

Range of Available Franchises

To give you an idea of the current scope of franchising, *Opportunities Canada* in their franchise and dealership guide[1], provides information on over 1500 different franchisor organizations in 32 product/service categories. The range of possibilities available to a prospective franchisee includes opportunities in the following areas:

- Accounting and financial services
- Automotive products and services
- Beauty, health, and personal services
- Building products and services
- Business related/communication services
- Car rental and limo services
- Computer products and services
- Convenience & grocery stores and bakeries
- Educational and training systems
- Employment and personnel services
- Fast food: takeout/sit-in
- Food retail: candy, coffee, yogurt, etc.
- Health aids and services and water treatment
- Hotels, motels, and campgrounds
- Interior decorating products and services
- Lawn care, landscaping, and hydroponic services
- Maid and janitorial services
- Maintenance, repair, restoration, and cleaning products
- Pet products and services
- Photography, art products, and services
- Printing, copying, and typesetting
- Publishing
- Real estate
- Recreation, sporting goods, and related services
- Restaurants: dining rooms/bars
- Retail apparel: footwear and fashion accessories
- Retail miscellaneous
- Security systems
- Support services: franchise and dealerships
- Travel
- Vending and dispensing machine systems
- Video retail

Within this broad spectrum of available opportunities, the most popular areas have been fast food (takeout/sit-in), food retail (candy, coffee, yogurt, etc.), automotive products and services, and business related/communication services.

---

[1] *Opportunities Canada*, Vol. 4, No. 2, Fall-Winter 1994-95.

At the individual franchiser level, the Top 10 franchise organizations in 1994 based on an evaluation by *Entrepreneur*[2] magazine were:

1. Subway — submarine sandwiches
2. McDonald's — hamburgers
3. Burger King Corp. — hamburgers
4. Hardee's — hamburgers
5. 7-Eleven Convenience Stores — convenience stores
6. Dunkin' Donuts — donuts
7. Mail Boxes Etc. — postal & business services
8. Choice Hotels Int'l — hotels & motels
9. Snap-On Inc. — hardware
10. Dairy Queen — soft-serve ice cream

LEGAL ASPECTS OF FRANCHISING

Canadian Legislation and Disclosure Requirements

Many states in the U.S. have laws and regulations governing franchise companies, but the same is not true for provinces in Canada. Only Alberta has a Franchise Act, though Ontario and Quebec have discussed the implementation of similar legislation.

The Alberta legislation did require franchisors wishing to sell franchises in that province to disclose the material facts involved in operating a franchise. This involved filing a prospectus as well as a set of audited financial statements with the Alberta Securities Commission. Some of the information the franchisor had to include in this document was:

1. A list of all company officers and directors
2. A brief history of the company
3. A list of major shareholders in the company
4. Description of any previous bankruptcies, of outlets or of officers and directors
5. Notice of any outstanding litigation against the company
6. Copies of all contracts to be signed by the franchisee
7. The amount of investment required by the franchisee
8. A list of all Alberta franchisees
9. A copy of the firm's financial statements

Many franchisors, however, complained that the Alberta legislation was incredibly onerous, it took a long time to prepare the required material, and the legal costs of complying were prohibitive for small, first-time franchisors. To address these concerns, the Alberta legislature passed a new Franchise Act in the spring of 1995, which relaxes some of the more stringent demands on franchisors. Instead of having to file documents with the Securities Commission, franchisors will now only have to give prospective franchisees a disclosure document containing much of the same information. It is also possible that franchisors will no longer need audited financial statements, only statements prepared in accordance with generally accepted accounting standards. This change will put more onus on franchisees, not only in Alberta but elsewhere in Canada as well, to take more responsibility for their business investments.

---

[2] *Entrepreneur*, Vol. 23, No. 1, January 1995. The evaluation is based on a number of factors including length of time in business and number of years franchising, number of franchised units and company-owned operating units, start-up costs, growth rate, percentage of terminations, and financial stability of the company.

In other provinces, franchisors are under no obligation to provide any specific information or file any material with a government agency or department; as a franchisee, you are on your own for the most part. If your potential franchisor does operate in Alberta, however, you should request a copy of the disclosure material they are obliged to provide to prospective franchisees in that province.

The U.S. Situation

Since 1979 the U.S. Federal Trade Commission (FTC) has required that every franchisor offering franchises in the U.S. have a *disclosure statement* ready to offer a prospective franchisee. A copy of any disclosure statement can be obtained from the Federal Trade Commission, Washington, DC 20580. This document discloses 20 categories of information:

1. Identifying information about the franchisor
2. Business experience of the franchisor's directors and key executives
3. The franchisor's business experience
4. Litigation history of the franchisor and its directors and key executives
5. Bankruptcy history of the franchisor and its directors and key executives
6. Description of the franchise
7. Money required to be paid by the franchisee to obtain or commence the franchise operation
8. Continuing expenses to the franchisee in operating the franchise business that are payable in full or in part to the franchisor or to a person affiliated with the franchisor
9. A list of persons who represent either the franchisor or any of its affiliates, with whom the franchisee is required or advised to do business
10. Real estate, services, supplies, products, inventories, signs, fixtures, or equipment which the franchisee is required to purchase, lease, or rent, and a list of any persons with whom such transactions must be made
11. Descriptions of consideration paid (such as royalties, commissions, etc.) by third parties to the franchisor or any of its affiliates as a result of a franchisee's purchase from such third parties
12. Description of any franchisor assistance in financing the purchase of a franchise
13. Restrictions placed on a franchisee's conduct of the business
14. Required personal participation by the franchisee
15. Information about termination, cancellation, and renewal of the franchise
16. Statistical information about the number of franchises and their rate of termination or failure
17. Franchisor's right to select or approve a site for the franchise
18. Training programs for the franchisee
19. Celebrity involvement with the franchise
20. Financial information about the franchisor

The FTC regulations also require that if the franchisor makes any claims regarding the level of earnings you might realize as a result of owning its franchise, a reasonable basis must exist to support the accuracy of these claims. When such claims are made, the franchisor must have prepared an "Earnings Disclosure Document" for prospective franchisees, explaining the basis and material assumptions on which the claims are made.

If the franchise you are investigating currently operates in the U.S., this information should be readily available.

The Franchise Agreement

Because two independent parties participate in a franchise relationship, the primary vehicle for obtaining central coordination and control over the efforts of both participants is a formal contract. This *franchise agreement* is the heart of the franchise relationship. It differs from the typical contract in that it contains restrictive clauses peculiar to franchising which limit your rights and powers in the conduct of the business. Franchisors argue that these controls are necessary in order to protect their trademark and to maintain a common identity for their outlets.

A franchise agreement should cover a variety of matters. There should be provisions that cover such subjects as:

- The full initial costs, and what they cover
- Use of the franchisor's trademarks by the franchisee
- Licensing fees
- Land purchase or lease requirements
- Building construction or renovation
- Equipment needs
- Initial training provided
- Starting inventory
- Promotional fees or allowances
- Use of operations manuals
- Royalties
- Other payments related to the franchisor
- Ongoing training
- Cooperative advertising fees
- Insurance requirements
- Interest charges on financing
- Requirements regarding purchasing supplies from the franchisor, and competitiveness of prices with those of other suppliers
- Restrictions that apply to competition with other franchisees
- Terms covering termination of the franchise, renewal rights, passing the franchise on to other family members, resale of the franchise, and similar topics

In considering any franchise proposition, you should pay a great deal of attention to the franchise contract. Since it is a key part of the relationship, it should he thoroughly understood. The rest of this section discusses the evaluation of an agreement for a single-unit franchise within a business format franchise system. It is important to realize, however, that this is not a "typical" franchise agreement; there is really no such thing. While agreements may follow a fairly standard approach in terms of format, they do not do so in terms of content. Every agreement is specially drafted by the franchisor to reflect its particular objectives and the future of the business.

Obligations Undertaken By the Franchisor

The obligations undertaken by the franchisor may include any or all of the following:

1. To provide basic business training to you and your employees. This includes training in bookkeeping skills, staff selection, staff management, business procedures, and the systems necessary to control the operation. In addition, the franchisor may provide you with training relating to the operational aspects of the business.
2. To investigate and evaluate sites for the location of your franchise. You will be advised as to whether or not the site meets the franchisor's standards and what sort of performance might be expected at that location. In addition you may be assisted in the design and layout of your franchise operation.

3. To provide either the equipment or the specifications for any necessary equipment and furniture you require.

4. To provide promotional and advertising material to you, and some guidance and training on marketing and promotional principles.

5. The franchisor may provide you with a statement indicating the amount of opening inventory required, and may make arrangements for you to purchase inventory either from the franchisor's own purchasing department or from particular suppliers established for this purpose.

6. The franchisor may provide you with on-site assistance for the opening of your franchise outlet. Quite often the franchisor will provide a team of two to three people to assist you in getting the business off the ground.

7. The franchisor may also provide business operating manuals explaining the details of operating the franchise system and a bookkeeping/accounting system for you to follow. There may also be additional support through such things as business consultation, supervisory visits to your premises, and staff retraining.

Obligations Imposed upon A Franchisee

Your obligations as a franchisee may include any or all of the following:

1. To build your franchise outlet according to the plan or specifications provided by the franchisor

2. To maintain construction and opening schedules established by the franchisor

3. To abide by the lease commitments for your franchise outlet

4. To observe certain minimum opening hours for your franchise

5. To pay the franchise fees and other fees specified in the franchise agreement

6. To follow the accounting system specified by the franchisor and to provide financial reports and payments of amounts due promptly

7. To participate in all regional or national cooperative advertising and to use and display such point-of-sale or advertising material as the franchisor stipulates (this would include having all your advertising materials approved by the franchisor)

8. To maintain your premises in clean, sanitary condition and redecorate when required to do so by the franchisor

9. To maintain the required level of business insurance coverage

10. To permit the franchisor's staff to enter your premises to inspect and see whether the franchisor's standards are being maintained

11. To purchase specific goods or services from the franchisor or specified suppliers

12. To train all staff in the franchisor's method and to ensure that they are neatly and appropriately dressed

13. Not to assign the franchise contract without the franchisor's consent

14. To maintain adequate levels of working capital and abide by the operations manual provided by the franchisor

These are only examples of some of the obligations you might expect to incur. There will probably also be clauses involving bankruptcy, transfer of the business, and renewal of the contract, and provisions for the payment of royalties and other financial considerations.

Franchise Fees and Royalties

In most cases you will be required to pay an initial franchise fee on signing the franchise agreement. This fee generally pays for the right to use the trade name, licences, and operating procedures of the franchisor, some initial training, and perhaps even assistance in site selection for your franchise outlet. The amount of the fee varies tremendously, according to the type of franchise business. For a large restaurant operation or hotel, for example, the fee may be as high as $50,000 or $60,000, but for a small service franchise (such as maid service or lawn care) it may be only $5000 to $10,000. This fee is not all profit for the franchisor, as it must go to pay for franchisee recruitment, training, assistance with site selection, and other services normally provided to you. Some franchisors will charge a separate training fee, but this is usually established merely to recover the cost of providing the training to you and your employees.

In addition to this initial fee, ongoing fees may also be provided for in the franchise agreement. These will generally consist of royalties payable for ongoing rights and privileges granted by the franchisor. The royalties fees are usually calculated as a percentage of the gross sales, not profits, generated by your franchise. They may be paid either weekly, monthly, or quarterly, and represent the main profit centre for most franchisors. These royalties must continue to be paid even though the franchise may be losing money. For a fast food franchise, typical royalties range from 3 percent to 8 percent. For some service franchises, the royalty may run from 10 to 20 percent or even higher.

While some franchisees come to resent having to continue to pay ongoing royalties to their franchisor, this payment may be preferable to the franchisor charging a higher initial fee to the franchisee. Ongoing royalty payments at least imply a continuing commitment to the success of the franchise by the franchisor, to the ultimate benefit of both parties.

As well as royalty fees, many franchise agreements require you to contribute a proportion of your business' gross revenues to a regional or national cooperative advertising fund. This contribution may be an additional 2 to 4 percent of gross sales. These payments are used to develop and distribute advertising material and to run regional and national advertising campaigns. These, too, are typically not a source of profit for the franchisor.

The administration of these advertising funds has often been the subject of considerable concern to franchisees and one of the areas of greatest dispute between franchisors and franchisees. The advertising fund should be maintained as a separate trust account by the franchisor and not intermixed with its general operating revenues. The purpose of this fund should be specified in the franchise agreement. In addition, the agreement should also state how and by whom the fund will be administered.

In addition to requiring you to support a regional or a national advertising program, a franchisor may require you to support your own *local* advertising. Typically you must spend a specific amount on a periodic basis, calculated either on the basis of a percentage of gross sales or in terms of a fixed amount. Local advertising devised by you will normally require the prior approval of the franchisor.

In some cases the franchisor also provides you with special services such as bookkeeping, accounting, and management consulting services which are billed on a fee-for-service basis. Before acquiring a franchise, you should be sure that you understand all the fees that will be payable, including any extra fees that may not be mentioned in the franchise agreement.

Purchase of Products and Supplies

A key element in the success of many franchise organizations is the sameness of each of the franchise outlets. Therefore, the franchisor will work to ensure the maintenance of a certain quality of product or service and to make sure that uniform standards are employed throughout their system. Consequently, many franchisors, in an attempt to exercise complete control over their operation, require you to purchase products and services from them or from designated sources. In some cases the approved suppliers may include affiliates of the franchisor. You may also be able to purchase items from other sources of supply, provided the franchisor has approved each of those sources in advance.

If the franchisor exerts tight control over such supplies, you should try to ensure beforehand that supplies are going to be readily available when required, that they are sold to you at fair market value and on reasonable terms, and that you have the ability to choose alternative sources for any non-proprietary items if the franchisor or the designated supplier is unable to provide them to you when required.

Many franchisors earn a profit from providing supplies to their franchisees. Often, however, because franchisors exercise enormous buying power they can supply goods and services at prices and under terms which are better than those you could negotiate for yourself. You should shop around to compare prices for comparable merchandise. If the prices being charged by the franchisor are out of line, this added cost can dramatically affect your business's future earnings.

Volume rebates are often paid to franchisors by suppliers of particular products. Rather than pocket the money themselves or distribute it back to their franchisees, some franchisors will contribute this to the advertising fund. As a potential franchisee you should ask how these rebates will be handled, as a considerable amount of money may be involved.

Leased Premises

Many franchise operations require the use of physical facilities such as land and buildings. Where these premises are leased rather than owned by the franchisee, there are a number of ways in which this lease arrangement can be set up:

1. The franchisor may own the land and/or buildings and lease it to you.
2. You may lease the land and/or building directly from a third party.
3. You may own the property, sell it to the franchisor, and lease it back under a *sale leaseback* agreement.
4. A third party may own the property and lease it to the franchisor, who then sublets it to you.

The franchise agreement should spell out who is responsible, you or the franchisor, for negotiating the lease, equipping the premises, and paying the related costs. If a lease is involved, its terms and renewal clauses should be stated and should correspond with the terms of the franchise. You must be careful not to have a 20-year lease on a building and only a 5-year franchise agreement, or vice versa.

Franchisors generally want to maintain control of the franchise premises. Accordingly they will often own or lease the property on which the franchise business is located, and then sublet these premises to you. In other situations the franchisor may assign a lease to you subject to a conditional reassignment of the lease back to the franchisor upon termination of the franchise for any reason.

With respect to other leasehold improvements, you may also be required to purchase, or lease from the franchisor or from suppliers designated by the franchisor, certain fixtures, furnishings, equipment, and signs that the franchisor has approved as meeting their specifications and standards.

Territorial Protection

In many cases the franchise agreement provision with respect to your territory and protection of that territory may be subject to considerable negotiation prior to inclusion in the agreement. You will generally want to have the franchisor agree not to operate or grant a franchise to operate another franchised outlet too close to your operation. This restriction may be confined to a designated territory, or may be confined to a predetermined geographic radius from your premises.

Franchisors, on the other hand, like to see exclusive territorial protection kept to a minimum. As a result, some franchisors may restrict the protection provided to you to a grant of first refusal to acquire an additional franchise within your territory, or may subject you to a performance quota in terms of a prescribed number of outlet openings in order to maintain exclusivity within your territory. Another approach taken by some franchisors is to limit exclusivity to a formula based on population, with the result that when the population within your territory exceeds a certain number, the franchisor may either itself operate, or grant a franchise to operate, an additional outlet in the territory.

Some questions you might like to have answered in the franchise agreement are as follows:

1. Exactly what are the geographic boundaries of your territory, and are they marked on a map as part of the contract?

2. Do you have a choice of other territories?

3. What direct competition is there in your territory, and how many more franchises does the franchisor expect to sell in that area within the next five years?

4. If the territory is an exclusive one, what are the guarantees of this exclusivity?

5. Even with these guarantees, will you be permitted to open another franchise in the same territory?

6. Can your territory be reduced at any time by the franchisor?

7. Has the franchisor prepared a market survey of your territory? (If so, ask for a copy of it and study it.)

8. Has the specific site for the franchise within the territory been decided on? (If not, how and when will this be done?)

Training and Operating Assistance

Virtually every franchise agreement deals with the question of training the franchisee. Training programs may involve training schools, field experience, training manuals, or on-location training.

The franchise agreement should have some provision for an initial training program for you, and should specify the duration and location of this training and who is responsible for your related transportation, accommodation, and living expenses. This initial training is generally provided for you and the manager of your franchise business. The franchisor will usually require you and your managers to complete the training program successfully prior to the opening of your franchise business. If for some reason you should fail to complete the training program, the franchisor often reserves the right to terminate the agreement and refund all fees, less any costs incurred so far.

Many franchise agreements also provide for start-up advisory training at the franchise premises prior to or during the opening of the business. This typically involves a program lasting a prespecified number of days. The agreement should indicate who is expected to bear the cost for such start-up training, including who will be responsible for the payment of travel, meals, accommodation, and other expenses of the franchisor's supervisory personnel.

The franchise agreement may also make reference to periodic refresher training. It should specify whether attendance at such programs is optional or mandatory. If they are mandatory, you should ensure that a specified maximum number of such programs is indicated for each year of the franchise agreement. The duration and location of these programs should also be specified.

Most franchisors want tight control over the day-to-day operations of the franchise, and accordingly they provide extensive operating assistance to their franchisees. This assistance is often in the form of a copyrighted operations manual that spells out, procedure by procedure, how you are expected to run the business. The manual will include such information as the franchisor's policies and procedures, and cover such details as the hours you must remain open, record-keeping methods and procedures, procedures for hiring and training employees, and, in a restaurant franchise, such matters as recipes, portion sizes, food storage and handling procedures, and menu mix and prices. The franchise agreement may also indicate that operating assistance will be provided in relation to:

1. The selection of inventory for your franchise business
2. Inspections and evaluation of your performance
3. Periodic advice with respect to hiring personnel, implementing advertising and promotional programs, and evaluating improvements in the franchise system
4. Purchasing goods, supplies, and services
5. Bookkeeping and accounting services
6. Hiring and training of employees
7. Formulation and implementation of advertising and promotional programs
8. Financial advice and consultation
9. Such additional assistance as you may require from time to time

Contract Duration, Termination, and Renewal

The duration of your franchise agreement may be as short as one year or as long as 40 to 50 years. However, the majority of franchise contracts run from 10 to 20 years. Most agreements also contain some provision for renewal of the contract. Be sure you understand these renewal provisions and what the terms, conditions, and costs of renewal will be. Renewal provisions commonly contain requirements for the payment of additional fees and upgrading of the franchise facilities to standards required by the franchisor at that time. The cost of upgrading is usually borne by the franchisee.

You should be aware, however, that not all agreements necessarily contain provisions for their renewal at the expiration of the initial term. Some agreements merely expire at the end of this terms, and the rights revert to the franchisor.

The part of the franchise agreement usually considered most offensive by many prospective franchisees are those sections relating to termination of the agreement. Franchisors typically wish to develop a detailed list of conditions in which you might be considered in default of the agreement. *Events of default* typically fall into two categories: (1) critical or material events which would allow for termination of the agreement without notice by the franchisor and (2) events upon which you would first be given written notice with an opportunity to correct the situation.

Most franchise agreements also allow the franchisor the right, upon termination or expiration, to purchase from you all inventory, supplies, equipment, furnishings, leasehold improvements, and fixtures used in connection with the franchise business. The method of calculating the purchase price of such items is entirely negotiable by the parties prior to the execution of the franchise agreement. This has been another area of considerable disagreement between franchisors and franchisees.

When renewing franchise agreements, many franchisors do not require the payment of an additional fee, but they may require franchisees to pay the current, and usually higher, royalty fees and advertising contributions. These increases, of course, reduce your income. In addition, the franchisor may require you to make substantial leasehold improvements, update signage, and make other renovations to your outlet in order to conform to current franchise system standards. These capital expenditures can be expensive, so it should be clear from the beginning what improvements might be required upon renewal.

Selling or Transferring Your Franchise

With respect to the transfer or sale of your franchise, most franchise agreements indicate that you are granted rights under the agreement based on the franchisor's investigation of your qualifications. These rights are typically considered to be personal to you as a franchisee. The contract will usually state that transfers of ownership are prohibited without the approval of the franchisor, but you should attempt to have the franchisor agree that such consent will not be unreasonably withheld.

For self-protection, you should be sure that the agreement contains provisions for the transfer of the franchise to your spouse or an adult child upon your death. Also, it should be possible to transfer the franchise to a corporation which is 100 percent owned by you and has been set up solely to operate the franchise. These transfers should be possible without the payment of additional fees.

Most franchisors, however, require transfer of your franchise to an external party who meets their normal criteria of technical competence, capital, and character. You may be able to enhance the marketability of your franchise by anticipating these and other problems in the initial negotiations.

Another common provision is for the franchisor to have a *right of first refusal* — the option to purchase your franchise in the event that you receive an offer from an independent third party to acquire your rights. In such a situation you may be required to first offer such rights back to the franchisor under the same terms and conditions offered by the independent third party. If the franchisor declines to acquire your rights within a specified period of time after receipt of your notice of such an offer, you can proceed to complete the sale or transfer to the third-party purchaser.

One problem with this right of first refusal is the response time the franchisor has to exercise this right. In some agreements the allowable period is several months, during which the third-party buyer is left on hold. In your original agreement, you should try to negotiate for a more reasonable period of 15 to 30 days for the exercise of this right of first refusal.

Some Examples

As mentioned above, the specific terms included in a franchise agreement can vary substantially from situation to situation. For example, under the terms of the Padgett Business Services of Canada Ltd. agreement for their accounting business services franchise, franchisees pay $34,500 for the franchise rights and a monthly royalty that begins at $50 but rises to $200 or 9 percent of gross sales by the end of the first year. For this fee the franchisee receives extensive support in the form of an initial month-long training program, use of a proprietary accounting software package, and marketing support including a defined territory and a number of initial leads.

In contrast, franchisees of Lick's Burger and Ice Cream Shops Inc. of Toronto can expect to pay about $375,000 to open a restaurant, including a franchise fee of $35,000. In addition, they must also pay 6 percent of their gross sales in royalties, as well as 2 percent to take part in Lick's advertising program and 1 percent to use the company's central computerized accounting system. To be considered for the Lick's program applicants have to meet rigid qualifications — including a satisfactory financial rating, good personal health, and a willingness to devote themselves to the franchise full-time. To be successful, applicants must be worth $200,000 to $250,000 net, with at least $150,000 of this in cash or liquid assets. Applicants also have to undergo a personal interview that includes psychological and other testing.

Microplay Video Games retail outlets buy, sell, rent, trade, and repair video games. A typical franchise has start-up costs that average about $150,000 including inventory, software, equipment, and a franchise fee of $37,500. Royalties range from zero for game consoles to 6 percent for games and repairs. Franchisees receive a week of comprehensive training plus the use of in-store trainers during the outlet's grand opening week. In addition, the company provides ongoing advice for operating the business and assists stores with local ad campaigns, as well as coordinating regional and national advertising programs.[3]

---

[3] For additional information on these franchises, see S. Noakes, "Number-Crunching Franchiser Aims Service at Entrepreneurs," *The Financial Post*, March 25, 1993, p. 29; E. Roseman, "Trials and Triumphs in a Far-Out Franchise," *The Globe and Mail*, February 7, 1994, p. B6; and "Microplay," *Canadian Business Franchise*, Canadian Franchise Association, 1995, p. 54.

A sampling of some popular franchisors indicating their initial franchise or dealership fee, royalty rate, required advertising contribution, and their approximate total average investment to open a typical outlet is shown in Table 4.1.

BUYING A FRANCHISE

Finding a Franchise Business

Perhaps the most common source of preliminary information regarding available franchises is newspaper advertisements. Major business newspapers such as *The Wall Street Journal*, *The Financial Post*, and *The Globe and Mail* all have special sections devoted to franchise advertisements. The "Business" or "Business Opportunities" section of the classified advertisements in your local newspaper can also be an important place to look for prospective franchise situations. Business journals and trade magazines may also contain ads for many franchise organizations. Recommendations from friends, trade shows and seminars, and business opportunity shows often held in our larger cities can also be excellent means of contacting franchisors.

Another important source of information is franchise directories, which list franchisors' names and addresses along with information on the type of franchise offered, the costs involved, and other useful information. Some useful directories are the *Franchise Annual* published by Info Press Inc. (728 Center St., Lewiston, NY 14092 or P.O. Box 670, 9Y Duke St., St. Catharines, Ont. L2R 6W8), *Opportunities Canada* published by the Type People Inc. (2550 Goldenridge Road, Unit 42, Mississauga, Ontario, L4X 2S3), and the *Franchise Opportunities Handbook* mentioned earlier, published by the U.S. Department of Commerce and available from Superintendent of Documents, U.S. Government Printing Office, Washington, DC 20402.

TABLE 4.1   A SAMPLING OF CANADIAN FRANCHISORS

Franchisor	Number of Units Owned	Number of Franchisees /Dealers	Initial Fee	Royalty	Advertising	Approximate Investment Required (cash and liquid assets)
Boston Pizza	1	92	$35,000	7%	2.5%	$550-650,000
Dollar Rent a Car	6	19	$25,000 min	7	2	Varies
Century 21 Real Estate	—	408	$20,000	6	$670/mo.	$70,000
Molly Maid	1	165	$14,000	6	2	$15,000
Dairy Queen of Canada	—	445	$30,000	4	3-6	$450,000
Magicuts	8	36	$25,000	7	1.5	$60-80,000
McDonald's Restaurants	252	240	$45,000	4	4	$600-800,000
Midas Muffler	35	209	$25,000	5	5	$225,000
Super 8 Motels	—	20	$20,000	4	3	$300-2,500,000
Second Cup	7	185	$20,000	9	2	$170-225,000
Tim Hortons	25	825	$25,000	3	4	$275-325,000
Kwik-Kopy	—	86	$20,000	6	3	$166,000

Source: Adapted from *Opportunities Canada*, Volume 4, No. 2, Fall-Winter 1994-1995.

Checking Out the Franchise Opportunity

After sifting through the various choices available, most prospective franchisees narrow their selection down to one or two possibilities. The next step is requesting a promotional kit from each of these franchisors. Normally this kit contains basic information about the company — its philosophy, a brief history, a listing of the number of outlets, where they do business, etc. Most kits also contain an *application form* requesting your name and address, and information about your past business experience, the value of your net assets, and other data; for the process to continue with the franchisor, you must complete it in detail. The form may have any one of a number of titles:

- Confidential Information Form
- Personal History
- Confidential Application
- Franchise Application
- Pre-interview Form
- Qualification Report
- Credit Application
- Application for Interview Form
- Request for Interview

Regardless of which of these titles is used, they are all different ways of describing the same thing and request much the same information. For example, you may be asked for:

1. Personal data such as your name, address, telephone number, age, health and physical impairments, marital status and number of dependents, and the name of any fraternal, business, or civic organizations to which you might belong

2. Business data such as your present business or corporation, your position, the name and address of your employer, how long you have been involved in this business, your present annual salary, and any previous business history you may have

3. References such as your present bank and the name and address of your bank manager, and any other references you may care to provide

4. Financial data such as your average annual income for the past five years, and a total declaration of your current assets and liabilities to establish your net worth

5. Additional data that relate to your particular interest in the franchise

The application form normally requires you to provide a deposit, typically in the range of $2000 to $5000. In most cases the form will state that this deposit will be credited toward the initial franchise fee without interest or deduction if the transaction should proceed. However, you should make sure that if you are turned down, all or most of this deposit will be refundable, especially if it is a large amount of money and the franchise is new and unproven.

If your application is approved, the franchisor will interview you to determine your suitability as a franchisee. The focus of this interview will be on assessing your capability according to various objective criteria that have been established by the franchisor. Every franchisor has its own established criteria based on previous experience with various kinds of people. For example, many franchisors will not consider absentee owners and refuse to grant franchises strictly for investment purposes. They feel that the success of their system rests on the motivation created by individually owned and managed outlets.

The personal characteristics desired by the franchisor will vary with the type of business. For example, a different level of education is necessary to operate a management consulting service than is needed to operate a carpet cleaning firm. Research on these selection criteria indicates that many franchisors tend to rank them in the following order:

1. Credit and financial standing
2. Personal ability to manage the operation
3. Previous work experience
4. Personality
5. Health
6. Educational background

While other factors may also be considered by particular franchisors, these criteria tend to dominate the selection process.

This interview is also an opportunity for you to raise questions about the franchisor's financial stability, trademark protection policy, the ongoing services provided to franchisees, information regarding any financial packages that may have been arranged with particular banks, the names and addresses of current franchisees, and any other questions that may occur to you. This is an opportunity for you and the franchisor to assess each other and see if you can work together on a long-term basis.

At this interview, the franchisor will also provide you with a copy of the franchise agreement. At this point, you must evaluate all the available information with the help of your accountant, your bank manager, and your lawyer in order to ensure that you feel comfortable with the franchisor and that you are happy your investment is secure. If you have any remaining questions or doubts, now is the time to resolve them. Then, if you are still not completely sure in your own mind that you wish to proceed, you should ask for a refund of your deposit.

Well-established and popular franchisors are unlikely to change their arrangements or legal documentation very much in response to a prospective franchisee's requests. They have successful systems in which many would-be franchisees would like to participate. For them, it's a seller's market.

If one of these franchisors accepts you as a franchisee, you may have to make up your mind very quickly. It is important to be decisive. If you are comfortable with the franchisor and the franchise agreement, you should be ready to sign. If not, you should ask for a refund and pursue other opportunities.

Some franchisors will expect you to sign the contract right away. Others wait until they have found a suitable location for your outlet, usually within a predetermined period of time. In some cases, it can take weeks, perhaps even months, for a suitable site to be found or a lease negotiated before you actually sign. It should also be remembered that popular franchisors often have long waiting lists of prospective franchisees, so that one or more years can pass before you will be in business.

Franchise Financing

One of the first steps in evaluating any franchise opportunity is to determine the total cost of getting into the business. This could include the initial franchise fee, real estate rental, equipment costs, start-up inventories and expenses, and initial working capital requirements. Then you must determine how much of this amount must be put up as an initial investment and what kind of terms might be arranged for handling the balance. Most franchisors expect the franchisee to put up 30 to 50 percent of the total franchise package cost as an initial investment. You must ask yourself whether you have enough unencumbered capital to cover this amount.

Financing of the remainder can sometimes be done through the franchisor, or the franchisor may have previously arranged a standardized financing package for prospective franchisees through one of the major banks or trust companies. Subway, the successful submarine sandwich franchise, offers its new franchisees financing via an in-house equipment leasing program. Moneysworth & Best Shoe Repair Inc. also has an in-house financing program for franchisees in conjunction with National Trust. These programs may be somewhat more expensive for the franchisee than arranging an independent bank loan, but they can be more convenient.

The initial investment required for a restaurant franchise can be substantial. A typical fast food take-out restaurant such as Koya Japan has an initial franchise fee of $25,000 and an average total investment of $160,000. The cost of a full service restaurant such as Swiss Chalet Chicken & Ribs includes a franchise fee of $75,000 and a total investment ranging from $1 million to $2 million. In these cases, equipment and leasehold improvements tend to make up the largest component of the total cost.

In the retail sector, the size of the total investment will vary depending on the nature and location of the outlet. For example, a video store like Jumbo Video will require a franchise fee of $40,000 and a total investment of roughly $400,000, with the franchisee having to provide $150,000 in cash. A computer store like Compucentre has a franchise fee of $25,000 with an average investment of $250,000, while a retail building supply dealership like Windsor Plywood has an initial fee of $35,000 and a total required investment upwards to $1 million. Most of these investments are typically in inventory.

The investment required for a service franchise is usually much lower. Many service franchises can be established for a total investment of less than $50,000. For example, Diet Centre, a weight loss clinic, has a franchise fee of $18,000 and a total average investment of $32,000. Similarly, Duraclean International offers a carpet and upholstery cleaning service for a franchise fee of $5,700 with a total investment of $11,000. A residential housecleaning and maid service franchise like Molly Maid can be established for a franchise fee of $14,000 and a total investment of $17,000. At the other extreme, opening a franchised hotel or motel may involve a total investment of several million dollars, although the initial amount of money required may be much less since the land and buildings for the hotel or motel can often be externally financed.

FUTURE TRENDS IN FRANCHISING

The U.S. Department of Commerce has identified a number of trends likely to emerge in the next several years in franchising across the U.S. and Canada. Among the most important of these are:

1. There will be growth in *conversion franchising*, the conversion of an independent business to a franchise. The idea is not new, and in the past has been used extensively in the franchising of real estate and travel agencies. The movement to conversion franchising is expected to be evident in many other areas, however, especially in construction, home repair and remodelling services, all types of business services, non-food retailing, and restaurants.

2. Women are expected to become involved in franchising in numbers larger than ever before, both as franchisors and as franchisees. Franchising offers new opportunities for women who are entering the professional and management ranks and want to be part of the business world or to invest in an independent business career. Starting their own businesses through franchising decreases the risk factor for women with little or no previous business experience. Furthermore, women often excel in businesses that cater specifically to the needs or interests of other women.

3. Changing consumer lifestyles and the new status of working women in society are expected to influence the growth of franchising, particularly in terms of non-food retail stores that provide a variety of services for the home. Accelerated growth is expected in franchise stores providing home furnishings, decorating, picture framing, and other types of accessories for the home. Growth is also expected to take place in all types of general merchandise, video, and electronic stores.

4. Computer technology is expected to have a dramatic impact on the service sector, especially franchising. The computer industry is establishing new businesses in the form of franchised retail stores and this trend is expected to continue. Although competition will

intensify and other distribution channels emerge, franchisors of computer stores will focus on two areas: (1) computer stores specializing in home computers, video games, software, and hardware, and (2) stores providing support services and systems for business.

5. Dental health care has become an integral part of franchising as franchised dental centres have spread to all regions of Canada and the U.S. This trend is expected to continue to develop rapidly as dental care expenditures rise and the application of modern business methods by dental franchisors provide increased efficiency, greater service, and lower fees, while meeting the needs of the huge, untapped dental patient market.

6. Franchised restaurants of all types are expected to continue to be the most popular sector of franchising. Increased activity is expected in the upscaling of franchised restaurants in terms of exterior and interior decor, service, and quality and variety of food items served. Franchisors of restaurants, especially those whose major product is pizza, have been among the fastest-growing, and this trend is expected to continue for the next few years.

7. Franchises that specialize in automotive repairs will continue to grow in many areas of the huge automotive "after-market." This trend will continue to expand through the next decade. Traditional sources of automotive repair are disappearing with the continuing decline of new-car dealerships and full-service gasoline service stations. In addition, the automobile population is growing annually in both number and variety and, on average, cars on the road are getting older. Franchise growth will be in specialized automotive centres providing services in tuneup, quick lube, muffler repair and replacement, transmissions, brakes, painting, electrical repairs, and general car care.

8. Other areas of franchising that bear watching over the next few years are automobile leasing, packaging and rapid delivery of parcels, home building, medical centres, temporary health services, and business brokers. More franchising is also expected in printing and copying services, weight control centres, and hair salons for both men and women.

9. Convenience stores, emphasizing speed and service, provide the multiple "fill-in" items that consumers need between their regular trips to the supermarket. Growing numbers of convenience stores are realizing extra sales by installing self-service gasoline pumps on their premises. Also, in order to increase their sales volume and compete with fast food restaurants, many convenience stores are offering a wide variety of take-out foods. This segment of the franchise industry is expected to continue to grow dramatically.

10. Businesses engaged in franchising educational services are becoming highly specialized. For example, increased leisure time has created a growing market for dietary and exercise training centres that has been successfully exploited by franchise systems. Franchisors have also entered the growing field of early childhood education with the establishment of daycare centres with modern learning and play equipment. Sales of this segment of the franchise industry, too, are expected to continue to increase dramatically.

EVALUATING A FRANCHISE — A CHECKLIST

The checklist shown in Figure 4.1 can serve as an effective tool for you to use in evaluating a franchise opportunity. Reading through the questions, you will notice that some of them require you to do a little homework before you can reasonably respond. For example, you and/or your lawyer will have to review the franchise agreement in order to assess the acceptability of the various clauses and conditions. You will also have to give some thought to how much capital you have personally and where you might raise additional financing.

Some questions call for some research. Ask the franchisor for the names and addresses of a number of current franchisees. Select a sample of them and contact them to discuss their views of the franchisor and the franchise agreement. Make certain your interview takes place without the franchisor or his representative present. Check the length of time that franchisee has operated in that particular location in comparison to the length of time that franchise has been in existence. If there is a difference try to determine what happened to the earlier franchisee(s). If you have been provided with pro forma financial statements or other information by the franchisor indicating the level of sales and financial performance you might expect, ask these franchisees to confirm that they are reasonably close to reality. In addition, what you may feel you require in terms of training, advertising and promotion support, and ongoing operating assistance may be a function of the type of franchise you are evaluating.

Make a copy of this checklist for each franchise you intend to evaluate. By using a similar outline to assess each opportunity, it will be much easier for you to compare them.

FIGURE 4.1 CHECKLIST FOR EVALUATING A FRANCHISE

THE FRANCHISOR

1. What is the name and address of the franchise company?

   Name _____

   Address _____

   _____

2. The franchise company is: Public _____ Private _____

3. What is the name and address of the parent company (if different from that of the franchise company)?

   Name _____

   Address _____

   _____

4. The parent company is: Public _____ Private _____

5. On what date was the company founded and when was the first franchise awarded?

   Company founded _____ First franchise awarded _____

6. How many outlets does the franchise currently have in operation or under construction? _____

   a. Of these outlets, how many are franchised and how many are company-owned?

   Franchised _____ Company-owned _____

   b. How many franchises have failed? _____

   c. How many of these failures have been within the past two years? _____

   d. Why did these franchises fail?

   Franchisor's reasons _____

   _____

   _____

   Franchisee's reasons _____

   _____

   _____

7. How many new outlets does the franchisor plan to open within the next 12 months? Where will they open?

   How many _____ Where _____

   _____

continued

Checklist for Evaluating a Franchise — continued

8. a. Who are the key principals in the day-to-day operation of the franchisor's business?

Name	*Title*	*Background*
_____	_____	_____
_____	_____	_____
_____	_____	_____
_____	_____	_____

b. Who are the directors of the company, other than those individuals named above?

Name	*Business Background*
_____	_____
_____	_____
_____	_____

c. Who are the consultants to the company?

Name	*Business Specialty*
_____	_____
_____	_____
_____	_____

THE FRANCHISE

1. Fill in the following data on each of several present franchisees.

Franchise 1

Owner _____

Address _____

_____

Telephone _____

Date started _____

Franchise 2

Owner _____

Address _____

_____

Telephone _____

Date started _____

Franchise 3

Owner _____

Address _____

_____

Telephone _____

Date started _____

2. Has a franchise ever been awarded in your area? Yes _____ No _____

a. If Yes, and it is *still in operation*, provide details.

Owner _____

Address _____

Telephone _____

Date started _____

Checklist for Evaluating a Franchise — continued

  b. If Yes, and it is *no longer in operation*, provide details.

Person involved _____

Address _____

Date opened _____

Date closed _____

Reason for failure _____

3. Is the product or service offered by the franchise:

a. Part of a growing market?	Yes _____	No _____
b. Needed in your area?	Yes _____	No _____
c. Of interest to you?	Yes _____	No _____
d. Safe for the consumer?	Yes _____	No _____
e. Protected by a guarantee or warranty?	Yes _____	No _____
f. Associated with a well-known trademark or personality?	Yes _____	No _____
g. Accompanied by a trademark that is adequately protected?	Yes _____	No _____

4. Will you be acquiring:

  a. A single-unit franchise? _____
  b. An area franchise? _____
  c. A master franchise? _____

5. The franchise is: Exclusive _____   Non-exclusive _____

6. What facilities will be required and will you have to own or lease?

  a. Business can be operated out of home?   Yes _____   No _____

  b. Facilities required:

	Yes	No	Own	Lease
Office	_____	_____	_____	_____
Retail outlet	_____	_____	_____	_____
Manufacturing facility	_____	_____	_____	_____
Warehouse	_____	_____	_____	_____
Other (specify)	_____	_____	_____	_____

7. Who will be responsible for:

	Franchisor	Franchisee
a. Location feasibility study?	_____	_____
b. Facility design and layout?	_____	_____
c. Construction?	_____	_____
d. Furnishing?	_____	_____
e. Arranging financing?	_____	_____

FRANCHISE COSTS

1. Is a forecast of expected income and expenses provided?   Yes _____   No _____

  a. If Yes, is it:

    i. Based on actual franchisee operations? _____
    ii. Based on a franchisor-owned outlet? _____
    iii. Based strictly on estimated performance? _____

  b. If Yes, does the forecast:

    i. Relate directly to your market area? Yes _____ No _____
    ii. Satisfy your personal goals? Yes _____ No _____
    iii. Provide for an acceptable return on investment? Yes _____ No _____
    iv. Provide for an adequate level of promotion and personal expenses? Yes _____ No _____

continued

Checklist for Evaluating a Franchise — continued

2. How much money will it require to get started in the business? Itemize.

Item	*Amount*
a. Franchise fee	$_____
b. Franchisor-provided services	_____
c. Supplies and opening inventory	_____
d. Real estate	_____
e. Machinery and equipment	_____
f. Furniture and fixtures	_____
g. Opening expenses	_____
h. Other	_____
Total Initial Investment	$_____(A)

3. How much other money will be required:
   a. To defray operating losses for first few months of operation? $_____(B)
   b. To cover your personal expenses for the first year of operation? $_____(C)

4. Total financial requirements (A + B + C = D) $_____(D)

5. How much of these total financial requirements do you personally have available? $_____(E)

6. If the franchisor provides any financial assistance:
   a. How much? $_____(F)
   b. What does this represent as a percentage of your total estimated costs?   _____ %
   c. What is the interest rate on this financing?   _____ %
   d. When does the money have to be paid back?   _____

7. Where will you be able to obtain the rest of the required funds?
   Specify sources from the following list:

a. Banks, credit unions or other financial institutions	$_____
b. Finance companies	_____
c. Friends, relatives, and neighbours	_____
d. Other private sources	_____
e. Leasing arrangements	_____
f. Suppliers' credit	_____
g. Government assistance programs	_____
h. Other (specify)	$_____
Total	$_____(G)

8. Total funds available from all sources (E + F + G = H)
   Grand Total $_____(H)

9. How do the funds available compare with your total estimated requirements? (D – H) $_____

THE FRANCHISE AGREEMENT

1. Have you obtained a copy of the franchise agreement?   Yes _____ No _____

2. Have you given a copy to your lawyer and accountant to review?
   Lawyer   Yes _____ No _____
   Accountant   Yes _____ No _____

Checklist for Evaluating a Franchise — continued

3. Does the agreement contain clauses that relate to the following areas and activities and are the specified terms and conditions acceptable or unacceptable to you?

	Yes	No	If Yes Acceptable	Unacceptable
a. Franchise fee	_____	_____	_____	_____
b. Commissions and royalties	_____	_____	_____	_____
c. Purchase of products and supplies	_____	_____	_____	_____
d. Lease of premises	_____	_____	_____	_____
e. Territorial protection	_____	_____	_____	_____
f. Training assistance	_____	_____	_____	_____
g. Termination	_____	_____	_____	_____
h. Renewal	_____	_____	_____	_____
i. Selling and transferring	_____	_____	_____	_____
j. Advertising and promotion	_____	_____	_____	_____
k. Operating assistance	_____	_____	_____	_____
l. Trademark protection	_____	_____	_____	_____

RUNNING YOUR FRANCHISE OPERATION

1. Does the franchisor provide you with an initial formal training program? Yes _____ No _____

If Yes: a. How long does it last? _____ days

b. Is cost included in the franchise fee? Yes _____ No _____ Partially _____

If No or Partially, specify how much you will have to pay for:

    i. Training course $ _____

    ii. Training materials   _____

    iii. Transportation   _____

    iv. Room and board   _____

    v. Other   _____

    Total Costs $ _____

c. Does the training course cover any of the following subjects?

    i.   Franchise operations   Yes _____ No _____

    ii. Sales   Yes _____ No _____

    iii. Financial management   Yes _____ No _____

    iv. Advertising and promotion   Yes _____ No _____

    v. Personnel management   Yes _____ No _____

    vi. Manufacturing methods   Yes _____ No _____

    vii. Maintenance   Yes _____ No _____

    viii. Operations   Yes _____ No _____

    ix. Employee training   Yes _____ No _____

    x. Other (specify) _____

    _____ Yes _____ No _____

2. How do you train your initial staff?

a. Is the training program provided by the franchisor? Yes _____ No _____

b. Does the franchisor make a staff member available from head office to assist you? Yes _____ No _____

c. What materials are included in the staff training program?

_____

_____

_____

continued

Checklist for Evaluating a Franchise — continued

3. Is there any requirement for you to participate in a continuing training program?
Yes _____ No _____
If Yes:

    a. Who pays the cost of this program? Franchisee _____ Franchisor _____

    b. If you have to pay for this continuing training, how much does it cost? $ _____

4. Is the product or service of the franchise normally sold by any of the following means?

    a. In customer's home — by appointment   Yes _____ No _____

    b. In customer's home — by cold-calling   Yes _____ No _____

    c. By telephone   Yes _____ No _____

    d. In a store or other place of business   Yes _____ No _____

    e. At customer's business — by appointment   Yes _____ No _____

    f. At customer's business — by cold-calling   Yes _____ No _____

    g. By direct mail   Yes _____ No _____

    h. Other (specify) _____ Yes _____ No _____

5. How do you get sales leads and customers?

    a. Provided by franchisor   Yes _____ No _____

    b. Self-generated   Yes _____ No _____

    c. Through advertising   Yes _____ No _____

    d. By direct mail   Yes _____ No _____

    e. By telephone   Yes _____ No _____

    f. Through trade shows   Yes _____ No _____

    g. Other _____ Yes _____ No _____

6. Give a brief profile of the types of customers you feel are the best prospects for the products or services offered by the franchise.

_____

_____

_____

7. a. What is the national advertising budget of the franchisor? $ _____

    b. How is this budget distributed among the primary advertising media?

TV	_____%
Radio	_____
Newspaper	_____
Outdoor	_____
Magazines	_____
Direct mail	_____
Other (specify) _____	_____
Total	**100%**

8. What kind of advertising and promotion support is available from the franchisor for the local franchisee?

	Yes	*No*	*If Yes, Cost*
a. Prepackaged local advertising program	_____	_____	$_____
b. Cooperative advertising program	_____	_____	$_____
c. Grand-opening package	_____	_____	$_____

9. Do you need the services of an advertising agency? Yes _____ No _____

Checklist for Evaluating a Franchise — continued

10. a. Who are your principal competitors? Name them in order of importance.

1. _____

2. _____

3. _____

b. Describe what you know about each and how each compares with your franchise.

Competitor 1

Owner _____

Address _____

_____

Description _____

_____

_____

Competitor 2

Owner _____

Address _____

_____

Description _____

_____

_____

Competitor 3

Owner _____

Address _____

_____

Description _____

_____

_____

11. What operating assistance is available from the franchisor if you should need it?

a. Finance and accounting   Yes _____ No _____

b. Advertising and promotion   Yes _____ No _____

c. Research and development   Yes _____ No _____

d. Sales   Yes _____ No _____

e. Real estate   Yes _____ No _____

f. Construction   Yes _____ No _____

g. Personnel and training   Yes _____ No _____

h. Manufacturing and operations   Yes _____ No _____

i. Purchasing   Yes _____ No _____

j. Other (specify) _____ Yes _____ No _____

12. Does the franchisor have a field supervisor assigned to work with a number of franchises?

Yes _____ No _____

If Yes: a. How many franchises are they assigned to?

b. Who would be assigned to your franchise?

Name _____

Address _____

_____

Telephone _____

STAGE

FIVE

ORGANIZING YOUR BUSINESS

One of the key issues you must resolve when starting your new venture is the legal form of organization the business should adopt. Making that decision means you should consider such factors as:

1. The complexity and expense associated with organizing and operating your business in one way or another
2. The extent of your personal liability
3. Your need to obtain start-up capital and operating funds from other sources
4. The extent to which you wish ownership, control, and management of your business to be shared with others (if at all)
5. The distribution of your business' profits and losses
6. The extent of government regulation you are willing to accept
7. Tax considerations and implications
8. The need to involve other principals in your venture

The most prevalent forms your business might take are:

- **An individual or sole proprietorship**
- **A partnership (general partnership or limited partnership)**
- **A corporation**

INDIVIDUAL OR SOLE PROPRIETORSHIP

The *individual* or *sole proprietorship* is the oldest and simplest form of business organization. As owner or proprietor, you have complete control over the conduct and management of your business. You alone are accountable for all business activities and their consequences. You assume the business' profits and are liable for its debts. You and the business are one and the same. The sole proprietorship is the most common form or organization for small businesses, particularly in the early stages of their development.

Advantages of Sole Proprietorship

- **Simple and inexpensive to start** A sole proprietorship is both simple and inexpensive to create and dissolve. It can be brought into existence with a minimum of legal formalities and terminated just as readily. Start-up costs are minimal — usually they are confined to registering your business name with the appropriate authorities and obtaining the necessary licences.

- **Individual control over operations** The operation of the business is coordinated in the mind and actions of a single individual. You are literally your own boss. If the business is not successful you are free to dissolve it. And if the business does well, you can have a strong personal sense of accomplishment.

- **All profits to the owner** If the business does well you will reap the benefits of your efforts; no one will share in the profits of the business. You work for yourself and determine your own destiny. In addition, if your business should incur a loss during its early stages, that loss is deductible from any other income you may have.

Disadvantages of Sole Proprietorship

- **Unlimited liability** Since the business and the proprietor are not recognized as being separate by law, you can be held personally liable for all the debts of your business. That means you may have to satisfy business debts with personal assets such as your house and car if the business is unable to meet its obligations. You may be able to protect some personal assets by putting them in your spouse's name before starting your venture but there is no real guarantee against domestic breakdown.

- **More difficult to obtain financing** The business' capital will be limited to what you, as the owner, can personally secure. This is typically less than $50,000 unless substantial security is available. With a sole proprietorship you are not in a position to share ownership with others who could contribute additional funds needed by the business.

- **Limited resources and opportunity** A sole proprietorship usually holds limited opportunity and incentive for employees, as it is not a form of ownership conducive to growth. One person can only do so much and may not have all the skills and knowledge necessary to run all phases of the business. Employees may have to be hired to perform these tasks. The life of the business in a proprietorship is limited to the life of the proprietor. If you should die, become ill, or encounter serious personal problems, your business is immediately affected, and unless other provisions are made, your business will die with you. This could lead to a forced sale of the business' assets by your beneficiaries, perhaps at a substantial loss.

PARTNERSHIP

A *partnership* is an association of two or more individuals carrying on a business for profit. The *principals* (partners) should jointly prepare a written partnership agreement outlining the following issues in terms that are clearly understood and mutually acceptable to all of them:

1. The rights and responsibilities of each partner
2. The amount and nature of their respective capital contributions to the business
3. The division of the business' profits and losses
4. The management responsibilities of each partner involved in the operation of the business
5. Provision for termination, retirement, disability, or death of a partner
6. Means for dissolving or liquidating the partnership

Partnerships fall into two categories: *general partnership* and *limited partnership*.

General Partnership

A *general partnership* is similar to a sole proprietorship except that responsibility for the business rests with two or more people, the partners. In a general partnership all the partners are liable for the obligations of the partnership and share in both profits and losses according to the terms of their partnership agreement.

Advantages of a General Partnership

- **Pooling of financial resources and talents** The partnership is useful for bringing together two or more people who can combine their skills, abilities, and resources into an effective group. Management of the business is shared among the principals.
- **Simplicity and ease of organization** A partnership, like a sole proprietorship, is easy and inexpensive to establish and is subject to a minimum amount of regulation.
- **Increased ability to obtain capital** The combined financial resources of all the partners can be used to raise additional capital for the business. Income from the partnership is taxed as part of the personal income of each of the partners.
- **Potential for growth** A partnership has a higher potential for growth than a proprietorship, since a valuable employee may be offered a partnership to dissuade him or her from leaving the firm. Growth, however, is still quite restricted compared to that possible to a limited company.

Disadvantages of a General Partnership

- **Unlimited liability** Partners are personally liable for all the debts and obligations of their business and for any negligence on the part of any of them occurring in the conduct of the business. This is similar to the situation with a sole proprietorship, except that the partners are liable both as a group and individually — i.e., not only for their own actions (*severally*) but also for the actions of all others in the partnership (*jointly*).
- **Divided authority** There is less control for an individual entrepreneur in a partnership with divided authority. There may be possible conflicts of views among partners which may be difficult to resolve and could affect the conduct of the business.

Limited Partnership

In a *limited partnership*, the partners' share in the liability of the business *is limited to the extent of their contribution to the capital* of the business. In such a partnership, however, there must also be one or more *general* partners, i.e., partners with *unlimited* liability.

The limited partners may not participate in the day-to-day management of the business of the partnership or they risk losing their limited-liability status. Also, a limited partner is entitled to interest on his or her capital of no more than 5 percent per year and some agreed-upon share of the profits. Limited partners have one major power — the ability to remove the general partner(s).

Advantages of a Limited Partnership

- **Limited liability** If properly established and registered the liability of the limited partners is restricted to the extent of their investment. Thus, you may find it easier to recruit investors.

Disadvantages of a Limited Partnership

- **Centralized management** In a limited partnership only a small subgroup of the owners — the general partners — have decision-making authority and can participate in the management of the business.

- **Difficulty in changing ownership** It is generally difficult to change ownership in a partnership, since the partnership must be dissolved and reconstituted every time a partner dies or wants to retire. So it is important that the procedure for dealing with this issue be laid out in a partnership agreement.

CORPORATION

The *corporation* is the most formal and complex of the various forms of business organization. A firm that is *incorporated* is a separate legal entity from its owners — that is, legally, it is regarded as a "person" with a separate, continuous life. As a legal person, a corporation has rights and duties of its own: it can own property and other assets, it can sue or be sued, and it files its own tax return. Ownership of a corporation is recognized through the purchase of *shares*, or *stock*, which can be held by as few as one or as many as thousands of *shareholders*.

A business need not be large to be incorporated. A sole proprietorship regularly earning in excess of $40,000 to $50,000 of taxable income annually probably should be incorporated.

Advantages of a Corporation

- **Limited liability** The owner or shareholder of a corporation is liable only for the amount he or she paid or owes for the shares. In case of bankruptcy, creditors are not able to sue shareholders for outstanding debts of the business.
- **Continuity of the business even if the owner dies** Since it is an entity under the law, a corporation is not affected by the death or withdrawal of any shareholder. The shares of its stock can be sold or transferred to other individuals without difficulty. This ease of transfer allows for perpetual succession of the corporation, which is not the case with a sole proprietorship or partnership.
- **Easier to raise capital** Incorporation makes it easier to raise capital, which is done by selling stock. In addition, corporations with some history and a track record can negotiate more effectively with outside sources of financing than either a proprietorship or a partnership.
- **Employee benefits** A corporation has a better opportunity to provide benefits to employees and stockholders in a variety of ways such as salaries, dividends, and profit-sharing plans.
- **Tax advantages** Being an independent entity in the eyes of the law, a corporation receives different tax treatment than either a proprietorship or a partnership, and is taxed separately on its business profits. This may provide you with some opportunity for tax deferral, income-splitting, or the reduction of your actual tax costs through the deductibility of certain personal fringe benefits.

Disadvantages of a Corporation

- **Cost** Corporations are more expensive to start and operate. Initially, incorporation can cost in excess of $1000 in legal and regulatory fees. In addition, a lawyer may charge upwards of $300 a year to maintain the registered office and keep the corporate *book*, i.e., the record of annual meetings, directors' meetings, etc.
- **Legal formalities** A corporation is subject to more-numerous and complicated regulatory requirements than a proprietorship or partnership. Corporations must typically file annual reports, hold annual meetings, and file federal and provincial tax returns. This can be very expensive and time-consuming for a small-businessperson, and may require the ongoing services of an accountant and a lawyer.
- **Inability to flow losses through** It is not uncommon for a new business to incur substantial start-up costs and operating losses during its first few years. These losses are "locked in" — a corporation must accumulate them for its own use in future years, and cannot use them to offset

income a shareholder may have from other sources. If your business should never become very profitable, it is conceivable that its losses could never be used to reduce your tax liability.

This is in contrast to a proprietorship or partnership, whose early losses would "flow through" to the owners of the business, to be deducted on their personal income tax returns in the year they were incurred. Therefore, it may be more beneficial financially not to incorporate, so you can offset other income for tax purposes. This can improve your overall cash flow when your business is just getting started and cash flow is most critical. You can always decide to incorporate later without any tax consequences.

- **Guarantee** Lenders often require a personal *guarantee*. This largely negates the advantage of limited liability.

REGISTRATION AND INCORPORATION — MAKING IT LEGAL

For a sole proprietorship, no formal, legal *registration* is required as long as the business is operated under your own name. However, if a specific business name like "Regal Dry Cleaners" or "Excel Construction" is used, or if more than one owner is implied by the use of "and Associates" or "and Sons" in conjunction with your name, your business must be logged with the Registrar of Companies or the Corporations Branch of the province in which the business is located. Registration is a relatively simple and inexpensive process that you can probably take care of yourself. Partnerships must be registered in a similar fashion.

Incorporation is a more complicated and considerably more expensive process that usually requires the services of a lawyer. If your business activities will initially be confined to a single province, you need only incorporate as a provincial company. Should your business plans include expansion to other provinces, however, you will be required to register in each province in which you wish to do business as an extra-provincial company, or register as a federally incorporated company.

Companies can be classified as either private or public. *Public companies* are those like Alcan and Great West Life which trade their shares on one of the country's public stock exchanges and with which most of us are familiar. They typically employ professional managers, external directors, and a number of shareholders who are the owners of the business.

Private companies, on the other hand, tend to have only one shareholder, or at most a small number of shareholders. There is some restriction on the transfer of their shares in their *articles of incorporation*, and their shares cannot be offered for sale to the public. A private corporation is sometimes called an *incorporated partnership*, because it usually consists of one, two, or three people who are personal friends, business associates, or family members, each of whom may play two or three roles, serving, for example, as an officer, director, and a shareholder of the company all at the same time.

Mondetta Clothing highlighted in Exhibit 5.1 is a good example of an incorporated partnership. The Modha brothers and the Bahl brothers share equally in the ownership of the company but have quite different responsibilities. Ash Modha is the company president and principal force behind the company's clothing designs. His brother, Prashant, is responsible for the financial affairs of the business while their cousins, Raj and Amit Bahl, look after sales and product distribution respectively.

If you choose to incorporate, a private corporation is probably the type you will establish.

CHOOSING A NAME

Like people, all businesses must have a name. The simplest procedure is to name the business after yourself — Harry Brown's Printing, for example. This type of name does not require formal registration for a sole proprietorship, but it does have disadvantages. For example, you might get

EXHIBIT 5.1

It's the stuff of dreams that before your 30th birthday you're flying to Europe on business. And your clothing is advertised in America's ultimate chic men's magazine, *GQ*, at a cost of $25,000.

But it's not a dream for 25-year-old Ash Modha, his brother Prashant, 27, and their partners, the Bahl brothers, Raj, 27, and Amit, 28. It's really happening. Their company, Mondetta Clothing, has been described by the American Association of Fashion as the hottest clothing company in Canada — likened to the hugely successful Paris-based sportswear company Faconnable.

It's more than a little miraculous that four young men who flogged T-shirts at Grand Beach in the summer of 1987 would wind up sending million-dollar orders to sewing factories in the Orient by 1994.

In the label-mad youth market there is no short distance to success, even for quality cotton T-shirts and sweat shirts with national flags on the fronts. The competition is everywhere — Levi's, Tommy Hilfiger, Polo, Klein, and in Europe, Faconnable.

The success of the company was achieved with the help of many. It's also a testament to the "never-say-we're-done" attitude of the four young principals and the creativity of president Ash Modha.

And above all, there is the all-important bonding of the two sets of brothers into what has become a team of four brothers and the support of their parents.

These laid-back, polite corporate chieftains carry on their world-wide business from offices in a modest, one-storey brownstone building on Winnipeg Avenue where 15 staff guide the internal workings of the company.

It's Monday afternoon at Mondetta and another 100-hour week has started for the young principals. Two black leased BMWs and a Jeep are parked outside the building. Company president and driving force Ash Modha is in Toronto to assess some new suppliers. His brother, Prashant — the numbers man who commutes from Edmonton where his wife is a doctor — is in for his week's work of x-raying the financial accounts. Raj Bahl, who covers sales, and his brother Amit Bahl, who handles distribution, are well into a 16-hour day gearing up for distribution of the spring and summer lines.

General manager Ron Yager, 41, is cutting through baffling customs bureaucracy for a sales rep on his way to Australia with samples.

Yager is the former marketing manager for Sport Maska. Says Yager, "My role here is keeping my good friends in the middle of the highway and out of the ditch."

Prashant says as the company grew the boys realized they were over their heads and needed someone with knowledge. "We needed that industry expertise and Ron has it," he says.

A smart move. Yager has been instrumental in acquiring some big-league licensing agreements for the company. Mondetta now has the rights to making and distributing clothing for World Cup Soccer; it already has the licensing rights to make products for all the universities in the United States and Canada. The Winnipeg Blue Bombers and Winnipeg Jets are on Mondetta's client list, and an agreement to make and distribute products in Italy is done. New markets in Japan and Australia are also opening, and final negotiations have been completed with Vicki Goetze, a professional golfer on the U.S. women's pro tour, for a line of sportswear under her name.

Yager says the strength in the company's line of youth clothing lies in the uncanny ability of Ash Modha to assess what is going on in Europe and to put the Mondetta touch on designs.

While Mondetta clawed its way into the marketplace on the strength and recognition of its "unification" national flags of the world, Yager now feels the Mondetta label on watches, gloves and 100 styles of knitwear and jeans is just as recognizable as the labels Levi's or Tommy Hilfiger in the Canadian market.

A significant move in the company's march to increasing its market share was made in 1992. Under the articulate leadership of Raj Bahl, the company negotiated direct sales agents in Ontario, Quebec and the Maritimes, and five in the United States, giving Mondetta a significant foothold in the huge American market. This action, which took place over a 14-month period, relieved the company of its dependence on the western provinces.

Kish Modha, Ash and Prashant's uncle, says, Mondetta's success formula is no secret.

"Those boys are a success because they are hard workers. Even when in university they were working from 4 p.m. to midnight at this business," he says.

For Amit, who started the original company in 1986 with Ash, the combination of the brothers is a powerful thing. "We are like real brothers. There are disagreements but we all have our own areas now instead of trying to run it all together."

Ash's ability to re-style other designs has been seminal to the success of Mondetta's lines.

Raj says, "That's because Ash goes to Europe and sees what's around and then gets our own stuff together; and 95 percent of our prototypes go to market so we have to be doing something right."

Reprinted with permission of Ritchie Gage.

people phoning you at home at all hours if you and your business' name are the same. In addition, your personal reputation may be tarnished should you experience some financial problems and be forced into receivership or bankruptcy. And if you should ever sell your business, your name would go with it, and the new owner's actions could reflect negatively on your reputation.

For businesses to be registered or incorporated, the most important consideration in selecting a name is that it be acceptable to the Registrar of Companies in your province. All provinces require that a search be conducted of proposed names. Any name that is similar to a name already registered will be rejected to avoid public confusion. It is not uncommon to have to submit several names before one is finally approved. To avoid this problem some individuals use a series of numbers rather than letters for the name of their corporation. On acceptance, the name is typically reserved for your exclusive use for 90 days, so that you can proceed with your registration or the filing of your articles of incorporation.

The best approach is usually to choose a distinctive name for the firm that *accurately describes* the type of business you plan to carry on. That is, a name like "Speedy Courier Service" or "Super-clean Automobile Washing" is probably much better than one like "Universal Enterprises" or "General Distributing." A good way to check out names is to go through the Yellow Pages or local business directories and get some idea of the range of names currently in use in your business area and perhaps some inspiration for a brilliant new possibility.

Names that are likely to be rejected and which should be avoided are those that:

1. Imply any connection with or approval of the Royal Family, such as names that include the word "Imperial" or "Royal"

2. Imply approval or sponsorship of the business by some unit of government, such as names containing "Parliamentary," "Premier's," or "Legislative"

3. Might be interpreted as obscene or not really descriptive of the nature of the firm's business

4. Are similar to or contractions of the names of companies already in business, even though they may be in a different field, such as "IBM Tailors" or "Chrysler Electronics"

The firm's name can become one of your most valuable assets if your business is successful, as has happened in the case of companies like McDonald's and Holiday Inn. Don't go for the first name that comes to mind. Think it over very carefully.

OTHER LEGAL REQUIREMENTS AND TAXES

Once you have determined the most appropriate form of organization for your business, you also need to consider a number of other legal and regulatory requirements that relate to such issues as the kinds of licences you may require, your obligations regarding the collection and payment of different employee contributions and taxes, and the current standards for employment that exist in your province.

Licences and Permits

You may require a municipal as well as a provincial licence to operate your business. Your need for the former depends on the location and nature of your business; requirements for the latter depend solely on the nature of your business.

Municipal

Not all types of businesses require a municipal licence. Every municipality regulates businesses established within its boundaries and sets its own licensing requirements and fees. In Winnipeg, for example, 114 types of businesses and occupations require a licence. In general, these are amusement operations or ones that may affect public health and safety. The licensing fees can be as high as several thousand dollars, but in most cases the fees are quite nominal — a few dollars.

In addition, all businesses — whether or not they require a licence — must conform to local zoning regulations and bylaw requirements. In fact, zoning approval is usually a prerequisite to licence approval. Companies operating in their own facilities in most cities must also pay a business tax, assessed as a percentage of the rental value of their business facilities.

Provincial

Various provincial authorities also require a licence or permit. For example, in Ontario all establishments providing accommodation to the public, such as hotels, motels, lodges, tourist resorts, and campgrounds, must be licensed by the province. Businesses planning to serve liquor, operate long-haul cartage and transport operations, process food products, produce optical lenses, or manufacture upholstered furniture or stuffed toys may also require licensing. You should check with the local authorities to determine the types of licences and permits your business might require.

Mandatory Deductions and Taxes

If your business has a payroll you will be required to make regular deductions from employees' paycheques for unemployment insurance, income tax, and the Canada Pension Plan. These deductions must be remitted to Revenue Canada every month.

In addition, you may also be required to pay an assessment to your provincial Workers' Compensation Board. The size of your payment will be based on the nature of your business and its risk classification as well as the estimated size of your annual payroll. These funds are used to meet medical, salary, and rehabilitation costs for any of your employees that may be injured on the job.

Depending on the nature of your venture, you may also be responsible for remitting taxes of various kinds to either the provincial or the federal government. Most provinces apply a retail sales tax to almost all products and services sold to the ultimate consumer. Exceptions in some provinces include food, books, children's clothing, and medicine. The size and the application of these taxes vary from province to province, but if your business sells to final consumers you must obtain a permit and are responsible for collecting this tax and remitting to the government on a regular basis. Provinces also impose a variety of other taxes you may be required to collect and pay, such as gasoline tax, fuel tax, tobacco tax, land transfer tax, corporations tax, and capital tax.

Federal taxes largely fall into the categories of the Goods and Services Tax (GST) and income taxes. The GST is levied on virtually all products and services produced in Canada or imported. There are some minor exemptions for certain types of products and for very small companies, so you should check and see whether these taxes apply in your business. If so, you will be required to obtain a licence and remit any taxes collected on a regular basis.

How income tax is collected depends on the form of organization of your business. Sole proprietorships and partnerships file income tax returns as individuals and the same regulations apply. Federal and provincial taxes are paid together and only one personal income tax form is required annually for both, although payments may have to be remitted quarterly on the basis of your estimated annual earnings.

Corporations are treated as a separate entity for income tax purposes and taxed individually. The rules, tax rates, and regulations that apply to corporations are very complex and quite different from those that apply to individuals. You should obtain professional advice or keep in touch with the local tax authorities to determine your obligations under the Income Tax Act and to keep the amount of tax you have to pay to a minimum.

Employment Standards

All provinces have standards for employment and occupational health and safety that must be adhered to by all businesses within their jurisdiction. These requirements deal with such matters as:

1. Hours of work
2. Minimum wages
3. Statutory holidays
4. Overtime pay
5. Equal pay for equal work
6. Termination of employment
7. Severance pay
8. Working conditions
9. Health and safety concerns

You should contact the office of your provincial Ministry of Labour or its equivalent and request a copy of the Employment Standards Act in effect in your province as well as a copy of the Guide to the Act. This will provide you with specific information on all of these topics, or you can use the services of an accountant or lawyer.

CONCLUSION

There is no pat answer to the question of the legal form of organization you should adopt. A lot will depend on such issues as the expected size and growth rate of your new venture, your desire to limit your personal liability, whether you plan to start the business on a part-time or a full-time basis, whether you expect to lose or make money from a tax point of view during your first one or two years of operation, your need for other skills or additional capital, and so forth.

One word of caution: if you are considering any type of *partnership* arrangement, be extremely careful. In hard reality, partners should fulfil at least one of two major needs for you: they should provide either needed *money* or needed *skills*. If you allow any other factors to overshadow these two essential criteria, you may be taking an unnecessary risk.

One of the primary reasons new venture teams often fail is ill-advised partnerships. Partnerships entered into principally for reasons of friendship, shared ideas, or similar factors can create considerable stress for both the partnership and the individuals involved. It has often been said that a partner should be chosen with as much care as you would choose an ideal spouse. However, in contemporary society, perhaps even greater care should be exercised, since a partnership may be even more difficult to dissolve than a marriage. An unhappy partnership can dissolve your business much faster than you can dissolve the partnership.

STAGE
SIX

PROTECTING YOUR IDEA

Many entrepreneurs are also inventors. One of the primary problems faced by these inventor/ entrepreneurs is how to protect the idea, invention, concept, system, design, name, or symbol that they feel may be the key to their business success. Legislators have long recognized that society should provide some protection for the creators of this "intellectual property." The laws they have developed provide a form of limited monopoly to the creators of intellectual property in return for their disclosure of the details of the property to the public.

Intellectual property is broken down into five components under the law:

1. Patents
2. Trademarks
3. Copyrights
4. Industrial designs
5. Integrated Circuit Topographies

Protection of your intellectual property can be expensive. While government costs may range from only a small fee for registration of a copyright to several hundred dollars for registration of a patent, many of the procedures can be quite complex and require you to obtain the services of a registered *patent agent*. This can increase the total cost of obtaining a patent to as much as $10,000, the cost depending on the complexity of the application. Therefore, it is important that you understand the advantages and disadvantages provided by this protection, and its likely impact on the success and financial viability of your business.

APPLYING FOR A PATENT

A *patent* is a government grant that gives you the right to take legal action, if necessary, against other individuals who without your consent make, use, or sell the invention covered by your patent during the time the patent is in force. Patents are granted for 20 years from the date on which the application was first filed and are not renewable. On expiration of its patent, a patented device falls into the *public domain* — i.e., anyone may make, use, or sell the invention.

115

To be patentable, your device must:

1. Have "absolute novelty"
2. Be useful
3. Not be easily thought of by anyone skilled in the area of the invention's application

A patent may be granted to the inventor of any new and useful product, chemical composition, machine, or manufacturing process.

Patents will *not* be granted for any of the following:

1. An improvement to a known device that would be obvious to a person familiar with the known device
2. An improvement to a known device whose only difference from the original is a change in size, shape, or degree
3. A device whose prime purpose is illegal or illicit
4. A device that has no useful function or that doesn't work
5. Printed material
6. An idea or suggestion that is not completely developed
7. A scientific principle
8. A method of doing business
9. New works of art
10. A medical treatment
11. Recipes for dishes or drinks
12. A previously unknown substance that occurs naturally
13. A computer program
14. A process that depends entirely on artistic skill and leads to an ornamental effect

A patent may only be applied for by the *legal owner(s) of an invention*. You cannot apply for a patent for an invention you may have seen in another country even though that invention may never have been patented, described, or offered for sale in Canada.

Patents are now awarded to the *first inventor to file an application* with the Canadian Patent Office, rather than on the basis of the "first to invent" system previously used in Canada. This means you should file as soon as possible after completing your invention (though not prematurely so that certain key elements or features of your idea will be missing from your application). It is also important that you not advertise or display or publish information on your invention too soon, as this may jeopardize your ability to obtain a valid patent later on. There is a one-year grace period for disclosure by an applicant but it is suggested that the following rule of thumb be adopted: *Your application for a patent should be filed before your product is offered for public sale, shown at a trade show, or otherwise made public.*

How to Apply

If your idea is patentable and you wish to obtain patent protection, you should take the following steps:

1. **Find a patent agent** The preparation and *prosecution* (assessment) of patent applications is quite complex. You should consult a patent agent trained in this specialized practice and registered to practise before the Commissioner of Patents. Though hiring such an agent is not mandatory, it is highly recommended. A list of such individuals can be found in the publication *List of Registered Agents*, available from Consumer and Corporate Affairs Canada, 50 Victoria Street, Place du Portage, Phase I, Hull, Que. K1A 0C9.

2. **Conduct a preliminary search** The first step your agent will recommend is a preliminary search of existing patents to see if anything similar to your idea has already been patented, in which case you may conclude the process immediately. This can save you a lot of time and money that might otherwise be spent pursuing a futile application. The search can be conducted at the Patent Office in Hull, Quebec or at your local public library.

3. **Prepare a patent application** A patent application consists of an abstract, a specification, and drawings.

    An *abstract* is a brief summary of the material in the specification. The *specification* is a document that contains (1) a complete description of the invention and its purpose and (2) *claims*, which are an explicit statement of what your invention is and the boundaries of the patent protection you are seeking. *Drawings* must be included whenever the invention can be described pictorially. Typically, all inventions except chemical compositions and some processes can be described by means of drawings.

4. **File your application** Filing your application means submitting it along with a petition asking the Commissioner of Patents to grant you a patent. In Canada, filing must be done within one year of any use or public disclosure of the invention.

    If your application is accepted, you will be required to pay an annual maintenance fee to keep it in effect. Independent inventors and small businesses whose gross annual revenues are less than $2 million pay lower maintenance fees than businesses classified as "other than small." Fees range from zero in the first year to $200 in years 15 to 19 of the patent's life.

5. **Request examination** Your application will not automatically be examined simply because you have filed it. You must formally request examination and submit the appropriate fee. This request can be made any time within seven years of your filing date.

    Filing an application and not requesting examination can be a cheap and effective way of obtaining some protection for your invention without necessarily incurring all the costs of obtaining a patent. For example, let's assume you want to protect your idea but don't wish to spend all the money required to obtain a patent while you assess the financial feasibility of your invention. Filing an application establishes your rights to the invention and publication of the application by the Patent Office informs other people of your claim to the product or process. Should they infringe on your invention after your application is published, you have seven years to decide whether to pursue the grant of a patent and seek retroactive compensation.

    Requesting an examination, however, is no guarantee that a patent will be granted. And if it is not, you will have no grounds to claim damages for infringing on your idea.

    The Canadian Patent Office receives over 35,000 applications a year, mostly from American inventors and companies. As a result, the examination process can be very slow, commonly taking two to three years to complete.

6. **If necessary, file amendment letters** Upon your requesting an examination, the patent examiner will assess your claims and either approve or reject your application. If your application is rejected, you can respond by filing an *amendment letter* with the Commissioner of Patents. The letter will be studied by the examiner. If the patent is not then granted, there may be a request for further amendments. This process will continue until either the patent is granted, your application is withdrawn, or your application is finally rejected.

    The fact that not all patent applications are successful is illustrated by the case of Charles Sitarz (see Exhibit 6.1), who has been able to obtain a U.S. patent for his "downspout receiver" but has yet to receive a patent in Canada after years of trying despite using the services of a patent agent and filing all the proper papers. In fact, many Canadian inventors apply for a U.S. patent first, since it is often easier to obtain.

EXHIBIT 6.1

On most houses, there are odd-looking pipes sticking out every which way, waiting to direct rainwater from downspouts connected to the roof gutters.

Downpipes are a fact of residential life, but that doesn't mean people have to like them — or put up with them.

Let's face it — they're a bother. They have to be disconnected every time the lawn is mowed. And if they cross a walkway, they have to be removed to prevent people from tripping over them. Then when the rain comes, they must be put back on again.

Charles Sitarz once knew all about that trouble. But he decided to do something about it.

A crane operator at CN Rail's Transcona shops by day, he operates Flow-Matic Ltd. from his workshop at night, where he makes a product that offers an alternative to the rain pipe two-step — the "downspout receiver."

It's a simple, but effective idea. The receiver itself is a cylindrical container about the size of a large coffee can, which is buried in the ground a certain distance away from the house.

When it rains, the water is led by the side pipes down another connecting pipe buried in the ground, which is connected to the receiver. When it is full, the water forces the top of the container open, distributing the water evenly around the grass. When the rain stops, the lid closes again, and excess water is drained through tiny holes in the bottom of the receiver.

"It just came to me in a flash one day," says Sitarz, who conceived the idea 15 years ago, just after he finished working for a company that installed eavestroughs.

"People kept asking me whether there was a way of eliminating those pipes that stick out from the house. At the time, I didn't have an answer.

"Then I got a job at CN, got married and built my own home. I put up my eavestroughs and my downpipes. But when I cut my grass they were always in the way. Then I remembered all those people asking me about those pipes, and I sat down one day and started thinking about how

I could get rid of those pipes. That's when it came to me."

Sitarz then used his 17 years of experience as a sheet metal worker to build an experimental model in 1975, which he installed at his own home. It worked so well that he made inquiries about registering his invention the following year.

Sitarz called a lawyer friend of his, who recommended he go to a patent lawyer. Little did they know that it was only the beginning of a 14-year governmental red-tape runaround.

"I gave him a working model that I had made out of a tobacco can," Sitarz recalls. "He told me it would take some time, because his office would have to do research on it. A little while later, he got in touch with me and said there shouldn't be much of a problem patenting it because there wasn't anything like it on the market."

Some months later, the downspout receiver was granted "patent-pending" status, and things looked positive. Sitarz says he was told that while the U.S. patent office might not pass it, there shouldn't be a similar problem in Canada.

If you have sensed this story is about to take an ironic turn, you're unfortunately correct.

"We filled out the proper papers and, sure enough, [the Canadian patent office] turned me down. Then my lawyer suggested we should try for an American patent anyway. So we did, and they granted me a patent. Meanwhile, I was still fighting for a patent on this side of the border."

To this day, the receiver's patent is still on hold, and Sitarz continues to scratch his head over the patent office's logic in not granting the patent.

"They're comparing it to a water sprinkler, but that doesn't make any sense to me. My invention works on gravity, not pressure like a water sprinkler does. I keep hoping that one day they'll contact me and say, 'Here's your patent,' but they haven't yet."

Excerpted from Bohdan Gembarsky, "Patent office rains on downspout device," *Winnipeg Free Press*, July 29, 1990, p. 16. By permission of Bohdan Gembarsky.

Protection Provided by Your Patent

As you can see, the patenting process is complex, costly, and time-consuming. If you have a patent application in process and are concerned that someone else may attempt to patent your invention, you may use the label "Patent Pending" or "Patent Applied For" to inform the public that your application for a patent has been filed. This, however, has no legal significance and does not mean that a patent will necessarily be granted. Of course, it is illegal to use this term if in fact no application is on file.

If your patent application is granted, the onus will be entirely on you to protect your rights under the patent, for the Patent Office has no authority to prosecute for patent infringement. If infringement occurs, you may (1) bring legal action to compel the offender to account for any profits made, (2) seek an injunction to prevent further use of your patent, or (3) obtain a court order for the destruction of any materials produced which infringe on your rights. This, however, can be a very expensive and time-consuming process, which may prohibit a small business from enforcing its rights.

A patent granted in Canada or the U.S. provides you with no protection outside the country in which it was originally granted. To obtain protection in other countries, you must register your patent in each country within the time limit permitted by law (typically one year from your initial application). You can apply for a foreign patent either from within Canada via the Canadian Patent Office, or directly through the patent office of the country or countries concerned. Under the terms of the Patent Cooperation Treaty, it is possible to file for a patent in as many as 43 countries, including the U.S., Japan, and most of Europe, by completing a single, standardized application which can be filed in Canada. Ask your patent agent about these procedures before you decide to file in another country.

You should realize that holding a patent on a worthy idea does not necessarily mean commercial success. Dan Knight and Rick Hilton, whose case is described in Exhibit 6.2, appear to have an interesting idea with their patented Golf Bag Cooler, but they may never even recover the cost of obtaining their patents. An invention succeeds by acceptance in the marketplace. Your patent may

EXHIBIT 6.2

Happiness is pulling a cold beverage out of your golf bag when the clubhouse is four fairways away.

Working up a sweat to get to golf course club-houses for a cool sip is what prompted Dan Knight and Rick Hilton to invent their Golf Bag Cooler.

It's a skinny tube that fits inside a golf bag and holds six cans. A spring made out of musical instrument wire pushes a fresh can of pop (or beer) to the top of the bag every time one is taken out.

"It was Rick's idea about five years ago. I had an old doodle art tube at home and we tried to come up with a calibrated spring for it," says Knight. "For a while, until we got the right spring, we thought we'd have to put a caution label on the tube in case it shot cans out."

What keeps the cans cold — even in 98 degree Fahrenheit weather — is the air space between two PVC tubes fit one into the other, and small hockey puck-like objects filled with freezable gel which fit in between the cans. "It was the spring and the disks which got us the patent," says Hilton. "There's lots of elongated tube coolers out there, but these two things made ours unique. We got the idea for the disks from a toy hockey puck which we drilled a hole into and filled with gel. We had to use a turkey baster."

They had to turn to engineering companies and a couple of professors at the University of Manitoba to find out what material to build the coolers out of. The parts are manufactured in Boucherville, Quebec and then shipped to Winnipeg.

But as any inventor soon learns, there are three stages to any invention — dreaming it up, getting the patent and then getting it on the market.

Knight and Hilton along with partner Russ Glow have American and Canadian patents on the Golf Bag cooler but they're still trying to find a market with which to share their slice of heaven.

Excerpted from Susie Strachan, "Dreaming of a cool million: inventors perceive need, seek to cash in on fulfilling it," *South Edition Free Press Weekly*, February 18, 1992. Courtesy of *Free Press Weekly*. Used by permission.

be perfectly valid and properly related to your invention but commercially worthless. Thousands of patents are issued each year that fall into this category. A patent does not necessarily contribute to the economic success of an invention. In some high-technology fields, for example, innovations can become obsolete long before your patent is issued, effectively making the patent worthless.

Holding a patent may improve your profitability by keeping similar products off the market, giving you an edge. But there is no guarantee you will be able to prevent all competition. Litigation, if it becomes necessary, can require considerable financial resources, and the outcome is by no means assured. A high percentage of patent infringements challenged in court result in decisions unfavourable to the patent holder.

However, there are many instances where patenting a product concept or idea has led to commercial success. James Croteau, a former hockey player, developed and patented a lightweight, shock-absorbent protective shirt, the Armadillo, to be worn under hockey jerseys to prevent back injuries (Exhibit 6.3). The Armadillo is now worn by a number of NHL superstars and being sold in seven countries around the world.

Bob Dickie of Spark Innovations Inc. has built his whole business around patentable products. He holds 80 patents for his inventions and thinks patent protection is crucial to business success in the 90s. Bob's first product was the FlatPlug, billed as the first innovation in electrical plug design in 75 years. The FlatPlug lies flat against the wall, unlike a conventional electrical plug which sticks out perpendicular to the wall. As a result, it doesn't waste space behind furniture and is more difficult for children to pry out. Bob got the idea when he saw his daughter reach through her crib bars for a conventional plug. FlatPlug is protected by eight U.S. and worldwide patents. Even the package — a cardboard sleeve that keeps the extension cord and the plug in place — is patented.

In 1991, Bob set up Paige Innovations Inc. to commercialize FlatPlug. Sales in 1993 were about $6 million in Canada and the U.S. The company went public on the Toronto Stock Exchange in May 1994 with a market capitalization of $40 million.

Bob has a number of strict criteria he feels product ideas have to meet in order to have commercial potential:

- **It must be ten times better** Rather than evolutionary improvements in product design, he looks for concepts with enough of a "story" to make distribution channels take serious notice.
- **It must be patentable** "If we can't get a patent, the business is absolutely dead," says Mr. Dickie.
- **It must be a mass-production item** High-volume products have a higher turnover, reducing much of the risk of holding inventory.
- **It should be smaller than a bread box** Small items are easier to make and less costly to design, package, and transport.
- **It must lend itself to distribution through existing channels** Going through established market lines speeds the acceptance of a new product.
- **It should have no government involvement** Sparks stays away from products that are motivated by or dependent on government support at any level.
- **It must be useful** Mr. Dickie only works with products that have long-term, practical usefulness. No novelties, fads or games.[1]

REGISTERING YOUR TRADEMARK

A *trademark* is a word, symbol, picture, design, or combination of these which distinguishes your goods and services from those of others in the marketplace. A trademark might also be thought of

[1] Adapted from Ellen Roseman, "Spark of Genius," *The Globe and Mail*, September 26, 1994

EXHIBIT 6.3

Niagara Falls, Ont., inventor James Croteau, who suffered a serious injury playing hockey when he was young, never could get over the fact that all of his hockey buddies seemed to have bad backs. So, in the early 1980s, he did something about it.

He created the Armordillo — a lightweight, shock-absorbent shirt to be worn under hockey jerseys to reduce back injuries.

Now the shirt is worn by players in the National Hockey League and has been patented in Canada, the U.S., Germany, Switzerland, Sweden, Holland, Britain, and France.

"What really urged me into developing it was meeting up with old hockey friends — they all had back problems," says Croteau.

That fact, along with his perforated disc which ended a budding hockey career, convinced him the backs of hockey players get a lot of abuse.

"I was one of the leading scorers and it [perforated disk] sort of crushed my dream of going into the NHL. It haunted me all through the years and I decided I was going to do something about it."

Going through six designers in more than 10 years, the former rock concert promoter finally found designer Carrie Winter, also of Niagara Falls, who developed the idea into a reality. "It was all trial and error and I tried so many different prototypes. I couldn't have done it without her," he says.

In order for the shirt to be accepted by athletes, there was a great deal to consider in its design.

For example, he says, player movement had to be unrestricted with a lightweight and comfortable shirt. One of the first models he tried was made of a hard plastic and weighed about 18 kilograms (40 pounds) — too heavy and limiting to make sense, he says.

The final design, made of a lightweight plastic weighing about 140 grams, disperses shock when a player is hit with a hockey stick or slammed into the boards, he says.

In 1983, Croteau got his patent and, four years later, formed Blue Armadillo Inc. to peddle his invention.

The obvious market to conquer was the NHL. He knew if he could get the shirt to the Professional Hockey Athletic Trainer's Society trade show in 1990, it would sell itself. But in order to be allowed into the trade show, it first had to be tested and recommended by three different people. He sent shirts to different pro hockey teams to be tested and a few players from the New York Rangers and the Los Angeles Kings took to it and now regularly wear it, he says.

He also went to other sporting goods trade shows where he would prove his faith in the shock-absorbency of the shirt by having a weightlifter hit him.

"He weighed about 225 pounds and he would get a board and hit me about 18 times — baseball swings. [They were] heavy blows, too," he says.

"From there, a lot of teams ordered it ... all the big superstars jumped on it right away."

After sinking about $375,000 into the project, Croteau is selling the shirts in seven countries around the world for about $50 each.

"I've gone all through Europe," he says. "I looked at where hockey was a popular sport."

Excerpted from "Hockey Player Wins with Protective Shirt," *The Financial Post*, July 3, 1993, p. S21.

as a "brand name" or "identifier" that can be used to distinguish the product of your firm. For example, both the name "McDonald's" and the symbol of the golden arches are (among others) registered trademarks of the McDonald's Corporation.

To *register* a trademark means to file it with a government agency for the purpose of securing the following rights and benefits:

1. Exclusive permission to use the brand name or identifier in Canada

2. The right to sue anyone you suspect of infringing on your trademark to recover lost profits on sales made under your trade name, and for other damages and costs

3. The basis for filing an application in another country should you wish to export your product

To be registrable, a trademark must not be so similar in appearance, sound, or concept to a trademark already registered, or pending registration, as to be confused with it. For example, the following trademarks would not be registrable: "Cleanly Canadian" for a soft drink (too close to Clearly Canadian, a fruit-flavoured mineral water); "Extendo" for a utility knife (too close to Exacto).

The value of a trademark lies in the goodwill the market attaches to it and the fact that consumers will ask for your brand with the expectation of receiving the same quality product or service as previously. Therefore, unlike a patent, a trademark should be registered only if you have some long-term plans for it that will result in an accumulation of goodwill.

It is possible for you to use a trademark without registering it. Registration is not mandatory and unregistered marks have legal status. But registration is advised for most commonly used identifiers, since it does establish immediate, obvious proof of ownership.

How to Register Your Trademark

In Canada it is possible for you to register your trademark before you actually use it, but the mark will not be validated until it is actually put into service. Registration of a trademark involves the following steps:

1. **A search of previous and pending registrations** As with a patent, a search should be conducted to determine that your trademark does not conflict with others already in use.

2. **An application to register your trademark** This involves filing an application for registration of your trademark.

Once your application is received, it is published in the *Trade Mark Journal* to see if anyone opposes your registration.

Even though registering a trademark is relatively simple compared with applying for a patent, it is recommended that you consult a *trademark agent* registered to practise before the Canadian Trade Marks Office.

Maintaining and Policing Your Trademark

It normally takes about a year from the date of application for a trademark to be registered. Registration is effective for 15 years, and may be renewed for a series of 15-year terms as long as the mark is still in use.

As with a patent, it is up to you to police the use of your trademark; the government provides no assistance in the enforcement of your trademark rights. It is your decision whether to take any legal action against an offender.

Registration of a trademark in Canada provides no protection of your trademark in other countries. If you are involved with or contemplating exporting to any other country, you should consider registering your trademark in that country.

OBTAINING COPYRIGHT

A *copyright* gives you the right to preclude others from reproducing or copying your original published work. Materials protected by copyright include books, leaflets, periodicals and contributions to periodicals, lectures, sermons, musical or dramatic compositions, maps, works of art, photographs, drawings of a scientific or technical nature, motion pictures, sound recordings, and computer programs. A copyright exists for the duration of your life plus 50 years following your death.

How to Obtain a Copyright

In Canada, there is no legal requirement that your work be registered in order to obtain copyright; it is automatically acquired upon creation of an original work. Nevertheless, you may wish to apply for voluntary registration. When your work has been registered, a certificate is issued that can, if necessary, be used in court to establish your ownership of the work.

The Protection Provided by Copyright

Your copyright enables you to control the copying and dissemination of your own works. This includes publishing, producing, reproducing, and performing your material. As with patents and trademarks, the responsibility for policing your copyright rests with you.

It is important to understand some of the limitations of copyright protection as well. For example, for purposes of copyright protection, the term "computer program" refers to "a set of instructions or statements, expressed, fixed, embodied or stored in any manner, that is to be used directly or indirectly in a computer in order to bring about a specific result." This means that a *specific* computer program such as Lotus 1-2-3 can be protected as a literary work but not the idea of *spreadsheet programs* in general. In addition, any accompanying documentation for a program, such as a user's guide, is considered a separate work and must be registered separately.

Unlike patents and trademarks, a copyright in Canada provides simultaneous protection in most other countries of the world.

PROTECTING INTEGRATED CIRCUIT TOPOGRAPHIES

The circuits incorporated into an integrated circuit (IC) are embodied in a three-dimensional hill-and-valley configuration called a topography. These designs are protected by the Integrated Circuit Topography Act. IC products, commonly called "microchips" or "semiconductor chips" are incorporated into a variety of consumer and industrial products. The protection associated with the design of a topography is entirely distinct from that of any computer program embodied in the chip. Computer programs are subject to protection under the Copyright Act.

What Protection Does the Act provide?

The legislation provides exclusive rights in regard to:
- reproduction of a protected topography or any substantial part of it
- manufacturing an IC product incorporating the topography or any substantial part of it
- importation or commercial exploitation of a topography, or of an IC product which embodies a protected topography or any substantial part of it
- importation or commercial exploitation of an industrial article which incorporates an IC product that embodies a protected topography

The Act provides for a full range of civil remedies including injunctions and exemplary damages. Protection for registered integrated circuit topographies is provided for approximately 10 years.

How to Protect an IC Topography

To protect an IC topography you must apply to the Registrar of Topographies. Applications for "commercially exploited" topographies must be filed within two years of the date of first commercial exploitation anywhere. The application may be rejected if the topography was first exploited outside Canada. Owners must be Canadian or nationals of countries having reciprocal protection agreements with Canada.

FOR MORE INFORMATION ON INTELLECTUAL PROPERTY

Further information on the protection of intellectual property can be obtained from:

Canadian Intellectual Property Office
Industry Canada
50 Victoria St.
Place du Portage, Phase 1
Hull, Quebec
K1A 0C9   Tel: (819) 997-1936

or contact your local Industry Canada, Canada Business Services Centre.

The deadlines for filing, the length of time for which protection is provided, and the current registration fees for several types of intellectual property are summarized in Table 6.1.

TABLE 6.1   INFORMATION ABOUT PROTECTION OF INTELLECTUAL PROPERTY IN CANADA

Type	Application Deadline	Period of Coverage	Initial Government Fees
Patents	File within 1 year of publication (file before publication for most other countries)	20 years from filing of application	$150
Trademarks	(None)	15 years; renewable indefinitely	$150
Copyright	(None)	50 years plus life of author	$ 35

CONCLUSION

As we have discussed, in addition to various *tangible* assets such as land, buildings, and equipment, your business may also own certain *intangible* assets, such as patents, trademarks, and copyrights. These can be just as important as, or even more important than, your tangible assets. And like tangible assets, with permission of their owner they can be bought, sold, licensed, or used by someone else.

Ideas that are not patentable, and are not otherwise protected, may be protected by contract law either by means of a written *non-disclosure agreement* or by treating them as *trade secrets*. This can be done by taking every precaution to keep valuable knowledge a secret and/or by placing specific provisions in any agreement you may have with your employees that they will neither disclose to anyone else nor use for their own purposes any trade secrets they may acquire while in your employ. The advantages of this type of protection may be even greater than those of patent protection. The success of this approach depends on your ability to control the access of outsiders to the information, as there are no *legal rights* in a trade secret. Typically, once confidential information has been publicly disclosed, it becomes very difficult to enforce any rights to it.

STAGE

CONDUCTING A FEASIBILITY STUDY

Part 1:
Technical and Market Assessment

So far, we have considered and evaluated your new venture primarily from a conceptual point of view. That is, we have concentrated on the following questions:

1. What product/service businesses would you be interested in pursuing?
2. How attractive are these venture ideas?
3. What options should you consider in getting into a business of your own?
4. How should your business be organized?
5. How can you protect your idea or concept?

Now, in Stage Seven, a step-by-step process will be presented to help you transform your *chosen* venture concept from the idea stage to the marketplace. This is accomplished by means of a *feasibility study*.

A feasibility study is the first comprehensive plan you need in contemplating any new venture. It proves both to yourself and others that your new venture concept can become a profitable reality. A typical feasibility study considers the following areas:

1. The concept for your venture
2. The technical feasibility of your idea
3. An assessment of your market
4. The supply situation
5. Cost-profit analysis
6. Your plans for future action

The first four of these topics will be discussed in this Stage; the last two will be addressed in Stage Eight. Much of the same information can be incorporated into your subsequent business plan (see Stage Ten) if it appears that your venture warrants commercial development.

YOUR VENTURE CONCEPT

It is critical that you be able to clearly and concisely explain, verbally, the principal concept underlying your venture — what sets it apart from other businesses of similar character. If you have difficulty explaining to other people precisely what it is your business proposes to do, it is a clear sign that your concept still needs development and refinement.

An idea is not yet a concept, only the beginning of one. A fully developed concept includes not only some notion as to the product or service the business plans to provide, but also a description of the proposed pricing strategy, promotional program, and distribution plans. It will also consider such aspects of the business as what is unique or proprietary about your product or service idea, any innovative technology involved in its production or sale, and the principal benefits it is expected to deliver to customers.

Developing a good description of your concept can be difficult. Many concepts are too broad and general, not clearly communicating the really distinctive elements of the venture — for example, "a retail sporting goods outlet" or "a tool and equipment rental store." Other concepts may use words like "better service," "higher quality," "new," "improved," or "precision machined," which are either ambiguous or likely to have different meanings for different people. It is much better to have a detailed, clear, definitive statement — for example, "a retail outlet providing top-of-the-line hunting and fishing equipment and supplies for the serious outdoors person" or "a tool and equipment rental business for the professional commercial and residential building contractor." Such descriptions are easier to visualize and allow the uninformed to really understand what it is you propose to do.

Your business concept is not necessarily etched in stone. It may need to change and evolve over time as you come to better understand the needs of the marketplace and the economics of the business. Sharpening and refining of your concept is normal and to be expected.

TECHNICAL FEASIBILITY

You should keep in mind that not all businesses are started on the basis of new or original ideas. Many, in fact, merely attempt to copy successful ventures. To simplify matters, all product and service ideas can be placed along a continuum according to their degree of innovativeness or may be placed into one of the following categories:

1. **New invention** This is something created for the first time through a high degree of innovation, creativity, and experimentation. Examples are fibre optics, laser surgery, and computer bubble memories.

2. **Highly innovative** This term means that the product is somewhat new and as yet not widely known or used. Examples are cellular phone systems and light rail transit train systems.

3. **Moderately innovative** This refers to a product which is a significant modification of an existing product or service or combines different areas of technology, methods, or processes. Examples include microprocessors used to control automobile fuel injection systems or single-person cars. The term could also refer to such ideas as the redesign of bicycles to make them easier to ride by handicapped or physically disabled people, thus developing a new market.

4. **Slightly innovative** This term means that a small, yet significant, modification is made to an established product or service, as in larger-scale or more exotic recreational water slides.

5. **"Copycatting"** This is simply imitating someone else's business idea.

The degree of innovation inherent in a business idea has strong implications for the risk, difficulty in evaluation, and profit potential of the venture. *Risk* refers to the probability of the product or service's failing in the marketplace. *Evaluation* is the ability to determine its worth or significance. *Profit potential* is the level of return or compensation that you might expect for assuming the risks associated with investing in this business.

In general, the following relationships hold:

1. New inventions are risky and difficult to evaluate, but if they are accepted in the marketplace they can provide enormous profits.

2. For moderately innovative and slightly innovative ideas, the risks are lower and evaluation is less difficult, but profit potential tends to be more limited.

3. In the "copycat" category, risks are often very high and profit potential tends to be quite low. Such businesses usually show no growth, or very slow growth, and there is little opportunity for profit beyond basic wages.

Every new product must also be subject to some form of analysis to ensure that the benefits promised prospective customers will indeed be delivered. In developing a working prototype or an operating model with this in mind, some of the more important technical requirements to consider are:

1. **Keep it as simple as possible** Keep it simple to build, to transport, to maintain, and above all to use.

2. **Make it flexible** There are many examples of products that were unsuccessful in the application for which they were originally developed but were able to be redesigned to satisfy the needs of an entirely different market.

3. **Build a product that will work as intended without failing** Quality assurance, or eliminating the need for regular and constant service, is becoming more important to consumers. They are more inclined than ever before to look for products that are durable, reliable, safe, and easily maintainable.

If a product does not meet these technical qualifications it should be reworked until it does.

One key approach for testing a new product is to subject it to the toughest conditions that might be experienced during actual use. In addition to this kind of test there may be standard engineering tests to which the product will have to be subjected to receive Canadian Standards Association (CSA) or Underwriters Laboratory certification. You might also undertake an evaluation of alternative materials from which the product might be made. Further assistance in conducting a technical evaluation may be available from various agencies of your provincial government as well as some colleges and universities.

MARKET ASSESSMENT

Assessing the potential market for your concept is a critical part of any feasibility study. At the very least, you need to demonstrate that a market does in fact exist, or there is not much point in developing a full-scale business plan. In some cases the potential market may be large and obvious; in others, considerable research and investigation may be required to demonstrate there is likely to be any significant level of demand. It is essential to determine that there is a sufficiently large market to make the concept financially viable.

Who is Your Customer?

In order to tailor your marketing program to the needs of your market, you must have a very clear idea of who your customers are likely to be. To do this you will need to conduct some thorough research in the marketplace. The more information you have about your target market, the better you will be able to develop a successful marketing plan.

The first thing to recognize is that the term "market" does not only refer to a single type of possible customer. A number of different types of markets exist such as:

1. The consumer market, consisting of individual users of products and services such as you and I.

2. The institutional market, consisting of organizations such as hospitals, personal care homes, schools, universities, and similar types of institutions.

3. The industrial market, comprised of other firms and businesses in your community and across the country.

4. The government market, consisting of various agencies and departments of the municipal, provincial, and federal governments.

5. The international market, composed of markets similar to the above examples outside the national boundaries of the country.

Very few businesses initially operate in all of these markets. Most analyze the possibilities available to them in each situation in order to determine which offers the best potential. This involves asking such broad questions as:

1. How big is the market?
2. Where is it located geographically?
3. How fast is it growing?
4. What organizations and/or individuals buy this kind of product or service?
5. Why do they buy it?
6. Where and how do they buy it?
7. How often do they buy it?
8. What are their principal requirements in selecting a product or service of this type?

This kind of assessment will serve to identify some broad areas of opportunity for you.

In addition to doing this broad analysis, you might also question whether within these major market types there are groups of potential buyers with different preferences, requirements, or purchasing practices. For example, toddlers, teenagers, business people, and older adults all have quite different clothing needs. A manufacturer must take these into account in developing and marketing their product line. Each of these groups should well be considered as a separate *target market*. This process of breaking large, heterogeneous consumer or industrial markets down into more homogeneous groups is known as *market segmentation*. Most markets can be segmented on the basis of a number of variables:

1. Their geographic location, such as part of a city, or town, county, province, region, or country.

2. Their demographic description such as age, sex, marital status, family size, race, religion, education level, and occupation. Non-consumer markets might be classified on the basis of their total purchases or sales, number of employees, or type of organizational activity.

3. A variety of sociological factors, such as their lifestyle, user status, usage rate, timing, and means of purchasing, and reasons for buying products or services similar to yours.

Figure 7.1 provides a framework you can complete to develop a *market profile* of your prospective customers.

Estimating Total Market Size and Trends

A large part of market assessment is determining the volume of *unit sales* or *dollar revenue* that might flow from a market and what proportion of this you might expect to capture. At first glance "unit sales" seems to mean simply how many potential customers there are in the market for your product/service. However, this would overlook the possibility that some customers may buy more than one unit of the product/service. Estimates of total market size must take these *repeat purchases* into account. Total demand is determined by multiplying the number of customers who will buy by the average number of units each might be expected to purchase. To determine the total market size in dollars, simply multiply this total number of units by the average selling price.

FIGURE 7.1 DEVELOPING A MARKET OR CUSTOMER PROFILE

1. Define your target customers in terms of geography, demographic characteristics, or other factors.

_____

_____

_____

_____

2. How many of these target customers are in your trading or relevant market area?

_____

_____

_____

_____

3. What are the principal factors these customers consider in the purchase of a product/service like yours?

_____

_____

_____

_____

4. Why will they buy your product rather than your competitors'?

_____

_____

_____

_____

Figure 7.2 provides a form you can complete to estimate the approximate total market size (past, present, and future) and the expected trends for your product/service type.

Customer and Market Research

SOURCES OF MARKET INFORMATION

There are a number of sources you might consult to get a handle on the approximate size of the market you are considering entering. Some of these sources are Statistics Canada publications; various industry reports, trade journals, and investment journals; and financial statements of your leading competitors. You must be careful to make some provision for error in your estimate of market size. Most of the information sources you will consult will not be able to provide complete up-to-date figures, and forecasts of future sales are always subject to error. Statistics Canada, for example, breaks the country up into 36 Census Metropolitan Areas (CMA). For each CMA there are a series of referenced maps providing an index for which it is possible to get a *tract number* for almost any neighbourhood in the country. From this tract number you can get a detailed breakdown of the number of people and their characteristics within a single local neighbourhood or for a combination of tracts comprising a region of a city or for the entire metropolitan area. This data can be a valuable resource providing a wide variety of information on a large number of geographic markets. The major drawback, however, is that it is largely derived from census data and may be

FIGURE 7.2 FORM FOR ESTIMATING MARKET SIZE

ESTIMATED TOTAL MARKET SIZE

1. DESCRIPTION OF PRINCIPAL MARKET

_____

_____

	19X0	19X1	19X2	19X3	19X4
Sales in units	_____	_____	_____	_____	_____
Sales in $000	_____	_____	_____	_____	_____

2. OVERVIEW OF MAJOR SEGMENTS

a. Description of segment: _____

_____

	19X0	19X1	19X2	19X3	19X4
Sales in units	_____	_____	_____	_____	_____
Sales in $000	_____	_____	_____	_____	_____

b. Description of segment: _____

_____

	19X0	19X1	19X2	19X3	19X4
Sales in units	_____	_____	_____	_____	_____
Sales in $000	_____	_____	_____	_____	_____

a little stale. This should not be surprising, given the constantly changing tastes of consumers and ongoing technological advancement.

Following are listings of some of the more popular sources of market information. Much of this material is available at your local public, college, or university library. In most situations the best place to start is with _the trade publications and trade associations for the industry in which your business will compete._

Trade Publications Just to give you an idea of the number and diversity of the trade publications produced in Canada, take a minute to review Table 7.1. It is by no means a listing of _all_ trade-oriented publications, merely a sampling of the range of material available to you. Depending on the nature of your new venture, any one or more of innumerable publications could represent a source of market-related information or a means for you to communicate with potential customers.

General Publications In addition to trade publications there are numerous general publications that can be extremely useful in compiling relevant market data. Some of the more important of these are listed in Table 7.2. In addition to all these publications, sources that you should look to for information include:

1. Your local chamber of commerce
2. Your city or municipal hall
3. Local or regional development corporations
4. District school board offices
5. Provincial government offices
6. Downtown business associations
7. Shopping centre developers

TABLE 7.1 SOME TRADE PUBLICATIONS PRODUCED IN CANADA

Aerospace & Defence Technology	Canadian Mining Journal	Jobber News
Applied Arts	Canadian Music Trade	Lighting Magazine
Architecture Concept	Canadian Oil & Gas Handbook	Luggage, Leathergoods &
Atlantic Fisherman	Canadian Pharmaceutical	Accessories
Aviation Trade	Journal	L'Automobile
Bakers Journal	Canadian Pool & Spa Marketing	Machinery & Equipment MRO
Bath & Kitchen Marketer	Canadian Premiums & Incentives	Masthead
Benefits Canada	Canadian Security	Medicine North America
Boating Business	Canadian Vending	Modern Purchasing
Bodyshop	Computer Dealer News	Motel/Hotel Lodging
Building Renovation	Construction Canada	Office Equipment & Methods
Business to Business Marketing	Cosmetics	Plant Engineering & Mainte-
CAD/CAM & Robotics	Dental Practice Management	nance
Canadian Apparel Manufacturer	Design Engineering	Plastics Business
Canadian Beverage Review	Eastern Trucker	Quill and Quire
Canadian Building Owner &	Electrical Equipment News	Sanitation Canada
Property Manager	Farm Equipment Quarterly	Service Station & Garage
Canadian Doctor	Fleur Design	Management
Canadian Food & Drug	Floor Covering News	Shopping Centre Canada
Canadian Forest Industries	Food in Canada	Software Report
Canadian Funeral News	Food & Drug Packaging News	Sports Business
Canadian Grocer	Footwear Forum	The Bottom Line
Canadian Hairdresser	Fur Trade Journal	The Business and Professional
Canadian Heavy Equipment	Gardenland	Woman
Guide	Gifts and Tablewares	The Western Investor
Canadian Hotel & Restaurant	Greenhouse Canada	Trade Asia Magazine
Canadian Industry Shows &	Group Travel	Transportation Business
Exhibitions	Hardware Merchandising	Visual Communications
Canadian Jeweler	Health Care	Water & Pollution Control
Canadian Machinery & Metal-	Industrial Distributor News	Woodworking
working	Industrial Product Ideas	

8. Advertising agencies
9. Newspaper, radio, and television stations
10. Competitors
11. Sales representatives and trade suppliers
12. Similar businesses in another location
13. Other business associates

CANADA BUSINESS SERVICE CENTRES

One prospective source of market information that should not be overlooked is your provincial Canada Business Service Centre (CBSC). The CBSCs are a collaborative effort between federal, provincial, and private sector organizations designed to provide business people with access to a wide range of information on government services, programs, and regulations. Each CBSC offers a broad range of products and services tailored to meet the needs of its particular clients. These include:

- a toll-free telephone information and referral service
- the Business Information System (BIS) database containing information on the services and programs of the participating departments and organizations
- faxables: condensed versions of the BIS products accessed through an automated FaxBack system

TABLE 7.2 OTHER PUBLISHED SOURCES OF MARKET INFORMATION

GENERAL

Gale Directory of Publication and Business Media
  Gale Research Company
  Book Tower
  Detroit, MI 48826

The Standard Periodical Directory
  Oxbridge Communications Inc.
  150 Fifth Avenue
  New York, NY 10011

Ulrich's International Periodicals Directory
  R. R. Bowker Company
  245 West 17th Street
  New York, NY 10011

Indexes to books and magazine articles on a wide variety of business, industrial, and economic topics:

Bibliographic Index: A Cumulative Bibliography
of Bibliographies
  H. W. Wilson Co.
  950 University Avenue
  New York, NY 10452

Business Periodicals Index
  H. W. Wilson Co.
  950 University Avenue
  New York, NY 10452

Canadian Business Index
  Micromedia Limited
  158 Pearl Street
  Toronto, Ontario
  M5H 1L3

A detailed listing of source books, periodicals, directories, handbooks, and other sources of information on a variety of business topics:

Sources of Information for Canadian Business
  Canadian Chamber of Commerce
  Suite 301
  200 Elgin Street
  Ottawa, Ontario
  K2P 2J7

Encyclopedia of Business Information Sources
  Gale Research Company
  Book Tower
  Detroit, MI 48826

Directory of Industry Data Sources
  Ballinger Publishing Co.
  54 Church Street
  Box 281
  Cambridge, MA 02138

A general guide to business publications:

Business Information: How to Find It, How to Use It
  Oryx Press
  2214 North Central Avenue
  Phoenix, AZ 85004-1483

Business Information Sources
  University of California Press
  2120 Berkeley Way
  Berkeley, CA 94720

Directories of business-oriented database retrieval systems:

On Line Business Information Guide
  John Wiley & Sons Inc.
  605 Third Avenue
  New York, NY 10158

Business Online: A Canadian Guide
  John Wiley & Sons Canada
  Professional & Trade Division
  22 Worcester Road
  Rexdale, ON
  M9W 1L1

INDUSTRY AND MARKET INFORMATION

Data on income, population, expenditures, etc. by major market area:

Survey of Buying Power (annual special issue of *Sales and Marketing Management*)
  Bill Communications, Inc.
  633 Third Avenue
  New York, NY 10017

Information on population size and growth, income, expenditures, prices, and similar data by market area:

Handbook of Canadian Consumer Markets
  Conference Board of Canada
  Suite 100
  25 McArthur Avenue
  Ottawa, Ontario
  K1L 6R3

Market Research Handbook
  Statistics Canada
  Ottawa, Ontario
  K1A 0T6

Canadian Markets: Complete Demographics for Canadian Urban Markets
  The Financial Post
  Maclean Hunter Limited
  777 Bay Street
  Toronto, Ontario
  M5W 1A7

A general listing of available federal government publications:

Subject List
  Supply and Services Canada
  Canada Communication Group Publishing
  Ottawa, Ontario
  K1A 0S9

COMPANY INFORMATION

Detailed information on most major corporations:

Thomas Register of American Manufacturers
  Thomas Publishing Co.
  1 Penn Plaza
  New York, NY 10001

Dun & Bradstreet Reference Book
  Dun & Bradstreet, Inc.
  99 Church St.
  New York, NY 10007

Corporate Directory
  Cambridge Information Group
  7200 Wisconsin Avenue
  Bethesda, MD 20814

  Moody's Manuals and Investor Services
  99 Church Street
  New York, NY 10007

Listings of Canadian manufacturers by location and product category:

Fraser's Canadian Trade Directory
  Maclean Hunter Limited
  777 Bay Street
  Toronto, Ontario
  M5W 1A7

Scott's Industrial Directories:
  • Western Manufacturers
  • Ontario Manufacturers
  • Quebec Manufacturers
  • *Atlantic Manufacturers*

Scott's Trade Directory: Metropolitan Toronto and Toronto Vicinity
  Scott's Directories Southam Ltd.
  Box 365
  75 Thomas Street
  Oakville, Ontario
  L6J 5M5

MARKETING INFORMATION

Listings of rates and other information on radio, television, consumer magazines, trade magazines, direct mail, and newspapers:

Standard Rate & Data Media Publications
  Standard Rate & Data Service
  3004 Glenview Road
  Wilmette, IL 60091

Canadian Advertising Rates & Data
  Maclean Hunter Research Bureau
  777 Bay Street
  Toronto, Ontario
  M5W 1A7

continued

Other Published Sources of Market Information — continued

A listing of agents and firms representing manufacturers of all types:

Verified Directory of Manufacturer's Representatives
Manufacturer's Agent Publishing Co.
663 Fifth Avenue
New York, NY 10022

Manufacturer's Agents National Association Directory of Members
Manufacturer's Agents National Association
2021 Business Center Drive
P.O. Box 16878
Irvine, CA 92713

Comprehensive listings of U.S. and Canadian meetings, conventions, trade shows, and expositions:

Conventions & Meetings Canada
Effective Communications Ltd.
5762 Highway 7
Markham, Ontario
L3P 1A8

World Convention Dates
CML Marked Letter Inc.
79 Washington Street
Hempstead, NY 11550

Directory of Conventions
Sales and Marketing Management Magazine
Bill Communications, Inc.
633 Third Avenue
New York, NY 10017

A comprehensive listing of mail order firms:

Mail Order Business Directory
B. Klein Publications
P.O. Box 8503
Coral Springs, FL 33065

Mail Order Product Guide
18 North Greenbush Road
Todd Pubus
West Nyack, NY 10994

Directory of Mail Order Catalogs
Grey House Publishing
Bank of Boston Building
Sharon, CT 06069

A comprehensive listing of all trade and professional associations in Canada:

Directory of Associations in Canada
Micromedia Ltd.
15B Pearl Street
Toronto, Ontario
M5H 1L3

TABLE 7.3 LOCATION OF CANADA BUSINESS SERVICE CENTRES (CBSC) ACROSS CANADA

Canada/British Columbia Business
Service Centre
601 West Cordova Street
Vancouver, British Columbia
V6B 1G1
Tel.: (604) 775-5525
Toll Free: 1-800-667-2272
Fax: (604) 775-5520
FaxBack: (604) 775-5515

Canada Business Service Centre
9700 Jasper Avenue, Suite 122
Edmonton, Alberta
Tel.: (403) 495-6800
Toll Free: 1-800-272-9675
Fax: (403) 495-7725

Canada/Saskatchewan Business Service Centre
122 - 3rd Avenue, North
Saskatoon, Saskatchewan
S7K 2H6
Tel.: (306) 956-2323
Toll Free: 1-800-667-4374
Fax: (306) 956-2328
FaxBack: (306) 956-2310
FaxBack: 1-800-667-9433

Canada Business Service Centre
330 Portage Avenue, 8th Floor
P.O. Box 981
Winnipeg, Manitoba
R3C 2V2
Tel.: (204) 984-2272
Toll Free: 1-800-665-1029
Fax: (204) 983-2187
FaxBack: (204) 984-5527
FaxBack: 1-800-665-9386

Canada/Nova Scotia Business Service Centre
1575 Brunswick Street
Halifax, Nova Scotia
B3J 2G1
Tel.: (902) 426-8604
Toll Free: 1-800-668-1010
Fax: (902) 426-6530
FaxBack: (902) 426-3201
FaxBack: 1-800-401-3201

Canada Business Service Centre
90 O'Leary Avenue
P.O. Box 8687
St. John's, Newfoundland
A1B 3T1
Tel.: (709) 772-6022
Toll Free: 1-800-668-1010
Fax: (709) 772-6090
FaxBack: (709) 772-6030

Canada Business Service Centre
Toronto, Ontario M5V 3E5
Tel: (416) 954-INFO (4636)
Toll Free: 1-800-567-2345
Fax: (416) 954-8597
FaxBack: (416) 954-8555
FaxBack: (800) 240-4192

Info entrepreneurs
5 Place Ville Marie
Plaza Level, Suite 12500
Montreal, Quebec
H3B 4Y2
Tel.: (514) 496 INFO (4636)
Toll Free: 1-800-322-INFO (4636)
Fax: (514) 496-5934
Info-Fax: (514) 496-4010
Info-Fax: 1-800-322-4010

Canada/New Brunswick Business Service Centre
570 Queen Street
Fredericton, New Brunswick
E3B 6Z6
Tel.: (506) 444-6140
Toll Free: 1-800-668-1010
Fax: (506) 444-6172
FaxBack: (506) 444-6169

Canada/Prince Edward Island Business Service
Centre
232 Queen Street
Charlottetown, Prince Edward Island
C1A 7K2
Tel.: (902) 368-0771
Toll Free: 1-800-668-1010
Fax: (902) 566-7098
FaxBack: (902) 368-0776
FaxBack: 1-800-401-3201

- pathfinders: a set of documents that provide brief descriptions of services and programs related to a particular topic (e.g., exporting, tourism)
- a collection of other business services which could include interactive diagnostic software, videos, business directories, how-to manuals, CD-ROM library search capability, and external database access

CBSCs are located in one major urban centre in each province. Table 7.3 contains a complete listing of the location of each Centre and the numbers for telephone referral and FaxBack service at each site.

THE INTERNET

Another place where you may be able to find a good deal of information about any idea you plan to pursue is the Internet. Not everything is available on the Net yet. In fact, it has been described as a "Work in Progress." But, with a little practice now even new users can skim the Net's millions of

Web pages and thousands of Usenet newsgroups for topics of general interest and also to home in on precise bits of specific data.

What has simplified the job of culling information from Web pages and Usenet groups is the development of a variety of "search engines" that enable the user to search rapidly through either a variety of searchable directories or the nooks and crannies of the Web itself to create indexes of information related to a particular topic in seconds.

Leading the way are Web-based engines like Lycos (http://www.lycos.com), Infoseek Guide (http://www.infoseek.com), Excite (http://www.excite.com), and Alta Vista (http://www.altavista.digital.com). These search engines send out software agents, or "spiders" that explore the entire Internet.

Complementing these databases are a number of searchable "directories" like Yahoo (http://www.yahoo.com), Magellan (http://www.mckinley.com), and PointCom (http://www.pointcom.com). These directories can be good jumping off points if you are looking for general information on a topic rather than very precise data. Broad subject areas such as travel, sports, or food are broken down into categories and sub-categories. The differences between the search engines and directories, however, is becoming clouded as each starts to take on more of the characteristics of the other.

Most search engines work in a similar way but usually do not come up with the same results. Alta Vista, for example, scans the full contents of Web pages and Usenet groups and probably provides the most detailed and minute references. Infoseek Guide, on the other hand, provides a less comprehensive search but may produce better results. To overcome such anomalies, a number of "metasearch" engines have been developed. Metacrawler (http://www.metacrawler.com), for instance, simultaneously loads search queries into nine leading engines and provides the combined results.

Most directories and search engines provide basic instructions as to how to initiate a search as part of their home page. For a beginner, it all starts with you entering a "query." A "query" consists of one or more key words — a company name, a city or country, or any other topic likely to appear either in the title or the body of a Web page. Most search programs employ Boolean logic, expanding or limiting a search by including "and," "but," and "or" as part of the search process. The more precise your query, the better. For example: if you are interested in a topic like antique automobiles, typing in "antique and automobiles" instead of just "automobiles" will direct you to information regarding older cars although you may also get sites for antique dealers in general and other related subjects.

With most search engines the process starts with the click of your mouse once you have entered your query. Within seconds, a list of matches is produced, usually in batches of 10, with a brief description and the home page address. A further click on one of the matches gets you to that page or Usenet group.

Because of the explosion in the number of Web-based search programs, it can be difficult to keep up with the latest services. Search (http://www.search.com) serves as a kind of one-stop shop for search engines while c/net, a news and information service (http://www.cnet.com), provides access to 250 search sites and directories. The most popular search engines can also be accessed from the home pages of the two most popular Web browsers, Netscape Navigator and Microsoft's Internet Explorer.

MARKET-TESTING YOUR IDEA

There are a number of methods for testing the market prospects of your idea. These include prototype development, obtaining opinions from prospective buyers, comparing your idea with competitors' offerings, conducting in-store tests, and demonstrating it at trade shows.

One or more of these techniques can be employed to assess how the market is likely to react to your concept or idea. Chips Klein, whose case is described in Exhibit 7.1, used a variety of methods before refining her Eye Maker to the point that she was happy with the design and felt it would be well received in the marketplace.

In 1981, Chips Klein, a cosmetics consultant and mother of three in Guelph, Ont., decided she had done her last contortion in front of a mirror to apply her eyeliner and mascara. She decided to become an inventor.

"I found I could do wonderful makeovers on clients because I could see their eyes from all sides — it was logical to develop a mirror that enabled me to see my own eyes the way a make-up artist can see them."

Klein, 40, wanted to create a three-way mirror that would reflect the tops and bottoms of eyelids as well as the direct view. To build her prototype, she experimented on her kitchen table with cardboard, plastic, tape and pieces of mirrored glass. The result was a miniature version of a professional beautician's three-way mirror.

With $10,000 for manufacturing and marketing, she and her husband, Paul, formed Chipco Canada Inc. Klein called her product "Eye Maker" and took her prototype to plastics and glass manufacturers to get the components made. Then she contracted the Vanier Centre for Women, a correctional institution in Brampton, Ont., to do assembly. She sent samples to major department stores and hairdressers' supply houses in time for the 1981 Christmas selling season, and sold out the first run of 5,000 mirrors, which retailed for $13 a piece.

"The feedback I got was that the concept was good but the models were too small," says Klein. "So we rolled back our profits of about $20,000, plus an additional $5,000 in personal savings, to develop a larger version."

By the end of 1982, Eye Maker sales reached $50,000. But Klein still wasn't happy with the design, so, in 1983, she took her invention to an industrial designer for refinements. A grant from the Ontario Ministry of Industry, Trade and Technology covered 80% of the $25,000

design fee. In that year she also stopped being a homemaker to pursue her business full-time.

Klein prepared a business plan for her bank manager in Guelph, Ont., but felt it was difficult to translate her product's potential into figures and projections.

"I wanted to be sure I could clinch the deal," says Klein. "Then I had a stroke of genius. There was a make-up manufacturers' convention in downtown Toronto in 1984, so I booked a suite at the hotel and sent invitations to the consultants to come see my product. The room was crammed with women who, what with the excitement created by the convention, were ecstatic with the mirror. I then called a Toronto branch bank manager to discuss the loan, and his jaw dropped when he saw the sales the mirror was generating. He called my bank in Guelph and I got a $40,000 line of credit immediately."

In 1986, Chipco Canada's sales totalled $120,000. Klein has also hired sales agents across Canada and the U.S. to increase her revenues. Representatives will push sales across Canada and help Chipco customers develop display units and in-store promotions.

Klein is now eyeing Europe, and has signed a deal with a distribution company in Germany. She is looking into cross-promotions with cosmetic firms based in Canada, and has introduced a thin, compact version of the Eye Maker which will retail for $8.50.

Because of the sales network and new products, Klein says she's been able to make a quantum leap in sales; she projects revenues of at least $1.1 million this year.

Excerpted from T. Nesdoly, "There are three sides to everything," *Small Business*, January/February 1988, pp. 30–33. By permission of the author.

First of all, Klein built a crude prototype to demonstrate the concept she had in mind. From this prototype she was able to get the necessary components produced and assembled so that she had samples to send to prospective department store buyers.

On the basis of the feedback Klein received, the product was substantially modified, and significant design improvements were made. This new version was shown to makeup consultants at a Toronto trade show or convention and the excitement created there was instrumental in her new business' getting successfully off the ground.

Developing a Prototype A *prototype* is a "working model" of your product. If you are considering selling a product that, when mass-produced, could cost you $5 per unit to manufacture, prototypes may cost you over $200 each. However, this would be an inexpensive investment, because with just one prototype you can get photographs, make up a brochure or circular, show the idea to prospective buyers, and put out publicity releases. You don't need a thousand or ten thousand units at this stage.

Even though you are only interested in producing, at most, a few units at this point, it is still important to get manufacturing prices from a number of (around five) different suppliers. You should find out how much it will cost to produce various quantities of the product (1000 units, 5000 units, 10,000 units) and what the terms, conditions, and costs of the production process would be. Once you have this information you will be able to approach buyers and intelligently and confidently discuss all aspects of the product.

Obtaining Opinions from Prospective Buyers A second way to test your product idea is to ask a professional buyer's personal opinion. For example, most major department stores and other retail chains are organized into departments, each department having its own buyer. After arranging to see the buyer representing the product area in which you are interested, arm yourself with the cost information you received from potential suppliers. Remember, a buyer is a very astute person. He or she has seen thousands of items before yours, and in most cases will be able to tell you if products resembling yours have ever been on the market, how well they sold, what their flaws were, etc. You can get a tremendous amount of free information from a buyer, so it is advisable to solicit his or her independent opinion before you become too involved with your product.

Comparing with Competitors' Products Most of us have only limited exposure to the vast array of products available in the marketplace and thus could end up spending a lot of money producing a "new" product which is already being marketed by someone else. Test your product idea by comparing it with other products already on the market, before you invest your money.

One-Store Test Another way to test your product is to run a *one-store test*. This can be done by arranging with a store owner or manager to put a dozen units of your product on display. The purpose of this test is to learn what the public thinks about your product. You can often get the store owner's cooperation, because the store doesn't have to put any money up front to purchase your product. However, there can be problems associated with such tests. If you are very friendly with the owner, he or she may affect the results of the test in your product's favour by putting it in a preferred location or by personally promoting it to store customers. You should request that your product be treated like any other, because you are looking for unbiased information.

Also, you should keep in mind that one store does not constitute a market; the one store in which you test may not be representative of the marketplace in general. Nevertheless, the one-store test is a good way to gather information on your product.

Trade Shows Another excellent way to test your product idea is at a trade show. It makes no difference what your field is — there is a trade show involving it. At a trade show you will have your product on display and you can get immediate feedback from sophisticated and knowledge-able buyers — people who know what will sell and what will not. There are approximately 15,000 trade shows in Canada and the U.S. every year, covering every imaginable product area. There is bound to be one that could serve as a reasonable test site for you.

CONDUCTING A CUSTOMER SURVEY

A critical factor in successfully launching a new venture is understanding who your customers are and what needs your product or service might satisfy. It is important to consider that not all potential customers are alike or have similar needs for a given product. For example, some people buy a toothpaste primarily to prevent cavities, while others want a toothpaste that promotes whiter teeth, fresher breath, or "sex appeal," or has been designed specifically for smokers or denture wearers. You have to determine which of these segments (i.e., cavity prevention, whiter teeth, etc.) your product or service can best satisfy.

As previously mentioned, most major markets can be broken down into more homogeneous groups or *segments* on the basis of a number of different types of variables. In developing a plan for your proposed business venture you must consider who your potential customers are and how they might be classified, as in the toothpaste example, into somewhat more homogeneous market segments. You should be clear in your own mind just which of these segments your venture is attempting to serve. A product or service that is sharply focussed to satisfy the needs and wants of a specifically defined customer group is typically far more successful than one that tries to compromise and cut across the widely divergent requirements of many customer types. Small businesses are often in a position to search for "holes" in the market representing the requirements of particular customer types that larger companies are unwilling or unable to satisfy.

In order to be successful, you should seek a *competitive advantage* over other firms — look for something especially desirable from the customer's perspective, something that sets you apart and gives you an edge. This may be the quality of your product, the speed of your service, the diversity of your product line, the effectiveness of your promotion, your personality, your location, the distinctiveness of your offering, or perhaps even your price.

To accomplish all this may require some basic market research. This might be thought of as one of the first steps in testing your product or service idea with potential customers.

Since you will want to provide as good a description of your offering as possible (preferably via a prototype), personal, face-to-face interviews are the best method for gathering the information. Figure 7.3 provides an outline for a survey you might conduct. It would be wise to interview at least 30 to 40 potential customers to help ensure that the responses you receive are probably representative of the marketplace in general. This approach can be used effectively for either consumer or industrial products/services.

This customer survey will provide you with important information that will allow you to further develop and fine-tune your marketing strategy. For example, if you discover that the most customers will pay for your product is $10, and you had planned on charging $12, you will have to reconsider your pricing strategy. Similarly, if customers prefer to purchase products like yours by

FIGURE 7.3   OUTLINE FOR A CUSTOMER SURVEY

Name of Customer _____

1. **NATURE OF THE CUSTOMER'S BUSINESS OR ROLE**

2. **CUSTOMER'S REACTION TO YOUR PRODUCT OR SERVICE**
   a. What advantages/benefits do they see?
   b. What disadvantages do they see?
   c. What questions do they raise?

3. **SPECIFIC NEEDS AND USES**
   a. What needs and uses do they have for a product such as yours?

4. **SELLING PRICE, SERVICE, AND SUPPORT**
   a. What do they believe would be an acceptable selling price?
   b. What level of service and support would they expect?
   c. What other terms would they expect?

5. **CURRENT PURCHASING PRACTICES**
   a. Where do potential customers currently buy this type of product (retailer, wholesaler, direct mail, broker, etc.)?

6. **NAMES OF COMPETITIVE FIRMS**
   a. What competing firms' products and services are they currently using?

mail, you will have to keep that in mind as you set up a distribution system. The responses to each of the questions posed in the survey should be analyzed and their impact on areas of marketing strategy noted. These will be brought together later in your preliminary marketing plan.

The Nature of Your Competition

Unless your product or service is a "new to the world" innovation, which is unlikely, it will have to compete with other products or services that perform a similar function. In the customer survey, your respondents probably identified the names of a number of firms that offer products or services designed to meet the same customer needs as yours. Now, you must ask specific and detailed questions concerning your likely competition. The answers will help you get a better understanding of the sales and market share you could achieve, and changes or improvements you should make in your marketing program (pricing, promotion, distribution, etc.).

You should also be on the lookout for areas where you can gain a sustainable competitive advantage. In other words: Can you provide the best-quality, the lowest-cost, the most innovative, or the better-serviced product?

Figure 7.4 provides a form to help you organize your evaluation. Fill out a copy of this form for each major competitor you have identified. Unfortunately, competitors will probably not cooperate in providing you with this information directly. Sources that can be useful in getting the information, however, include published industry reports, trade association reports and publications, corporate annual reports, and your own personal investigation.

Developing a Sales Forecast

Sales forecasting is the process of organizing and analyzing all the information you have gathered to date in a way that makes it possible to estimate what your expected sales will be. For your business plan, these figures for your first year of operation should be monthly, while the estimates for subsequent years can be quarterly. A serious miscalculation many aspiring entrepreneurs make is to assume that because their new product or service appeals to *them*, other consumers will buy it as well. It is important to be aware of this tendency. This type of thinking is often reflected in what is known as the "2 percent" syndrome. This syndrome follows a line of reasoning such as,

FIGURE 7.4 FORM FOR ANALYZING YOUR COMPETITORS

Name of Competitor _____ **Estimated Market Share** _____%

1. PRODUCT OR SERVICE

    a. How does the company's product or service differ from other products and services in the marketplace? _____

    _____

    _____

    _____

    b. Do they offer a broad or narrow product line?_____

    _____

    c. Do they emphasize quality?_____

2. PRICE

    a. What is their average selling price?_____

    b. What is their profit margin?_____

    c. What type of discounts do they offer?_____

d. Do they emphasize a low selling price?_____

3. PROMOTION

  a. How much do they spend on advertising and trade promotion?_____

  b. How well known are they (brand recognition)?_____

  c. Through which media do they advertise?_____

  _____

  d. What other types of promotion do they use?_____

  _____

  e. How many salespeople do they have?_____

4. DISTRIBUTION/LOCATION

  a. What type of distribution intermediaries do they use (brokers, company sales force, direct to wholesaler, etc.)?_____

  _____

  _____

  b. Where are they located?_____

  c. Is location very important in this industry?_____

5. MARKETING STRATEGY

  a. Does the company cater to any particular segment of the market?_____

  _____

  b. Does the company offer some unique product or service that makes it different from other competitors?_____

  _____

  _____

  c. Do they offer a particularly low price?_____

  d. What is the principal factor that accounts for the success of this firm?_____

6. MARKET POSITION

  a. What is their market share?_____

  b. Have their sales been growing? Stable? Declining?_____

  _____

  c. How successful are they?_____

  _____

7. MAJOR STRENGTHS AND WEAKNESSES

  a. What are their major strengths?_____

  _____

  _____

  b. What are their major weaknesses?_____

  _____

  _____

"The total market for a product is $100 million. If my firm can pick up just 2 percent of this market, it will have sales of $2 million per year."

There are, however, two things wrong with this line of reasoning. The first is that it may be extremely difficult for you to capture 2 percent of this market unless your business has a unique competitive advantage. The second is that a 2 percent market share may still be unprofitable, since competing firms with greater market share may benefit from *economies of scale* — smaller unit cost due to mass-production — and other cost advantages unavailable to your firm.

There are a number of external factors that can affect your sales. These include:

- seasonal changes
- holidays
- special events
- political activities and events
- general economic conditions
- weather
- fashion trends and cycles
- population shifts
- changes in the retail mix

In addition, there are a number of internal factors that must be considered as well, such as:

- level of your promotional effort
- your ability to manage inventory levels effectively
- the distribution channels you decide to use
- your price level relative to the competition
- any labour and personnel problem you might encounter.

It is impossible to predict all these situations but you should try to take them into account in developing your sales forecast.

One approach to gaining some insight into your business' potential market is to follow the example laid out in Figure 7.5. Refer to the *market profile* you developed in Figure 7.1. How do you feel your prospective customers would decide whether or not to buy your offering. This estimate should also consider the likely frequency and volume of a typical customer's purchases over a certain period of time.

In implementing this process, you should think about how prospective customers will likely hear about the opportunity to buy your product/service, whether from a salesperson, from an advertisement, or through a chain of middlemen. Estimates can then be made of how many of the people you have described are good prospects, and consequently what your total sales volume might be. This can be an "armchair" procedure involving the use of some library references or personal knowledge of similar businesses. The estimate of market potential developed using this method can be quite crude; however, it is important that you think your way through such a process and not sidestep it in favour of simply hoping a market exists for you.

Selecting a Location

It is often said that the three most important factors in the success of any retail business are "location, location, and location." Every new business faces the problem of where to locate its facilities. This problem is much more critical to retailers than to other types of businesses. Much of their business typically comes from people who are walking or driving by. As a consequence, a customer's decision to shop or not shop at a particular store may depend on such factors as what side of the street you are on, ease of access and egress, availability of parking, or similar concerns. This means that in determining the best location for your business you will have to concern yourself with a variety of issues.

FIGURE 7.5   DEVELOPING A SALES FORECAST

1. Provide a summary overview of typical individuals, companies, or organizations that are likely prospects for your product/service offering as described in the market profile you prepared in Figure 7.1. Ask yourself such questions as: How old would these customers be? Where do they live? In what types of activities would they participate? What primary benefits are they looking for in my product or service? Etc.

_____

_____

_____

_____

_____

2. How many of the people or organizations you have described as good prospects are in your trading area?

_____

_____

_____

3. Describe how you feel these individuals or organizations would go about deciding whether to purchase your product/service rather than a competitor's offering. Would these potential customers be principally concerned with price, convenience, quality, or some other factor?

_____

_____

_____

_____

4. How often would prospective buyers purchase your product or service? Daily? Weekly? Monthly? Etc. Where would they look for it or expect to buy it? What kind of seasonal or other patterns are likely to influence sales? How will holidays or other special events affect sales patterns within a month? A year?

_____

_____

_____

_____

5. How much (in dollars and/or units) would a typical customer purchase on each buying occasion?

_____

_____

6. How would your customers likely hear about your product/service offering? Through newspapers? TV or radio advertisements? Word of mouth? Salespeople? Middlemen? Etc.

_____

_____

_____

continued

Developing a Sales Forecast — continued

7. From the above information, estimate your expected annual sales in terms of *dollars* and/or *number of units:*

a. By week for each month for the first year of operation of your business.

	Week 1	Week 2	Week 3	Week 4
January	_____	_____	_____	_____
February	_____	_____	_____	_____
March	_____	_____	_____	_____
April	_____	_____	_____	_____
May	_____	_____	_____	_____
June	_____	_____	_____	_____
July	_____	_____	_____	_____
August	_____	_____	_____	_____
September	_____	_____	_____	_____
October	_____	_____	_____	_____
November	_____	_____	_____	_____
December	_____	_____	_____	_____

b. By month for each of the next two years.

	2nd year	3rd year
January	_____	_____
February	_____	_____
March	_____	_____
April	_____	_____
May	_____	_____
June	_____	_____
July	_____	_____
August	_____	_____
September	_____	_____
October	_____	_____
November	_____	_____
December	_____	_____

1. **Zoning Regulations** Zoning bylaws govern the kind of activities that can be carried on in any given area. Classifications vary from locality to locality, but many municipalities categorize activities as residential, commercial office, commercial retail, institutional, and industrial. When considering a location, make certain the business activities you plan to pursue are permitted under the zoning restrictions for that area.

2. **Municipal Licences and Taxes** Businesses must typically buy a municipal business licence. In the city of Winnipeg, for example, more than 115 types of businesses require a licence, which costs from $15 to over $2000. In general, businesses in some amusement fields or that affect public health and safety require a licence.

   Businesses, like homeowners, must usually pay a "business tax" — a tax assessed as a percentage of the rental value of the premises or on the basis of a standard assessment per square foot of space utilized. These requirements vary from municipality to municipality.

3. **Municipal Services** You should make sure that municipal services such as police and fire protection, adequate sewer and water supplies, public transit facilities, and an adequate road network are available to meet your business' requirements.

4. **Other Considerations** Other things to consider are such site-specific issues as:
    1. Cost
    2. The volume and timing of traffic past the location
    3. The nature of the location, whether on a downtown street, in a strip mall, or in an enclosed mall
    4. The nature of the area surrounding your location and its compatibility with your business
    5. The kind and relative location of surrounding businesses
    6. The volume of customer traffic generated by these other firms and the proportion that might "spin off" to your store
    7. The growth potential of the area or community
    8. The number and location of curb cuts and turnoffs

Figure 7.6 provides a rating form you can use to help choose the most favourable location for a retail business.

FIGURE 7.6 RATING FORM FOR SELECTING A RETAIL LOCATION

FACTOR A: PRIMARY ACCEPTANCE OR REJECTION FACTORS
(RATE YES OR NO)

	Location No.			
	1	2	3	4
1. Will municipal zoning allow the proposed business?	___	___	___	___
2. Does this site meet the minimum operating needs of the proposed business?	___	___	___	___
3. Do existing buildings meet minimum initial needs?	___	___	___	___
4. Is the rent for this location within your proposed operating budget?	___	___	___	___
5. Is the rent for this location, with or without buildings, reasonable?	___	___	___	___

One "No" answer may be sufficient reason not to proceed with further investigation unless some modification can be achieved.

FACTOR B: SITE EVALUATION
(USE PERCENTAGE SCALE 0 TO 100)

	Location No.			
	1	2	3	4
6. How does this location compare with the best possible location available?	___	___	___	___
7. What rating would you give the present buildings on the site?	___	___	___	___
8. How would you rate the overall environment of this location with the best environment existing within your trading area?	___	___	___	___
9. How would you rate the availability of parking for automobiles?	___	___	___	___
10. How would you rate the nature and quantity of combined foot and auto traffic passing your location?	___	___	___	___
11. What is the improvement potential of this location?	___	___	___	___
Total	___	___	___	___

FACTOR C: TREND ANALYSIS
(COMPARE THE ANSWER FOR EACH LOCATION AND RANK EACH BY NUMBER FROM AMONG THOSE REVIEWED — I.E., 1ST, 2ND, 3RD, OR 4TH)

	Location No.			
	1	2	3	4
12. Has the location shown improvement through the years?	___	___	___	___
13. Is the owner and/or landlord progressive and cooperative?	___	___	___	___

continued

Rating Form for Selecting a Retail Location — continued

	Location No.			
	1	**2**	**3**	**4**
14. What major patterns of change are affecting this location?	___	___	___	___
a. Streets: speed limits, paving	___	___	___	___
b. Shopping centres	___	___	___	___
c. Zoning	___	___	___	___
d. Financial investment	___	___	___	___
e. Dynamic leadership and action	___	___	___	___
f. Type of shopper or other potential customer	___	___	___	___
15. What businesses have occupied this location over the past 10 years?	___	___	___	___
16. Have the businesses identified in question 15 (above) been successful?	___	___	___	___
17. Why is this location now available?	___	___	___	___
18. Are a number of other suitable locations available?	___	___	___	___
FACTOR D: PRICE-VALUE DETERMINATION				
19. What is the asking rent for each location?	___	___	___	___
20. What numerical total for each site is developed through questions 6 to 11?	___	___	___	___
21. Is there a "No" answer to any of questions 1 to 5?	___	___	___	___
22. Do the answers to questions 12 to 18 develop a pattern which is:	___	___	___	___
a. Highly favourable?	___	___	___	___
b. Average?	___	___	___	___
c. Fair?	___	___	___	___
d. Questionable?	___	___	___	___
e. Not acceptable?	___	___	___	___
Rank each location according to numerical totals and preferences as to subjective Factors C and D.	___	___	___	___

Adapted from M. Archer and J. White, *Starting and Managing Your Own Small Business* (Toronto: Macmillan Company of Canada, 1978), pp. 38–40. Reproduced by permission.

Most of these same location factors also apply to service businesses, although perhaps not to the same degree. If your service business requires you to visit prospective customers at their home or place of business, a central location providing easy access to all parts of your market area may be preferred.

Location has a quite different meaning for manufacturing firms. Manufacturers are principally concerned about locating their plant where their operations will be most efficient. This means considering such issues as the following:

1. General proximity to primary market areas
2. Access to required raw materials and supplies
3. Availability of a suitable labour force
4. Accessibility and relative cost of transportation and storage facilities
5. Availability and relative cost of power, water, and fuel supplies
6. Financial incentives and other inducements available from municipal, provincial, or federal government agencies

The importance of each of these factors in the location decision will depend on the nature of your manufacturing business and your own preferences and requirements.

Buying or Leasing Facilities

Many new businesses already own or decide to purchase the land and building in which their ventures are located or the machinery and equipment they will require to operate. With today's extremely high costs, however, this may not be a wise decision. The majority of new firms are not principally in the business of speculating in real estate and should not acquire their own property. During their early stages most businesses tend to be short of cash and many have failed because they had their capital tied up in land and buildings when it could have been more effectively used to provide needed working capital for the business itself. In addition, a business that owns its own building may be more difficult to sell at a later date, since a smaller number of potential buyers will have enough capital to buy both the business and the property.

If you are planning to rent or lease your facilities it is probably a good idea to have your lawyer review the terms and conditions of the agreement. You will want to ensure satisfactory arrangements in such matters as:

1. **The duration of the agreement** A business lease can last a year, three years, five years, or any other mutually agreed-upon term. A short-term lease may be preferable if your situation is likely to change soon. However, the lease conditions can be a valuable asset of your business, and a short-term lease may reduce the sale value of your business (if you ever sell it) because of loss of the goodwill associated with maintaining your present location. The ideal lease arrangement should enable you to stay in the location for some time, in case your venture is successful, but give you the flexibility to move after a reasonable period of time if it doesn't work out.

    You also need to consider the terms and conditions for renewing the lease. Are there provisions for automatic renewal? Is there a maximum to any rent increase applied upon renewal of your lease?

2. **The rent** Rental costs for commercial property are commonly stated in terms of the annual cost per square foot of floor space. For example, a 1500 square foot location rented for $8 per square foot will cost $12,000 a year, or $1000 per month. This may be a *net lease*, in which you pay a single monthly fee which is all-inclusive (rent, utilities, maintenance costs, property taxes, etc.), or a "net-net-net" or *triple net lease*, in which you pay a base rent plus a share of all the other expenses incurred by the landlord in operating the building. In the latter situation your operating costs may fluctuate each year because of changing tax, maintenance, insurance, and other costs.

    In retail shopping malls, *participating* (or *percentage*) *leases* are common. Instead of a fixed monthly rent, the landlord receives some percentage of your sales or net profit. There are several types of participating leases. You may pay either a percentage of the total monthly sales of your business, a base rent plus some percentage of your gross sales, or a percentage of your net profit before interest and taxes. Shopping centre leases can be quite complex documents, so be certain to check with your accountant and lawyer before committing yourself.

3. **The ownership of any additions or improvements you might make to the facilities** Under the terms of most leases, all improvements and fixtures that you add to the premises are considered as belonging to the landlord. They immediately become part of the building and cannot be removed without his or her consent. If you need to install expensive fixtures to launch your business, you should try right up front to negotiate permission to remove specific items.

4. **Any restrictions on the use of the property** Most leases specify the kind of business activity you can carry on in the location. Before signing, you should think not only about the activities you now plan to engage in, but also about those you might wish to engage in in the future. Many leases also contain a non-competition clause to protect you from competitive firms' coming into the premises and taking away your business.

5. **Whether you are permitted to sublet some or all of the property to a third party** This is commonly permitted, but only with the prior written consent of the landlord, and it is subject to any use restrictions and non-competition clauses in your agreement.

   A closely related issue is your ability to assign any remaining time left on your lease to another party. If you decide to sell your business, this can be an attractive part of the package. In some cases, assignment of the lease is not permitted; in others, an assignment may be acceptable with the prior written consent of the landlord, which may then not be unreasonably withheld.

6. **The nature of any default and penalty clauses** The lease will spell out the situations which constitute a breach of its conditions and the recourse available to the landlord. Obvious grounds for default include failure on your part to pay the rent, the bankruptcy of your business, violation of the use conditions or non-competition clauses, and so on. Should you default on the lease, the landlord may be able to claim accelerated rent for the time remaining on the lease. For example, if you were to move out two years before your lease expires, the landlord may claim the full two years' rent. In this situation, however, the landlord legally must try to limit his or her damages by renting out your space to another party as soon as possible.

   Your lease may or may not contain a *penalty clause* limiting your exposure should you breach the lease. A penalty of three months' rent is common in many situations, although the landlord will want you or the directors of an incorporated business to sign personal guarantees for the amount of the penalty.

Of course, building your own facility enables you to more carefully tailor the property to the specific requirements of your business but tends to be a much more costly alternative.

Home-Based Businesses

For many kinds of businesses, working out of the home has become a very popular and attractive option. There are a number of advantages to running your business out of your home, the most obvious of which is the cost.

Not only can you save on the rent for your business premises by operating in this manner; Revenue Canada will also let you write off part of your home expenses for income tax purposes. Possible writeoffs are utility costs, mortgage interest, municipal taxes, and other expenses related to maintaining that part of your premises used for your business. You can also save on the cost and time of travelling to and from work every day, and you have greater flexibility in planning and organizing your work and personal life. In addition, a home-based business may have a number of other benefits such as letting you wear more comfortable clothes and giving you more time to look after and be with your family.

There are, however, a number of disadvantages.

1. It takes a lot of self-discipline to sustain a regular work schedule and resist distractions from family, friends, television, and other sources. You may find that there are too many interruptions to work effectively, that you tend to mix work with family life too much, or become distracted by household chores. Conversely, you may find it very difficult to get away from your work when you would like to, since it is so close at hand, and you may have trouble quitting after a full day.

2. Suppliers and prospective customers may not take you as seriously. You may have to rent a post office box or make other arrangements to give the appearance of operating from a more conventional commercial location.

3. The space available in your home may not be appropriate for your business, and you may not have access to facilities and equipment such as computers and fax machines that you need to conduct your business effectively.

4. If your house is in a typical residential area, operating a business from your home will probably contravene local zoning bylaws.

    It is true that most municipal governments have become reasonably flexible in this regard and do not go looking for violations; they will, however, respond to complaints from immediate neighbours and others in the vicinity. It is probably a good idea to check with these people before starting any kind of visible business activity from your home. Activities that may lead to complaints are posting a large sign on the front lawn, constant noise, a steady stream of customers, suppliers, or others in and out of your home, or the clutter of parked vehicles in your yard or on the street.

In the end, operating a home-based business is really a very personal decision. From a legal perspective, you can probably do what you want, as long as no one complains. However, this mode of operation is not suitable for all types of businesses, and for many people may not be a comfortable decision.

Fleshing Out Your Marketing Program

The purpose of this section is to bring together what you have learned about the total market potential for your product or service, customer attitudes toward your particular offering, and the nature of the competitive environment you will be facing. The goal is to put down on paper a preliminary marketing strategy or plan for your new venture concept. This involves making some decisions regarding what you feel is an appropriate *marketing mix* for your business. Put simply, the principal ingredients of your marketing program that must be blended together to form your overall strategy can be grouped under the following headings:

1. Product or service offering
2. Pricing program
3. Promotional plans
4. Method of distribution

Product or Service Offering

The product area involves the planning and development of the product or service you are planning to offer in the marketplace. This involves defining the breadth and depth of your offering, the length of your line, how it will be packaged and branded, the variety of colours and other product features, and the range of complementary services (delivery, repair, warranties, etc.) that will be made available to the customer.

Pricing Program

Your pricing strategy involves establishing the right base price for your offering so that it is appealing to customers and profitable to you. This base price may be adjusted to meet the needs of particular situations, such as to encourage early acceptance of your offering during its introductory stages, to meet aggressive or exceptional competition, to provide for trade, functional, seasonal, and other discounts, or to introduce your product/service into new market situations.

One of the most commonly used strategies by retailers and small manufacturers is *markup pricing*. The cost of your product or service is determined and used as the base, and then a markup is added to determine what your selling price should be. *Markups* are generally expressed as a percentage of the selling price — for example, a product costing $2.50 and selling for $5 has a 50 percent markup.

To illustrate, let's assume you've come up with a new formula for an automobile engine treatment that will be sold through auto parts jobbers to service stations for use in consumers' cars. Table 7.4 illustrates what the price markup chain for this product might look like.

TABLE 7.4 PRICE MARKUP CHAIN

	Per Bottle	Markup
Direct factory costs	$1.00	
Indirect factory costs	0.50	
Total factory cost	$1.50	
Manufacturer's markup	0.50	25%
Manufacturer's selling price	$2.00	
Jobber's markup	0.50	20%
Jobber's selling price	$2.50	
Service station markup	2.50	50%
Service station selling price	$5.00	

As you can see, in this illustration a product with a factory cost of $1.50 has a retail selling price of $5 to the final consumer. The markup percentages shown here are merely examples of a typical situation, but in most wholesale and retail businesses standard markups tend to prevail in different industry sectors. Food products and other staple items usually have a low unit cost and high inventory turnover, so the markups tend to be fairly low, 15 to 25 percent: products such as jewelry and highly advertised specialty products typically have higher markups, perhaps as much as 50 or 60 percent or even more.

This type of markup pricing is simple and easy to apply and can be very successful if all competitors have similar costs of doing business and use similar percentages. On the other hand, this approach does not take into account variations in the demand for the product that may occur with a different final price. For example, how much more or less of the engine treatment would be sold at a price of $4 or $6 rather than the $5 price determined by the standard markup chain?

Most manufacturers do not employ markup pricing in the same way that many wholesalers and retailers do. However, if you plan to manufacture a product that will be sold through wholesalers and various types of retail outlets, it is important for you to know the markups these distributors will likely apply to your product. For instance, in the above example if the manufacturer of the engine treatment thinks $5 is the right retail price, he or she can work backwards and determine that it must be able to sell profitably to the jobbers for $2 in order to succeed. If that is not possible, perhaps the overall marketing strategy for the product should be reconsidered.

In addition to establishing a base price for your product or service line, you may permit some customers to pay less than this amount in certain circumstances or provide them with a discount. The principal types of discounts are quantity discounts, cash discounts, and seasonal discounts. *Quantity discounts* are commonly provided to customers who buy more than some minimum quantity or dollar value of products or services from you. This discount may be based either on the quantity or value of each individual order (non-cumulative) or on the total value of their purchases over a certain period of time, such as a month (cumulative).

Cash discounts are based on the typical terms of trade within an industry and permit the customer to deduct a certain percentage amount from the net cost of their purchases if payment is made in cash at the time of purchase or full payment is made within a specified number of days. Different types of businesses have their own customary cash discounts. For example, a typical discount is expressed as "2/10 net 30." In this situation, a customer who is invoiced on October 1 for an outstanding bill of $2000 need only pay $1960 if payment is made before October 10. This is a 2 percent cash discount for making payment within the 10 days. Otherwise the full face value of the invoice ($2000) is due by October 31 or 30 days after the invoice date.

Seasonal discounts of 10 percent, 15 percent, 20 percent, or more on your normal base price may be offered to your customers if their purchases are made during your slow or off-season. This gives you a method of moving inventories that you may otherwise have to carry over to the following year or of providing your dealers, agents, and other distributors with some incentive to stock up on your products well in advance of the prime selling season.

Promotional Plans

The budget that you allocate for the promotion of your new venture must be distributed across the following activities:

1. Advertising
2. Personal selling
3. Sales promotion
4. Public relations

The distribution of your expenditures should be made to obtain the maximum results for your particular circumstances. It is impossible to generalize about the optimum distribution of your dollars to each of these activities. Different businesses use quite different combinations. Some companies put most of their money into hiring a sales force and their sales promotion program; others put most of their budget into a media advertising campaign. The proper combination for you will depend on a careful study of the relative costs and effectiveness of each of these types of promotion and the unique requirements of your business.

We often think of promotion as being directed strictly toward our final prospective customer, and in fact the largest share of most promotional activity is channelled in that direction. However, promotion can also be used to influence your dealers, your distributors, and other members of your distribution channel. This may persuade them to adopt your offering more rapidly and broaden the breadth of your distribution coverage.

ADVERTISING

Advertising is one of the principal means you have of informing potential customers about the availability and special features of your product or service. Properly conceived messages presented in the appropriate media can greatly stimulate demand for your business and its offerings. A wide range of advertising media are available to carry your messages, of which the most important are those listed in Table 7.5. Which of these media you should choose for your advertising program will depend on the consumers you are trying to reach, the size of the budget you have available, the nature of your product or service, and the particular message you hope to communicate.

Advertising on the Internet One form of advertising that is rapidly increasing in popularity is the use of the Internet. The World Wide Web is open for business and small firms, particularly retail businesses, are jumping aboard in ever increasing numbers. Before joining this throng, however, you should consider whether a Web presence will really serve your business interests. If so, you need to formulate a clear strategy or plan, rather than just developing another Web page to join the thousands that already exist on the Net.

Should you decide to proceed with implementing a Web site, remember that the Web is not a passive delivery system like most other media but is an active system where the user expects to

TABLE 7.5 THE MOST IMPORTANT ADVERTISING MEDIA

1. **MAGAZINES**
   a. Consumer magazines
   b. Trade or business publications
   c. Farm publications
   d. Professional magazines

2. **NEWSPAPERS**
   a. Daily newspapers
   b. Weekly newspapers
   c. Shopping guides
   d. Special-interest newspapers

3. **TELEVISION**
   a. Local TV
   b. Network TV
   c. Special-interest cable TV

4. **RADIO**
   a. Local stations
   b. Network radio

5. **DIRECTORY**
   a. Yellow Pages
   b. Community
   c. Special-interest

6. **DIRECT MAIL ADVERTISING**
   a. Letters
   b. Catalogues

7. **OUTDOOR ADVERTISING**
   a. Billboards
   b. Posters

8. **TRANSPORTATION ADVERTISING**
   a. Interior car cards
   b. Station posters
   c. Exterior cards on vehicles

9. **POINT-OF-PURCHASE DISPLAYS**

10. **ADVERTISING NOVELTIES AND SPECIALTIES**

participate in the experience. Your virtual storefront must be genuinely interesting and the interactivity of the Web should be used to your advantage to attract and hold the ongoing interest of your target consumers.

Opening a successful Web site is not as complicated as it may appear but it can be expensive to do the job right. You can do it yourself or enlist the expertise of a multimedia production house. Production costs depend entirely upon the size and interactivity of your site, running anywhere from $500 on the cheap to $100,000 for a full-blown corporate site. Maintenance costs are minimal but materials and other aspects of the site's operation should be updated regularly, such as once a month. To find out more about Canadian multimedia houses, a listing is provided at http://www.ideaguy.com.

Once your page is developed, it is important that you get a domain name and file a registration request. You will also want a reliable Web server to house your site. Try to get as many links leading to your site as possible by listing with directories, hotlinks, and so on where consumers will be able to find you quite easily. You might also give some consideration to joining a Cybermall.

PERSONAL SELLING

Personal selling involves direct, face-to-face contact with your prospective customer. A personal salesperson's primary function is usually more concerned with obtaining orders than informing your customers about the nature of your offering as in the case of advertising. Other types of salespeople are principally involved in providing support to different components of your business or filling routine orders rather than more persuasive kinds of selling. The basic steps involved in the selling process are as follows:

1. **Prospecting and qualifying** Identifying prospective customers
2. **The sales approach** The initial contact with the prospective customer
3. **Presentation** The actual sales message presented to a prospective customer
4. **Demonstration** of the capabilities and features or most important characteristics of the product or service being sold

5. **Handling any objections or concerns** the prospective customer may have regarding your offering

6. **Closing the sale** Asking the prospective customer for the order

7. **Postsales activities** Follow-up to determine if customers are satisfied with their purchase and to pursue any additional possible sales

SALES PROMOTION

Sales promotion includes a broad range of promotional activities other than advertising and personal selling that stimulate consumer or dealer interest in your offering. While advertising and personal selling tend to be ongoing activities, most sales promotion is sporadic or irregular in nature. Sales promotion includes activities related to:

1. Free product samples

2. Discount coupons

3. Contests

4. Special deals and premiums

5. Gifts

6. Special exhibits and displays

7. Participation in trade shows

8. Off-price specials

9. Floats in parades and similar events

As you can see, sales promotion consists of a long list of what are typically non-recurring activities. They are intended to make your advertising and personal selling effort more effective and may be very intimately involved with them. For example, your advertising may be used to promote a consumer contest, or certain special deals and incentives may be offered to your salespeople to encourage them to increase their sales to your dealers or final consumers. These activities can be an effective way for businesses with a small budget and some imagination to reach potential sales prospects and develop a considerable volume of business.

PUBLIC RELATIONS

Public relations relates to your business' general communications and relationships with its various interest groups such as your employees, stockholders, the government, and society at large, as well as your customers. It is concerned primarily with such issues as the image of you and your business within the community rather than trying to sell any particular product or service. Publicity releases, product introduction notices, news items, appearances on radio and television, and similar activities are all part of your public relations program.

Method of Distribution

Your *channel of distribution* is the path your products or service take to market. Physical products typically follow one or more complex paths in getting from the point at which they are produced into the hands of their final consumer. These paths involve the use of several different kinds of wholesalers and retailers who perform a variety of functions that are essential to making this flow of products reasonably efficient. These functions include buying, selling, transporting, storing, financing, risk-taking, and several others.

Distribution channels consist of channel members who are independent firms that facilitate this flow of merchandise. There are many different kinds and they have quite different names, but the functions they perform may not be that dramatically different. For example, wholesalers are generally classified according to whether they actually take title or ownership of the products they handle (*merchant wholesalers*) or not (*agents*). Merchant wholesalers are further classified as *full-service, limited-function, drop shippers, truck wholesalers,* and *rack jobbers*. Agents are commonly referred to as *brokers, manufacturer's agents, selling agents, food* or *drug brokers*, etc. For a small manufacturer all of these types of wholesalers, alone or in combination, represent possible paths for getting their product to market.

Retailers, too, cover a very broad spectrum, starting with the large department stores that carry a broad product selection and provide an extensive range of customer services, through specialty stores such as electronics, men's clothing, and furniture stores, on down to discount department stores, grocery stores, drug stores, catalogue retailers, and convenience stores. All represent possible members that could be included in your channel of distribution.

In addition to opportunities for marketing your products or services in conjunction with these traditional and conventional distribution channel members, you should not overlook more unconventional possibilities for reaching your potential customers. For example, over the past few years we have seen tremendous growth of various forms of non-store retailing, including:

1. Mail order catalogues
2. Direct response advertising on television, and in newspapers and magazines
3. Direct selling door to door
4. Party plan or home demonstration party selling
5. Direct mail solicitations
6. Vending machines
7. Trade shows
8. Fairs and exhibitions

You should also be aware of market opportunities that may exist for your venture in foreign markets. These may be accessed by direct exporting, using the services of a trading company, licensing or franchising a firm in that market to produce and sell your product or service, setting up a joint venture with a local firm, or some similar strategy.

MANAGING THE SUPPLY SITUATION

A key factor in the success of any new venture is some assurance of continuing access to critical supplies of raw material and component parts at reasonable prices. Many new businesses have floundered due to changing supply situations that impacted their ability to provide products of acceptable quality or drastically increased their costs of production. These conditions are seldom correctable and tend to be terminal for the smaller firm. It is critical that you investigate the range of possible sources for these key elements well in advance of starting your venture.

Assessing your supply situation requires an understanding of the manufacturing cycle for your product or service and an in-depth appreciation of the market for equipment, materials, and parts. One strategy being followed by more and more smaller firms is to subcontract their production requirements instead of making their own products. This strategy has a number of significant advantages:

- Your business can use the subcontractor's money instead of having to raise the funds to build your own production facilities.
- You can take advantage of the expertise and technical knowledge possessed by the subcontractor without having to develop it yourself.
- Using a subcontractor may enable you to bring your business on stream more rapidly. There is no need to delay while your production facilities are being built and broken in.

- You can concentrate your time on developing a market for your products and running your business rather than on trying to produce a satisfactory product.

- You may be able to benefit from the reputation and credibility of the subcontractor; having your products produced by a firm with an established reputation will rub off on your business.

- A reliable subcontractor can also keep you up to date with technical advances in that field so that your products don't become obsolete.

- Perhaps the most important advantage of using a subcontractor is that it establishes your costs of production in advance, reducing the uncertainty and unpredictability of setting up your own facilities. A firm, fixed price contract from a reliable subcontractor nails down one of your most important costs of doing business and facilitates your entire planning process.

As you can see, there are a number of strong advantages to subcontracting certain aspects of your operations but that does not necessarily mean this strategy should be employed in all situations. There are a number of disadvantages that should be considered as well:

- The cost of having a job done by a subcontractor may not be as low as if you did the work yourself. The subcontractor may have antiquated equipment, high cost, unionized labour, or other problems to deal with that make their operations very expensive. Subcontractors also factor in some margin of profit for themselves into a job. The end result may be a total production cost which would make it very difficult for you to successfully compete.

- Your business may be jeopardized if the subcontractor should fail to meet commitments to you or divulge critical trade secrets about your product or process.

In any case, sometimes a suitable subcontractor is just not available. If you want your product produced, you may have no alternative but to do it yourself.

Regardless of the approach you decide to take, to cover your supply situation there are a number of key factors that have to be considered. These include:

- Delivered cost (total cost including transportation, etc.)
- Quality
- Delivery schedules
- Service level

All have to be at an acceptable level in order for you to have confidence your supply situation is under reasonable control.

STAGE
EIGHT

CONDUCTING A FEASIBILITY STUDY

Part 2: Cost and Profitability Assessment

In addition to determining the size and nature of the market for your new venture idea, it is also important to consider the financial components of your business. The costs associated with operating your business may include labour, materials, rent, machinery, etc. Collecting potential sales and cost information should put you in a better position to make reasonably accurate financial forecasts that can be used not only as a check on the advisability of proceeding with the venture but also for raising capital, if required.

DETERMINE YOUR START-UP FINANCIAL REQUIREMENTS

The process of financial analysis begins with an estimate of the funds required to set up your business. Start-up financial requirements can be broken down into two components:

1. **One-time expenditures** that must be made before your business can open its doors. This includes such expenses as the purchase or lease of furniture, fixtures, and equipment; utility deposits and fees; and pre-opening advertising and promotion expenses. In the case of retailing and manufacturing businesses these requirements can be considerable, while a service business may not require a very large initial expenditure to get started. You can determine your one-time financial requirements by completing Figure 8.1.

2. **Operating expenses** such as payments for owner and employee wages, raw materials, rent, supplies and postage, and other expenses that must be made until the business begins to show a profit. Many new businesses take several months or even years before they operate "in the black." Sufficient funds should be available to cover a *minimum* of two to three months' operation and provide a cash reserve for emergency situations. As a typical situation, your cash requirements may be reduced if your business gets started with firm orders in hand, or even a down payment from some customers, which may start to generate considerable cash flow from the moment you open your doors. On the other hand, a business that is going to build up slowly, or a high tech business requiring a lot of initial research and development, may need to have sufficient working capital available to carry it for four or six months or even longer. You can estimate the funds required to cover these initial operating expenses by completing Figure 8.2.

Insufficient financing is a major cause of new business failure, so you should be certain you have sufficient financing to cover both your estimated one-time and your initial operating expenses.

DEVELOP SHORT-TERM FINANCIAL PROJECTIONS

Pro Forma Income Statement

The next step is to estimate your total expected revenue and expenses for at least the first year of operation of your business. This projected operating statement, or *pro forma income statement*, should show:

1. Your predicted sales volume for the first year of operation of your business
2. How much it will cost to produce or purchase the products you will sell
3. Your fixed monthly operating expenses such as rent, utilities, insurance premiums, and interest costs
4. Your controllable monthly operating expenses such as advertising and promotion expenses, wages and salaries, and delivery expenses
5. Your expected net operating profit or loss

FIGURE 8.1 FORM FOR ESTIMATING ONE-TIME START-UP FINANCIAL REQUIREMENTS

Item	Total Original Cost	Estimated Cash Required
1. Land	$_____	$_____
2. Buildings	_____	_____
3. Improvements		
a. Mechanical	_____	_____
b. Electrical	_____	_____
c. Construction	_____	_____
4. Machinery and Equipment	_____	_____
5. Installation of Equipment	_____	_____
6. Shop Tools and Supplies	_____	_____
7. Office Equipment and Supplies	_____	_____
8. Vehicles	_____	_____
9. Starting Inventory	_____	_____
10. Utility Hookup Fees and Installation	_____	_____
11. Licenses and Permits	_____	_____
12. Pre-opening Promotion	_____	_____
13. Accounts Payable	_____	_____
14. Cash for Unexpected Expenses	_____	_____
15. Other Cash Requirements	_____	_____
Total Estimated One-Time Cash Requirements (1+ … +15)		$_____

FIGURE 8.2 FORM FOR ESTIMATING START-UP OPERATING EXPENSES

Item	Estimated Monthly Expense	x	Number of Months* to Breakeven	=	Total Cash Required
1. Owners' Salaries	$_____		_____		$_____
2. Employee Salaries, Wages, and Benefits	_____		_____		_____
3. Rent	_____		_____		_____
4. Promotion Expenses	_____		_____		_____
5. Supplies and Postage	_____		_____		_____
6. Vehicle Expenses	_____		_____		_____
7. Telephone	_____		_____		_____
8. Other Utilities	_____		_____		_____
9. Insurance	_____		_____		_____
10. Travel	_____		_____		_____
11. Legal and Other Professional Fees	_____		_____		_____
12. Interest	_____		_____		_____
13. Maintenance	_____		_____		_____
14. Other Expenses	_____		_____		_____
Cash Required for Operating Expenses (1+ ... +14)					$_____
A. Total Cash Required to Cover Operating Expenses	$_____				
B. Total One-Time Cash Requirements (From Figure 8.1)	$_____				
C. Total Cash or Operating Line of Credit Required For Start-up (C=A+B)	$_____				

* Two to three months *minimum* are typical here.

One means of developing a pro forma income statement for your business is to follow the Desired Income Approach suggested by Szonyi and Steinhoff.[1] This approach enables you to develop financial projections on the basis of the actual operating performance of firms similar to the business you are contemplating. It also suggests that your business should provide you with not only a return for the time you will spend running the business but also a return on the personal funds you have to invest to launch the business. For example, you could keep your present job or obtain another one and earn a salary working for someone else. You could also invest your money in common stocks, bonds, guaranteed income certificates, or other investments, where it would yield some kind of return. Both possibilities should be kept in mind in determining your expected minimum level of acceptable profit performance of your new venture.

To illustrate this approach, assume you are considering the possibility of opening a retail store of some kind, perhaps a jewelry store. You have determined that you require a minimum annual return of $30,000 to cover your time as well as provide a reasonable return for the investment you will have to make in the business. This represents your "desired income" level. By referring to Dun & Bradstreet Canada information or Statistics Canada catalogues you can obtain comprehensive

[1] A. J. Szonyi and D. Steinhoff, *Small Business Management Fundamentals*, 3rd Canadian ed. (Toronto: McGraw-Hill Ryerson, 1988), pp. 58-65.

financial data on jewelry stores as well as dozens of other different lines of business. Similar data is also available from the Business Development Bank of Canada, industry trade associations, and several other sources.

Combining this information about your desired level of income with some of this published data will enable you to develop a pro forma income statement. The additional information you require is:

- **The average inventory turnover for this type of business** is the number of times a typical firm's inventory is sold each year. If the business carries an inventory of $25,000 and its overall cost of goods sold is $150,000, inventory turnover is six times per year.

- **The average gross margin** is the difference between the firm's net sales and cost of goods sold, expressed as a percentage. For example, if the business' net sales are $200,000 while cost of goods sold total $140,000, its gross margin is $60,000 or 30 percent.

- **Net profit as a percentage of sales** is relatively self-explanatory. It can be determined either before or after the application of any federal or provincial income taxes. In the case of the Dun & Bradstreet statistics, this data is shown after taxes.

Developing the Statement

With this data and an estimate of your desired profit, you can construct a pro forma income statement for an unincorporated jewelry store. Checking the Key Business Ratios (from Statistics Canada, *Operating Results, Retail Jewellery Stores*, Cat. No. 63-609, Table 2, p. 3) provides us with the following information:

Inventory turnover	1.03 times per year
Gross margin	45.9% of sales
Net profit as a percentage of sales	14.1%

Figure 8.3 illustrates how this data, along with the information that the desired profit is $30,000 (including salary and return on investment), can be used to develop a pro forma income statement. This statement indicates the minimum level of sales your business will have to generate in order to provide your desired level of profitability. Sales above this level will probably provide a higher level of profits while lower sales will likely mean you will not make as much money as you had hoped. It is assumed in this evaluation that your business will be operated as efficiently as, and in a similar manner to, other jewelry stores across the country.

FIGURE 8.3 SAMPLE PRO FORMA INCOME STATEMENT FOR SMALL RETAIL STORE

SMITH JEWELRY STORE
PRO FORMA INCOME STATEMENT
For the year ending [date]

Net sales		$212,766 **(A)**
Less: Cost of goods sold:		
Beginning inventory	$111,753	
Plus: Net purchases	115,106	
Goods available for sale	$226,859	
Less: Ending inventory	117,753	
Cost of goods sold		115,106 **(B)**
Gross margin		$ 97,660 **(C)**
Operating expenses		67,660 **(D)**
Net Profit (Loss) Before Income Tax		**$ 30,000** **(E)**

All the figures in this statement have been computed from our ratio data and estimate of desired level of income. For example:

1. Our $30,000 desired profit is inserted on line (E).

2. Profits for a small, unincorporated retail jewelry store are reasonably good at 14.1 percent of sales. This includes compensation for the owner(s) of the business as well as any return on their initial investment. In order to determine the sales level required to provide our desired level of profitability, we divide $30,000 by 0.141 to obtain our estimate of the required level of $212,766 for net sales on line (A).

3. Our statistics indicate that jewelry shops typically have a gross margin of 45.9 percent of net sales. In our situation this would provide a gross margin estimate of $97,660 on line (C).

4. The difference between our estimated net sales and gross margin has to provide for our cost of goods sold. In this example our cost of goods sold will be $212,766 - $97,660 = $115,106 on line (B).

5. Jewelry stores have a very low level of inventory turnover in comparison with most other retail businesses. A typical retail firm will turn its inventory over from five to seven times per year while our statistics indicate a turnover ratio of only 1.03 times for our jewelry store. This means we need to have more money tied up in inventory to support our esti- mated level of net sales than most other retailers. Our projected average inventory level can be determined by dividing our cost of goods sold by the inventory turnover rate or $115,106/1.03 = $111,753.

6. The difference between our expected gross margin and the net operating profit (before tax) necessary to provide our desired income level represents our total operating expenses on line (D). In this case $97,660 - $30,000 = $67,660 should be available to cover such expenses as employees' salaries, rent, insurance, promotion, interest, and similar expenses.

This pro forma statement shows you the level of sales, investment in inventory, and similar information you need to know in order to generate the indicated level of desired income you feel you need to obtain from the business.

The statement constructed in Figure 8.3 is based upon the distinct financial characteristics of a small, unincorporated retail jewelry business and relates only to that situation. A pro forma income statement for a store in another line of business could look very different due to variations in inventory turnover, gross margin percentage, and other factors reflecting the different charac- ter of that business.

This is even more true if we are considering the start-up of a service business or a manufac- turing company. Service firms, like drycleaners and management consultants, typically do not carry an inventory of goods for resale and so don't have a "cost of goods sold" section on their income statement. Manufacturing companies, on the other hand, may have several types of inven- tory — raw materials, work in process, and finished goods. Appropriate levels for all three types of inventories should be determined and reflected in the projected income statement. The state- ment also tries to determine the value of raw materials and components, direct labour, factory overhead, and other inputs required to manufacture a product suitable for sale. This "cost of goods manufactured" replaces the cost of goods sold component on the pro forma statement.

Determining Reasonable Operating Expenses

So far, our pro forma income statement has lumped all our business' projected operating expenses together under a single heading. For example, Figure 8.3 shows our overall, estimated operating expenses to be $67,660. This means that all operating expenses must be covered by this amount if we are to achieve our desired level of profitability.

Similar statistical sources to those used to obtain the data for our overall pro forma statement can be used to obtain a breakdown of the operating expenses for our type of business. For example, Statistics Canada Catalogue 63-609 provides data on the operating results of retail jewelers by sales size and by province or region of the country. Reviewing this publication provides the following breakdown of operating expenses as a percentage of sales for an average firm:

Advertising	1.5%
Business taxes and licences	0.5%
Delivery, freight	1.0%
Depreciation	1.5%
Employees' wages and benefits	10.8%
Insurance	1.0%
Interest	2.0%
Supplies	1.5%
Professional fees	0.5%
Rent	5.5%
Property taxes	0.5%
Repairs and maintenance	1.0%
Telephone and utilities	1.5%
Travel and entertainment	1.0%
Other expenses	2.0%*

* Numbers have been rounded to simplify calculations for illustrative purposes.

These expenses total approximately 32 percent of sales. If we translate these percentages to our pro forma statement, we can obtain an approximation of the detailed breakdown of our operating expenses in dollar terms. Our finalized pro forma income statement would look like Figure 8.4.

This complete pro forma income statement can now serve as part of your plan for outlining the requirements of your proposed new business venture or as a guide or schedule to monitor the ongoing performance of your new business during its early stages.

A typical pro forma income statement form that you can use for projecting the first-year operating performance of your new business is illustrated in Figure 8.5.

Forecast Your Cash Flow

Your next step is to bring the operating profit or loss you have projected closer to reality by developing a *cash flow forecast*. Failure to plan for their future cash requirements is one of the principal reasons small businesses don't survive; an accurate cash flow forecast can be your best means of ensuring continued financial solvency.

In a typical small business, sales revenue and expenses vary throughout the year. Your cash flow forecast tries to predict all the funds that you will receive and disburse within a certain period of time — e.g., a month, quarter, or year — and the resulting surplus or deficit. It allows you to estimate the total amount of cash you actually expect to receive each period and the actual bills that have to be paid. At times your cash inflows will exceed your outflows; at other times your cash outflows will exceed your inflows. Knowing your expected position and cash balance will enable you to plan your cash requirements and negotiate a line of credit with your bank or arrange other external financing.

Your completed cash flow forecast will clearly show to the bank loans officer what additional working capital, if any, your business may need and demonstrate that there will be sufficient cash on hand to make the interest payments on a line of credit or a term loan for purchasing additional machinery or equipment or expanding the business.

FIGURE 8.4 SAMPLE COMPLETED PRO FORMA INCOME STATEMENT WITH BREAKDOWN OF OPERATING EXPENSES

SMITH JEWELRY STORE
PRO FORMA INCOME STATEMENT
For the year [date]

Net Sales			**$212,766 (A)**
Less: Cost of goods sold:			
Beginning inventory		$111,753	
Plus: Net purchases		115,106	
Goods available for sale		$226,859	
Less: Ending inventory		111,753	
Cost of Goods Sold			115,106 **(B)**
Gross Margin			**$ 97,660 (C)**
Less: Variable expenses:			
Employees' wages and benefits	$22,979		
Supplies	3,191		
Advertising and promotion	3,191		
Delivery, freight	2,128		
Travel and entertainment	2,128		
Professional fees	1,063		
Other expenses	4,255		
Total Variable Expenses		**$ 38,935 (D)**	
Less: Fixed expenses:			
Rent	$11,702		
Telephone and utilities	3,192		
Property taxes	1,064		
Business taxes	1,064		
Repairs and maintenance	2,128		
Depreciation	3,192		
Interest	4,255		
Insurance	2,128		
Total Fixed Expenses		**$ 28,725 (E)**	
Total Operating Expenses			**$ 67,660 (F)**
Net Operating Profit (Loss) Before Income Tax			**$ 30,000 (G)**

Estimate Your Revenues

In most small businesses, not all sales are for cash. It is normal practice to take credit cards or to extend terms to many customers. As a result, the revenue from a sale may not be realized until 30 days, 60 days, or even longer after the actual sale is made. In developing your cash flow forecast you must take into account such factors as:

- Your ratio of cash to credit card or credit sales
- Your normal terms of trade for credit customers
- The paying habits of your customers
- Proceedings from the sale of any auxiliary items or other assets of the business

Sales should only be entered on the cash flow forecast when the money has actually been received in payment.

FIGURE 8.5 FORM FOR TYPICAL PRO FORMA INCOME STATEMENT FOR A SMALL COMPANY

YOUR COMPANY NAME
PRO FORMA INCOME STATEMENT
For year ending _____
[first year]

Gross sales $_____

Less: Cash discounts   _____

Net Sales $_____ **(A)**

Less: Cost of goods sold:

   Beginning inventory $_____

   Plus: Net purchases   _____

   Total goods available for sale   _____

   Less: Ending inventory   _____

   Cost of Goods Sold   _____ **(B)**

Gross Margin (or Profit) (C = A – B) $_____ **(C)**

Less: Variable expenses:

   Owner's salary $_____

   Employees' wages, salaries, and benefits _____

   Supplies and postage   _____

   Advertising and promotion   _____

   Delivery expense   _____

   Bad debt expense   _____

   Travel   _____

   Legal and accounting fees   _____

   Vehicle expense   _____

   Miscellaneous expenses   _____

   Total Variable Expenses $_____ **(D)**

Less: Fixed expenses:

   Rent $_____

   Utilities (heat, light, power)   _____

   Telephone   _____

   Taxes and licences   _____

   Depreciation or Capital Cost Allowance   _____

   Interest   _____

   Insurance   _____

   Other Fixed Expenses   _____

   Total Fixed Expenses $_____ **(E)**

Total Operating Expenses (F = D + E) $_____ **(F)**

Net Operating Profit (Loss) (G = C – F) $_____ **(G)**

Income Tax (estimated) $_____ **(H)**

Net Profit (Loss) After Income Tax (I = G – H) $_____ **(I)**

Determine Your Expenditures

To estimate your cash outflow you must consider:

- How promptly you will be required to pay for your material and supplies. It is not uncommon that a new business will have to pay for its inventory and supplies up front on a cash on delivery (COD) basis until it establishes a reputation for meeting its financial commitments. Then it may be able to obtain more favourable credit terms from its trade suppliers. These terms of trade should be reflected in the cash flow forecast. For example, if you have to pay your suppliers' invoices right away, the cash payouts would be reflected in the cash flow forecast during the same month in which the purchases were made. However, if you have to pay your suppliers' invoices within 30 days, the cash payouts for July's purchases will not be shown until August. In some cases, even longer-term trade credit can be negotiated, and then cash outlays may not be shown for two or even three months after the purchase has been received and invoiced. You must know:

- How you will pay your employees' wages and salaries (weekly, biweekly, or monthly).

- When you must pay your rent, utility bills, and other expenses. For example, your rent, telephone, utilities, and other occupancy costs are normally paid every month. Other expenses like insurance and licence fees may be estimated as monthly expenses but not treated that way for cash flow purposes. Your insurance premium of $1200 annually may have to be paid in three instalments: $400 in April, August, and December. That is how it must be entered on the cash flow worksheet. Your license fees might be an annual expense incurred in January of each year and would be reflected as part of your estimated disbursements for that month.

- The interest and principal payments that you must make each month on any outstanding loans.

- Your plans for increasing your inventory requirements or acquiring additional assets.

Reconciling Your Cash Revenues and Cash Expenditures

Figure 8.6 is an outline for a typical cash flow forecast which will enable you to project your anticipated cash surplus or shortfall at the end of each month of your first year of operation. At the beginning of each month it shows the cash balance carried over from your previous month's operations. To this it adds the total of the current month's revenues and subtracts the total of the current month's expenditures to determine the adjusted balance to be carried forward to the next month. In summary form this relationship can be demonstrated by the following formula: Forecasted Cash Flow in Month (x) = Cash Balance Carried Over from Month (x-1) + Expected Revenue in Month (x) – Estimated Expenditures in Month (x). Cumulative cash surpluses or shortfalls will be clearly evident well in advance of their actual occurrence. Knowing this information in advance can assist you in scheduling your initial capital expenditures, monitoring your accounts receivable, avoiding temporary cash shortages, and will enable you to plan your short-term borrowing requirements well in advance.

Pro Forma Balance Sheet

One more financial statement should also be developed — a *pro forma balance sheet* listing what you forecast your business will own (assets) minus what it will owe to other people, companies, and financial institutions (liabilities) to determine its net worth at any particular point in time. A typical pro forma balance sheet is illustrated in Figure 8.7.

Current assets would include an estimate of your expected average accounts receivable, start-up inventory requirements, available cash, and similar items. *Fixed assets* are typically items like buildings, fixtures, machinery and equipment, automobiles, and other capital items which you will need to operate your business and that typically get used up over a number of years, and therefore must be *depreciated* in value gradually.

FIGURE 8.6 TYPICAL CASH FLOW FORECAST FOR A SMALL COMPANY

12-MONTH CASH FLOW PROJECTIONS

	Month 1	Month 2	Month 3	Month 4	Month 5	Month 6	Month 7	Month 8	Month 9	Month 10	Month 11	Month 12	Year 1 TOTAL
Cash Flow From Operations (during month)													
1. Cash Sales													
2. Payments for Credit Sales													
3. Investment Income													
4. Other Cash Income													
A. TOTAL CASH FLOW ON HAND	$	$	$	$	$	$	$	$	$	$	$	$	$
Less Expenses Paid (during month)													
5. Inventory or New Material													
6. Owners' Salaries													
7. Employees' Wages and Salaries													
8. Supplies and Postage													
9. Advertising and Promotion													
10. Delivery Expense													
11. Travel													
12. Legal and Accounting Fees													
13. Vehicle Expense													
14. Maintenance Expense													
15. Rent													
16. Utilities													
17. Telephone													
18. Taxes and Licences													
19. Interest Payments													
20. Insurance													
21. Other Cash Expenses													
B. TOTAL EXPENDITURES	$	$	$	$	$	$	$	$	$	$	$	$	$
Capital													
Purchase of Fixed Assets													
Sale of Fixed Assets													
C. CHANGE IN CASH FROM PURCHASE OR SALE OF ASSETS	$	$	$	$	$	$	$	$	$	$	$	$	$
Financing													
Payment of Principal of Loan													
Inflow of Cash From Bank Loan													
Issuance of Equity Positions													
Repurchase of Outstanding Equity													
D. CHANGE IN CASH FROM FINANCING	$	$	$	$	$	$	$	$	$	$	$	$	$
E. INCREASE (DECREASE) IN CASH $(E = A - B + C + D)$	$	$	$	$	$	$	$	$	$	$	$	$	$
F. CASH AT BEGINNING OF PERIOD $(F = F^o \text{ or } G^{-1})$	$	$	$	$	$	$	$	$	$	$	$	$	$*
G. CASH AT END OF PERIOD $(G = F + E)$	$	$	$	$	$	$	$	$	$	$	$	$	$
MEET MINIMUM CASH BALANCE	Acceptable	Acceptable	Acceptable	Acceptable	Acceptable	Acceptable	Acceptable	Acceptable	Acceptable	Acceptable	Acceptable	Acceptable	Acceptable

* This entry should be the same amount as for month 1 at the beginning of the year. All other rows will be the total for the entire year.

Current liabilities are debts you expect to incur that will fall due in less than 12 months. These usually include bills from your suppliers for the supplies and raw materials you will need for your initial inventory, short-term loans from banks and other financial institutions, any portion of your long-term debt that must be repaid during your initial year of operation, and so on. *Long-term liabilities* include outstanding mortgages on land and buildings, notes on machinery and equipment, loans made to the business by you, your partners, and other stockholders, and any other outstanding loans of a long-term nature.

To help choose among several business options you might consider evaluating them on the basis of their expected *return on investment* (ROI). For example, will the rate of return on the money you will have invested in your business be greater than the rate of return you might expect on your money if you invested it elsewhere? ROI can be determined by dividing your expected net profit (before tax) for the first year (as determined in Figure 8.5) by the expected net worth of your business at the end of the year (from Figure 8.7). For example,

$$\text{ROI} = \frac{\text{Net Profit (Before Taxes)}}{\text{Net Worth}}$$

A ratio of 10 to 25 percent might be sufficient to provide for the future growth of your business. If your expected return is less than this, your money could probably be better used elsewhere.

DETERMINE YOUR BREAKEVEN POINT

As your preliminary financial forecasts begin to clarify the size of the potential opportunity you are investigating, there is one other key question to explore: What sales volume will be required for your business to break even? This *breakeven point* indicates the level of operation of the business at which your total costs equal your total revenue. The breakeven point is important, because it indicates when your business begins to make a profit. If your sales level is less than the breakeven point, your business will suffer a loss.

The breakeven point is affected by several factors — among them your fixed and variable costs and your selling price. *Fixed costs* are those that remain constant regardless of your level of sales or production. *Variable costs* vary directly with the amount of business you do. For example, your rent is a fixed cost, because it remains the same regardless of your level of sales. Your cost of goods sold, however, is variable, because the amount you spend is directly related to how much you sell. Fixed costs typically include insurance, licences and permits, property taxes, rent, and similar expenses. Variable costs include supplies, salaries and wages, raw material, utilities, and delivery expenses. Variable costs are usually determined on a per-unit or per-dollar of sales basis.

The breakeven point can be determined algebraically. The basic formula is:

$$\text{Breakeven Point (Units)} = \frac{\text{Total Fixed Costs}}{\text{Contribution Margin per Unit}}$$

where:

Contribution Margin per Unit = Selling Price per Unit − Variable Cost per Unit

The following simple hypothetical example may help illustrate the breakeven concept. Suppose a recently graduated college student has an opportunity to rent a kiosk near a popular beach area to sell ice cream cones. It will cost him $500 per month to rent the kiosk, including the cost of utilities. In order to set up his business he borrows $1000 to acquire the necessary freezers and other fixtures, a loan that has to be paid back at a rate of $100 per month.

FIGURE 8.7 TYPICAL PRO FORMA BALANCE SHEET FOR A SMALL COMPANY

YOUR COMPANY NAME
BALANCE SHEET
as of _____

ASSETS

Current Assets

Cash	$_____	
Accounts receivable	_____	
Inventory	_____	
Other current assets	_____	
Total current assets		_____ (A)

Fixed Assets

Land and Buildings	$_____	
Furniture and fixtures	_____	
Equipment	_____	
Trucks and automobiles	_____	
Other fixed assets	_____	
Total fixed assets		_____ (B)
Total Assets (C = A + B)		$_____ (C)

LIABILITIES

Current Liabilities (debt due within 12 months)

Accounts payable	$_____	
Bank loans/other loans	_____	
Taxes owed	_____	
Total current liabilities		_____ (D)

Long-Term Liabilities

Mortgages payable	$_____	
Loans from partners or shareholders	_____	
Other long-term loans	_____	
Total long-term liabilities		_____ (E)
Total Liabilities (F = D + E)		$_____ (F)

NET WORTH (CAPITAL)

Total Net Worth (G = C − F)		_____ (G)
Total Liabilities and Net Worth (H = F + G)		$_____ (H)

He plans to sell his ice cream cones for $1 each. He estimates that his direct costs of supplies for each cone he sells will be:

Ice cream	$0.50
Cones	0.05
Napkins, etc.	0.05
Total Cost	$0.60

Rather than plan for a regular salary, he has decided to pocket any net profit the business might earn as his income.

In this example the student receives $1 for each ice cream cone he sells but must use supplies worth $0.60 (his variable cost) to earn it. Therefore, he keeps $0.40 (this $0.40 is called his *contribution margin*) to cover his fixed costs (in this case, his rent is his only fixed cost). His contribution margin per unit can then be expressed as follows:

$$\text{Contribution Margin per Unit} = \text{Selling Price} - \text{Total Variable Cost}$$
$$= \$1 - \$0.60$$
$$= \$0.40$$

For determining the number of ice cream cones he will have to sell each month to break even, the formula is as follows:

$$\frac{\text{Total Fixed Costs}}{\text{Contribution Margin per Unit}} = \text{Breakeven Volume (units)}$$

or, in this case:

$$\frac{\$500}{\$0.40} = 1250 \text{ ice cream cones per month}$$

Therefore, the student must sell a minimum of 1250 ice cream cones each month in order to cover his fixed costs of doing business. Even at this level of operation, he does not earn any income for himself. It is only after his sales exceed this level that the business starts to generate sufficient revenue to provide him with some compensation for his time and effort. In addition, this calculation does not consider any interest charges on the $1000 he had to borrow to start the business. These charges would normally be considered a fixed cost as well.

The value of breakeven analysis is that it can be used to determine whether some planned course of action — for example, starting a new business, opening a new store, or adding a new item to your product line — has a chance of being profitable. Once you have estimated the breakeven point for the action, you are in a better position to assess whether such a sales volume can be achieved and how long it will take to reach it.

It is essential that you determine the breakeven level of operation for your business before you proceed very far with its implementation. Bankers and other financial people will expect to see this information as part of the financial documentation for your venture. In addition, if it appears that the breakeven volume is not achievable, the business idea is probably destined to fail and should be abandoned before any money is invested.

PLAN FOR FUTURE ACTION

Figure 8.8 provides a detailed framework that you can use to conduct a comprehensive feasibility assessment of your own new venture idea. When you have completed this evaluation, you need to give some thought to where you go from here. Does the business look sufficiently viable to proceed with the development of a comprehensive business plan? Have you identified all the potential flaws and pitfalls that might negatively impact your business? What role do you expect to play in the growth of the venture? Do you plan to produce and market the concept yourself, or do you hope to sell or license the idea to someone else? How much external money do you need and where do you think you can obtain it? These are the kinds of issues that need to be carefully considered and resolved before you will be in a position to move forward.

In most cases, the next stage is to write out a complete *business plan*. This, however, requires a major commitment of time, effort, and money. Make sure your feasibility study indicates that your concept is clearly viable and that a reasonable profit can be expected.

And don't be too disappointed if your feasibility assessment indicates that your concept is not likely to be profitable. Think of all the time and money you have saved by not going forward with the implementation of a business that has a low probability of succeeding. That's why a preliminary assessment is so essential.

FIGURE 8.8 OUTLINE FOR FEASIBILITY STUDY

YOUR CONCEPT

1. Describe the principal concept underlying your product or service idea.

_____

_____

_____

_____

_____

2. What is unique or distinctive about your idea? How does it differ from similar concepts already being employed in the marketplace?

_____

_____

_____

_____

3. Who will be the primary customers of your concept and what are the principal benefits your concept will deliver to them?

_____

_____

_____

_____

4. How innovative is your concept? How would you categorize it along the continuum from "copycatting" to being an entirely new invention?

_____

_____

_____

5. Is your idea technically feasible? Have you built a working model or prototype? Will you have to obtain Canadian Standards Association (CSA) approval or other permissions, before the concept can be marketed?

_____

_____

_____

_____

PRELIMINARY MARKETING PLAN

Products and Services

1. What products or services will you sell? (Be specific.)

_____

_____

_____

_____

_____

continued

Outline for Feasibility Study — continued

2. What additional customer services (delivery, repair, warranties, etc.) will you offer?

_____
_____
_____
_____
_____

3. What is unique about your total product or service offering?

_____
_____
_____
_____
_____

Customers

1. Define your target customers. (Who are they?)

_____
_____
_____
_____
_____

2. How many target customers are in your trading area?

_____
_____
_____
_____
_____

3. Why will they buy your product?

_____
_____
_____
_____
_____

Competition

1. Who are your principal competitors? What is their market position? Have their sales been growing? Stable? Declining?

a. _____
_____

b. _____
_____

c. _____
_____

d. _____
_____

Outline for Feasibility Study — continued

2. How does your concept differ from each of these other products or services?

_____

_____

_____

_____

Location

1. What location have you selected for your business?

_____

_____

_____

_____

_____

2. Why did you choose that location?

_____

_____

_____

_____

_____

Pricing

1. Describe your pricing strategy.

_____

_____

_____

_____

2. Complete the following chain of markups from manufacturer to final customer:

Cost to manufacture	_____ (A)
Manufacturer's markup	_____ (B)
Manufacturer's selling price (C = A + B)	_____ (C)
Agent's commission (if applicable)	_____ (D)
Wholesaler's cost (E = C + D)	_____ (E)
Wholesaler's markup	_____ (F)
Wholesaler's selling price (G = E + F)	_____ (G)
Retailer's markup	_____ (H)
Retailer's selling price (I = G + H)	_____ (I)

3. How do your planned price levels compare to your competitors'?

_____

_____

_____

_____

continued

Outline for Feasibility Study — continued

Promotion

1. What will your primary promotional message to potential customers be?

   _____

   _____

   _____

   _____

   _____

2. What will your promotion budget be?

   _____

   _____

   _____

   _____

   _____

3. What media will you use for your advertising program?

   _____

   _____

   _____

   _____

   _____

4. Will you have a cooperative advertising program? Describe it.

   _____

   _____

   _____

   _____

   _____

5. Describe your trade promotion program.

   _____

   _____

   _____

   _____

   _____

6. Describe any publicity, public relations, or sales promotion program you will have.

   _____

   _____

   _____

   _____

   _____

Outline for Feasibility Study — continued

Distribution

  1. How do you plan to distribute your product? Direct to the consumer? Through traditional distribution channels? Through specialty channels such as exhibitions, mail order, or trade shows?

  _____

  _____

  _____

  _____

  _____

  2. Will you employ your own sales force or rely on the services of agents or brokers? How many?

  _____

  _____

  _____

  _____

  _____

  _____

THE SUPPLY SITUATION

  1. What raw materials or component parts will you require to produce your product or service? What volume of these materials will you require? Who will be your major source of supply? Do you have alternative supply arrangements or other sources that can meet your requirements?

  _____

  _____

  _____

  _____

  2. What will be the cost of these materials and components? Are prices guaranteed for any length of time? Are volume or quantity discounts available? What credit terms will your suppliers make available to you?

  _____

  _____

  _____

  _____

  3. Describe your manufacturing requirements. Will you manufacture the product yourself or use subcontractors? What will it cost to establish your own manufacturing facility?

  _____

  _____

  _____

  _____

  4. If you are planning to use subcontractors, what alternatives are available? What are their capabilities and comparative costs? Will you have to incur any other costs — e.g., for moulds, etc.? Do any of these contractors provide additional services?

  _____

  _____

  _____

  _____

continued

Outline for Feasibility Study — continued

COST/PROFITABILITY ANALYSIS

1. What do you estimate your costs would be and the funds required to get your business successfully launched?

   a. Complete the following chart to determine your one-time financial requirements.

   Estimated One-time Start-up Financial Requirements

Item	Total Original Cost	Estimated Cash Required
1. Land	$_____	$_____
2. Building	_____	_____
3. Improvements:		
I Mechanical	_____	_____
II Electrical	_____	_____
III Construction	_____	_____
4. Machinery and equipment	_____	_____
5. Installation of equipment	_____	_____
6. Shop tools and supplies	_____	_____
7. Office equipment and supplies	_____	_____
8. Vehicles	_____	_____
9. Starting inventory	_____	_____
10. Utility hookup and installation fees	_____	_____
11. Licences and permits	_____	_____
12. Pre-opening advertising and promotion	_____	_____
13. Accounts payable	_____	_____
14. Cash for unexpected expenses	_____	_____
15. Other cash requirements	_____	_____
Total Estimated One-Time Cash Requirements (1+ ... +15)		$_____

   b. Do you have this much money available or have some ideas as to where you might be able to obtain it?

2. What do you estimate your sales will be, by product or service category, for your first 12 months? What will it cost you to produce those products or provide that service? What do you estimate your gross margin will be for each product or service? How does this compare with the norm for your industry? What operating expenses for such items as rent, travel, advertising, insurance, and utilities do you expect to incur? What profit do you estimate your business will show for its first 12 months?

   Complete the following pro forma income statement for your first year of operation.

3. How are your sales and expenses expected to vary throughout the year? What proportion of your sales will be for cash? On credit? What credit terms, if any, will you provide to your customers? What credit terms do you expect to receive from your suppliers? What other expenses will you have to pay on a regular, ongoing basis?

   a. Complete the following table to estimate your cash flow surplus or deficit for each month of your first year in business.

Outline for Feasibility Study — continued

PRO FORMA INCOME STATEMENT

For the period ending _____

			Month											
		1	2	3	4	5	6	7	8	9	10	11	12	Total
Gross sales															
Less Cash discounts															
Net Sales	**(A)**														
Cost of goods sold:															
Beginning inventory															
Plus: Net purchases															
Total goods available for sale															
Less: Ending inventory															
Cost of Goods Sold	**(B)**														
Gross Margin (C = A – B)	**(C)**														
Less: Variable expenses															
Owner's salary															
Employees' wages and salaries															
Supplies and postage															
Advertising and promotion															
Delivery expense															
Bad debt allowance															
Travel															
Legal and accounting fees															
Vehicle expenses															
Miscellaneous expenses															
Total Variable Expenses	**(D)**														
Less: Fixed expenses															
Rent															
Utilities (heat, light, water, power)															
Telephone															
Taxes and licences															
Depreciation or Capital Cost Allowance															
Interest															
Insurance															
Other Fixed Expenses															
Total Fixed Expenses	**(E)**														
Total Operating Expenses (F = D + E)	**(F)**														
Net Operating Profit (Loss) (G = C – F)	**(G)**														
Income Taxes (estimated)	**(H)**														
Net Profit (Loss) After Income Tax (I = G – H)	**(I)**														

continued

TWELVE-MONTH CASH FLOW PROJECTIONS

	Month 1	Month 2	Month 3	Month 4	Month 5	Month 6	Month 7	Month 8	Month 9	Month 10	Month 11	Month 12	Year 1 TOTAL
Cash Flow From Operations (during month)													
1. Cash Sales													
2. Payments for Credit Sales													
3. Investment Income													
4. Other Cash Income													
A.TOTAL CASH FLOW ON HAND	$	$	$	$	$	$	$	$	$	$	$	$	$
Less Expenses Paid (during month)													
5. Inventory or New Material													
6. Owners' Salaries													
7. Employees' Wages and Salaries													
8. Supplies and Postage													
9. Advertising and Promotion													
10. Delivery Expense													
11. Travel													
12. Legal and Accounting Fees													
13. Vehicle Expense													
14. Maintenance Expense													
15. Rent													
16. Utilities													
17. Telephone													
18. Taxes and Licences													
19. Interest Payments													
20. Insurance													
21. Other Cash Expenses													
B. TOTAL EXPENDITURES	$	$	$	$	$	$	$	$	$	$	$	$	$
Capital													
Purchase of Fixed Assets													
Sale of Fixed Assets													
C. CHANGE IN CASH FROM PURCHASE OR SALE OF ASSETS	$	$	$	$	$	$	$	$	$	$	$	$	$
Financing													
Payment of Principal of Loan													
Inflow of Cash From Bank Loan													
Issuance of Equity Positions													
Repurchase of Outstanding Equity													
D. CHANGE IN CASH FROM FINANCING	$	$	$	$	$	$	$	$	$	$	$	$	$
E. INCREASE (DECREASE) IN CASH	$	$	$	$	$	$	$	$	$	$	$	$	$
F. CASH AT BEGINNING OF PERIOD	$	$	$	$	$	$	$	$	$	$	$	$	$*
G. CASH AT END OF PERIOD	$	$	$	$	$	$	$	$	$	$	$	$	$
MEET MINIMUM CASH BALANCE	Acceptable	Acceptable	Acceptable	Acceptable	Acceptable	Acceptable	Acceptable	Acceptable	Acceptable	Acceptable	Acceptable	Acceptable	Acceptable

* This entry should be the same amount as for month 1 at the beginning of the year. All other rows will be the total for the entire year.

Outline for Feasibility Study — continued

    b. Can you arrange for more favourable terms from your suppliers, accelerate the collection of your outstanding accounts receivable, negotiate a line of credit with your bank, or take other action to enable your business to continue to operate if cash flow is insufficient?

4. What do you estimate your total fixed costs will be for your first year of operation? What did you estimate your average gross margin to be as a percentage of your total sales in preparing your pro forma income statement in question 2? (This amount is also known as your *contribution margin per dollar of sales.*)

Compute your breakeven level of sales by means of the following formula:

$$\text{Breakeven Point (\$ sales)} = \frac{\text{Total Fixed Costs}}{\text{Contribution Margin per \$ of Sales}}$$

When do you expect to attain this level of sales? During your first year of business? Your second year? Your third year?

PLANS FOR FUTURE ACTION

1. According to your feasibility study, what were the strong points and weak points of your new venture idea? Can the weak points and potential problems be successfully overcome?

_____

_____

_____

_____

2. Does the feasibility assessment indicate that the business is likely to be profitable? Does it look sufficiently attractive that you should write a comprehensive business plan? What other information do you have to obtain, or what additional research do you have to do, in order to develop this plan?

_____

_____

_____

_____

3. If you decide not to proceed with the development of a business plan, indicate the reasons why.

_____

_____

_____

_____

STAGE
NINE

ARRANGING FINANCING

Quite a number of sources of financing are available to established businesses. However, there are very few sources of *seed capital* for ventures that are just getting off the ground and have no track record. Obtaining such capital can require persistence and determination. Usually you must submit a formal proposal to a prospective lender, in which you outline your plans, needs, and schedule of repayment. Many financing proposals have to be revised several times before receiving a positive response. In addition, you may have to be prepared to combine financing from several sources in order to raise all the funds you require.

The major sources of funds for small-business start-ups are personal funds, "love money," banks, government agencies and programs, and venture capital.

MAJOR SOURCES OF FUNDS

Personal Funds

The first place to look for money to start your business is your own pocket. This may mean cleaning out your savings account and other investments, selling your second car, postponing your holiday for this year, cashing in your RRSPs, extending your credit cards to the limit, mortgaging the cottage, taking out a second mortgage on the family home, or any other means you may have of raising cash.

"Love Money"

Once you have scraped together everything you can from your resources and personal savings, the next step is to talk to other people. Additional funds may come from your friends, family, and close personal relations. This is known as "love money."

Recent estimates indicate that, in fact, love money makes up more than 90 percent of the new business start-up capital in Canada. This personal funding is necessary because banks and other conventional sources usually will not lend money without extensive security. For example, Peter Oliver, whose case is described in Exhibit 9.1, was able to launch his successful chain of restaurants in Toronto only with the financial support of his wife's parents.

The biggest risk with this source of capital is that if your new business fails and the investors lose money, it can create considerable hard feelings among family and friends. This possibility can be reduced if you lay out all the terms and conditions of the investment in advance, just as you would for any other investors. You should explain the nature of your business, your detailed implementation plans, the risks associated with the venture, and other relevant factors. In fact, it is best if you give both yourself and your investors some measure of comfort by translating your understanding into a formal legal agreement, as Peter Oliver did with his in-laws. If the money is provided to you as a loan, another important reason for putting it into writing is that if, for some reason, you are unable to repay the money and your investor must write it off, the amount of a properly documented loan becomes a capital loss for income tax purposes and can be offset against any capital gains, thereby providing the investor with the potential for some tax relief from the loss.

This most basic kind of financing is often not enough to get the business started, but it is important for external funding sources to see that you and your family are prepared to invest most of your personal resources in the venture. Without a strong indication of this type of individual commitment, it will be extremely difficult to raise any other money. Why should someone not directly involved in the business risk money in your business if you are not prepared to put your own assets on the line?

Banks

Banks are the most popular and widely used *external* source of funds for new businesses. A visit to the local banker becomes almost a mandatory part of any new venture start-up situation. Banks historically have provided debt financing in the form of self-liquidating, short-term loans to cover small businesses' peak working capital requirements, usually in the form of an *operating loan* or *line of credit*.

An operating loan extends credit to you up to a prearranged limit *on an ongoing basis*, to cover your day-to-day expenses such as accounts receivable, payroll, inventory carrying costs, office supplies, and utility bills. If you happen to be in a highly seasonal or cyclical business, for

---

EXHIBIT 9.1

"I've always wanted something I could build into something bigger," says Peter Oliver, explaining why in 1978 he gave up a lucrative career as a real estate agent, and opened Oliver's Old Fashioned Bakery in uptown Toronto. The something bigger is what the 38-year-old has today — four restaurants with anticipated 1987 sales of $12 million and gross profits of 8% to 12%. He also owns two of the four buildings that house his restaurants.

Oliver's success would not have been so swift without the financial support of his wife's parents. They provided the $40,000 down payment on the first building,, which was renovated with another $40,000 from Oliver's savings. In exchange for their investment, Oliver guaranteed his in-laws a minimum 12% annual return as well as half ownership in the building. The money has earned them almost 20% every year,

and the building has escalated in value from $160,000 to an estimated $1 million....

In the beginning he had no formal agreement with his in-laws. But as time went on and they invested more money in his company, proper documents were drawn up, both to arrange bank financing and give everyone concrete evidence of their investment. After nine years, Oliver has built a small empire on a base of love money. And his in-laws have made a superb return on their investments. Oliver sums it up beautifully: "They got a helluva deal," he says, "and I got a helluva deal."

Excerpted from Larry Gaudet and Tony Leighton, "Setting out with buoyant backing," *Canadian Business*, October 1987, pp. 76–77. By permission of the authors.

example, such a "line of credit" can be used to purchase additional inventory in anticipation of your peak selling period.

Operating loans, however, can have some restrictions. For example, your banker may prohibit you from taking retained earnings out of your company during the early stages of your business. In addition, he or she may even veto the purchase of machinery, equipment, and other fixed assets above a certain amount.

Banks also provide *term loans* to small businesses — loans for the purchase of an existing business or to acquire fixed assets such as machinery, vehicles, and commercial buildings, which typically must be repaid in three to ten years. The "term" is usually linked to the expected lifespan of the asset. Three to four years is common for a truck or computer, while the term of a loan to acquire a building could be considerably longer.

You should realize that business bank loans, both operating and term loans are *demand* loans so that regardless of the term, the bank can and will demand they be paid back if it feels the company is getting into trouble. While this usually only occurs when the business has real problems, there is the potential for difficulties; what the banker may perceive as a serious situation may only be perceived as a temporary difficulty by the owner of the business.

Frank Toews and Stephen Boyd, whose case is described in Exhibit 9.2, are typical new business owners. After some initial frustration, both were able to obtain financing from a bank or trust company to acquire their new franchise businesses. Note, however, that 30 to 40 percent of the total financing they required had to come from their personal resources, e.g., personal savings and equity they had built up in their homes. This is typical of most bank financing.

The bank may ask for your personal guarantee of these loans as well as a pledge of collateral security for the full value of the loan or more. This means that even though your business might be incorporated, your personal liability is not necessarily limited to your investment in the business; you could lose your house, car, cottage, and other personal assets if the business should fail and you are unable to repay your loans to the bank.

In order to qualify for a loan you must have sufficient equity in your business and a strong personal credit rating. Banks do not take large risks. Their principal considerations in assessing a loan application are the safety of their depositors' money and the return they will earn on the loan. It is critical that you take these factors into account in preparing your loan proposal and try to look at your situation from the banker's point of view.

Government

Governments at all levels in Canada have developed a proliferation of financial assistance programs for small business. Most of these programs are aimed at companies in more advanced stages of their development who are looking to grow and expand, but quite a number can be utilized by firms in the start-up stage. These programs are too numerous to describe in any detail, but let us briefly look over several of the more important ones.

Business Improvement Loans

New and existing businesses whose gross revenues are less than $5 million may be eligible to obtain term loans from chartered banks or other lenders to purchase or upgrade fixed assets and have the loan guaranteed by the federal government under the Small Business Loans Act (SBLA). These loans are provided at a reasonable rate of interest (prime plus 3% for floating rate loans) plus a 1.25% lender fee payable to the bank. These loans may be used for any number of purposes, such as the purchase or renovation of machinery and equipment and the purchase or improvement of land and buildings for business purposes. The maximum loan size is $250,000, of which as much as 90% can be guaranteed by the government. Contact your local bank or call (613) 954-5540.

EXHIBIT 9.2

Want to buy a franchise but aren't sure if you can raise the money? Consider the experiences of two franchisees who found sources of funding to make their dreams come true.

Frank Toews worked as a high-school teacher in Paris, Ont., for 21 years. In 1986 he bought a Mmmarvellous Mmmuffins franchise from a Toronto franchisor.

Toews' bank agreed to pay 60% of the franchise's overall cost. For the remaining sum, he tapped into both his own savings and the federal government's Small Business Loans Act program, using his own home as collateral.

Toews' first store prospered and paid off [his] startup costs so he decided to buy a second franchise last year. But when he went to the Royal Bank of Canada — which had financed his first store — he was turned down. "We found that frustrating," Toews acknowledges, pointing out that his net worth was higher than it had been the first time he'd sought funding from the bank. So he decided to shop around.

After a number of rejections, the Toronto Dominion Bank agreed to finance his second franchise. However, the TD did a thorough investigation of Toews before it agreed to pay 60% of the cost. The rest he made up out of savings and profits from his first store. "In this economic climate, it's a matter of judgment calls on

the part of the banks. Don't let yourself get discouraged easily," he says.

Stephen Boyd is a former management accountant. In 1988, he bought a franchise from Moneysworth & Best Shoe Repair Inc.; last year, he purchased his second. Both are located in Halifax. A Moneysworth & Best franchise costs from $125,000 to $150,000.

Boyd was unable to interest his bank in financing the first store, largely because the franchise chain was not well known in the Maritimes. So he opted for Moneysworth & Best's in-house financing program. With this program and $30,000 of his own savings, Boyd successfully opened his first outlet. Still, he is not overly enthusiastic about the in-house program because it is more expensive than bank financing. "[National Trust] has pegged on a couple more points above what the banks would," says Boyd of the company that backs the in-house program. When it came to financing his second store last year, Boyd was able to get bank financing, which covered 70% of the cost. The rest of the money came from $35,000 in savings and equity from his home.

B. Livesey, "How two franchisees found funds," *Financial Times of Canada*, April 22, 1991, p. A5. By permission of Bruce Livesey, a Toronto-based freelance journalist.

INDUSTRIAL RESEARCH ASSISTANCE PROGRAM (IRAP)

Provides technical and financial assistance to firms to develop their technical capability. Call (613) 993-1790.

PROGRAM FOR EXPORT MARKET DEVELOPMENT (PEMD)

A 50–50 cost-shared program to help new exporters introduce their products in foreign markets. Call Foreign Affairs and International Trade, (613) 996-9134.

CANADIAN INTERNATIONAL DEVELOPMENT AGENCY (CIDA)

CIDA's Industrial Cooperation Program promotes joint ventures and technology transfer with developing countries and encourages Canadian companies to participate in sustainable development projects in these countries. Call (819) 997-5456.

BUSINESS DEVELOPMENT BANK OF CANADA (BDC)

The BDC is a federal Crown corporation that provides a wide range of financial, management counselling, and information services to small business. Its financial services complement those of the private sector by providing funds for business projects that are not available from the commercial banks and other sources on reasonable terms. The BDC will provide term loans for the acquisition of fixed assets or to replenish working capital, loan guarantees for loans from private sector institutions, and in some situations will provide equity capital by purchasing shares in the business.

BDC also runs the Financial Planning Program, which has three separate components:

1. Financial matchmaking through an information service which tries to match potential investors with individuals like you who may be seeking equity financing

2. Do-it-yourself business planning packages on such topics as arranging financing, analyzing financial statements, credit and collection tips, and forecasting and cash flow budgeting

3. Assistance in preparing financial proposals

The BDC is also a major source of small-business counselling through its Counselling Assistance to Small Enterprises (CASE) program.

PROVINCIAL FINANCIAL ASSISTANCE PROGRAMS

Most of the provincial governments provide a range of grants, loans, and other forms of assistance to small business. For example, many provinces have financial assistance programs similar to the Business Start Program offered in Manitoba. It provides a guarantee for loans up to $10,000, along with an educational component to assist new entrepreneurs in getting their businesses off the ground. These are much too extensive to discuss here, but you can obtain specific information on the programs offered in your area by contacting the following government agencies:

British Columbia

> Ministry of Small Business, Tourism, and Culture
> 1117 Wharf Street
> Victoria, B.C.
> V8W 2Z2
> Fax: (604) 356-8248
> Phone: (604) 356-6363

Alberta

> Alberta Economic Development and Trade
> Small Business and Tourism Division
> Sterling Place
> 9940 - 106th Street
> 6th Floor
> Edmonton, Alberta
> T5K 2P6
> Fax: (403) 297-6168
> Phone: (403) 297-6284
> and
> 999 - 8th Street
> 5th Floor
> Calgary, Alberta
> T2P 1J5

Saskatchewan

> Department of Economic Development
> 1919 Saskatchewan Drive
> Regina, Saskatchewan
> S4P 3V7
> Phone: (306) 787-2232

Manitoba

Manitoba Industry, Trade, and Tourism
Business Resource Centre
155 Carlton Street
5th Floor
Winnipeg, Manitoba
R3C 3H8
Fax: (204) 945-1354
Phone: (204) 945-7738

Ontario

Ministry of Economic Development and Trade
900 Bay Street
Toronto, Ontario
M7A 2E1
Fax: (416) 325-6688
Phone: (416) 325-6666

Quebec

Ministère de l'Industrie du Commerce, de la Science et de la Technologie
710 Place d'Youville
9th Floor
Quebec City, Quebec
G1H 4Y4
Fax: (418) 644-0118
Phone: (418) 691-5950

Place Mercantile
10th Floor
770 Sherbrooke Street West
Montreal, Quebec
H3A 1G1
Fax: (514) 873-9913
Phone: (514) 982-3000

New Brunswick

Department of Economic Development and Tourism
670 King Street
5th Floor
P.O. Box 6000
Fredericton, New Brunswick
E3B 5H1
Fax: (506) 444-4586
Phone: (506) 453-2850

Nova Scotia

Economic Renewal Agency
World Trade and Convention Centre
1800 Argyle Street
7th Floor
P.O. Box 955
Halifax, Nova Scotia
B3J 2V9
Fax: (902) 422-2922
Phone: (902) 421-8686

Prince Edward Island

Department of Economic Development and Tourism
Shaw Building
P.O. Box 2000
Charlottetown, P.E.I.
C1A 7N8
Fax: (902) 368-4224
Phone: (902) 368-4240

Newfoundland

Department of Industry, Trade and Technology
Confederation Annex
4th Floor
P.O.Box 8700
St. John's, Newfoundland
A1B 4J6
Fax: (709) 729-5936
Phone: (709) 729-5600

Northwest Territories

Department of Economic Development and Tourism
Corporate and Technical Services
P.O. Box 1320
Yellowknife, N.W.T.
X1A 2L9
Fax: (403) 873-0101
Phone: (403) 920-3182

Yukon Territory

Yukon Economic Development
211 Main Street
Suite 400
P.O. Box 2703
Whitehorse, Y.T.
Y1A 2C6
Fax: (403) 668-8601
Phone: (403) 667-5466

FOR MORE INFORMATION

For detailed information on specific federal or provincial government programs, you might check out the following publications at your local library:

Government Financial Assistance Programs in Canada

Butterworths
25 Clegg Road
Markham, Ontario
L6G 1A1

Industrial Assistance Programs in Canada

CCH Canadian Ltd.
6 Garamond Court
Don Mills, Ontario
M3C 1Z5

Government Assistance Programs and Subsidies
Canada Pack
P.O. Box 358
Richmond Hill, Ontario
L4C 4Y6

Venture Capital

Venture capital involves equity participation in a start-up or growing business situation. Conventional venture capital companies, however, really don't offer much opportunity for firms still in the concept or idea stage. These investors are generally looking for investment situations in proven firms requiring in excess of $1,000,000 and on which they can earn a 40 to 50 percent annual return. While these companies will often accept high-risk situations, most new venture start-ups don't meet their primary investment criteria. There are, however, a number of venture capital firms that may be prepared to consider smaller investments. Some of them are listed in Exhibit 9.3. However, keep in mind that of 100 proposals considered by a typical venture capital firm, only four or five are selected for investment purposes. Therefore, the probability of receiving any financial assistance from this source is very slim. For more information, however, you can contact the Association of Venture Capital Companies at (416) 487-0519.

A new business start-up probably has a better chance of obtaining equity capital from small, private venture capitalists — often called "angels" — or provincially supported venture capital programs. There may be doctors, dentists, lawyers, accountants, and other individuals within your community whom you can approach for investment funds. Many of these people may be looking for situations where they can invest small sums (less than $50,000) with the possibility of earning a larger return than that offered by more-conventional investments, and they are often prepared to invest in start-up situations.

A number of communities and organizations have programs to bring entrepreneurs together with private investors. York University and the MIT Alumni Club of Toronto as well as other organizations sponsor "enterprise forums," in which small companies get an opportunity to tell their story before a group of prospective investors and other experts. The city of St. John's, for example, runs the Investment Opportunities Project (IOP), which attempts to match cash-hungry entrepreneurs with investors throughout the province; and the provincial chambers of commerce across Canada operate a national program called the Canada Opportunities Investment Network (COIN). COIN charges about $200 to sign up for a year. If your needs match up with an investor's profile, COIN sends the angel information on your company, which may lead to a face-to-face meeting and further consideration of your proposal.

Leon Rudanycz, who is profiled in Exhibit 9.4, is a typical "angel." He had a very successful business of his own, sold it, and used some of the proceeds to invest in other people's ideas. These investments gave him a way to keep involved, to continue to participate in the growth and development of these businesses, to contribute to major company decisions, and an opportunity to make a good financial return on his investments.

Obtaining money from private venture capital sources, however, may pose certain problems for you. You will probably have to give up at least partial ownership and control of your business. In addition, venture capitalists usually have limited resources, so additional funds may not be available if required later. Finally, as amateur investors, these people may not have the patience to wait out the situation if things don't work out as quickly as you originally planned.

EXHIBIT 9.3

A SELECTION OF CANADIAN VENTURE CAPITAL COMPANIES

BG ACORN CAPITAL FUND
Toronto (416) 362-9009
Focus: all sectors

CANADIAN VENTURE FOUNDERS
Oakville, Ont. (905) 842-9770
Focus: environmental and high-tech/information management

DGC ENTERTAINMENT VENTURES CORP.
Toronto (416) 972-0098
Focus: entertainment, communications, primarily Ontario-based

BUSINESS DEVELOPMENT BANK (VENTURE CAPITAL DIVISION)
Offices in Montreal (514) 283-2121, Ottawa (613) 995-0234, Toronto (416) 973-0031, Vancouver (604) 666-7815.

FONDS DE SOLIDARITÉ DES TRAVAILLEURS DU QUÉBEC (FTQ)
Montreal (514) 383-8383
Focus: all sectors, preference for small and medium-size businesses in Quebec

GRIEVE HORNER BROWN & ASCULAI
Toronto (416) 362-7668
Focus: technology related to health care, information processing, communications

HELIX INVESTMENTS (CANADA) LTD.
Toronto (416) 326-1025
Focus: technology

HORATIO ENTERPRISE FUND L.P.
Toronto (416) 488-8783
Focus: Toronto-area telecommunications services, education

INNOVATECH GRAND MONTREAL
Montreal (514) 864-2929
Focus: information technology, biotech, pharmaceuticals, telecommunications

INNOVATION ONTARIO CORP.
Toronto (416) 326-1025
Focus: all sectors, high-tech R&D ventures based in Ontario

MDS DISCOVERY VENTURE MANAGEMENT INC.
Vancouver (604) 872-8464
Focus: medical and biotechnology

MDS HEALTH VENTURES INC.
Etobicoke, Ont. (416) 675-7661
Focus: health care and biotech

NATIVE VENTURE CAPITAL CO. LTD.
Edmonton (403) 488-7101
Focus: Alberta ventures operated by aboriginal peoples

NOVACAP INVESTMENTS INC.
Montreal (514) 282-1383
Focus: medium- and high-tech manufacturing

SASKATCHEWAN GOVERNMENT GROWTH FUND
Regina (306) 787-2994
Focus: Saskatchewan-based ventures

SOCCRENT
Jonquière, Que. (418) 548-1155
Focus: aluminum, forest products

SOCIÉTÉ EN COMMANDITE CAPIDEM QUÉBEC ENR.
Quebec City (418) 681-1910
Focus: manufacturing

SOQUIA
Quebec City (418) 643-2238
Focus: agri-food technology

VENCAP EQUITIES ALBERTA LTD.
Calgary (403) 237-8101
Focus: all sectors

VENTURES WEST MANAGEMENT INC.
Vancouver (604) 688-9495
Focus: technology

VISION CAPITAL FUND
Winnipeg (204) 925-5450
Focus: all sectors, Manitoba-based preferred

WESTPORT CAPITAL INC.
Toronto (416) 979-5675
Contact: D. T. Waite

WORKING VENTURES CANADIAN FUND
Toronto (416) 929-7777
Contact: Ron Begg

EXHIBIT 9.4

How do you find an angel? You might hear about him from your lawyer, from an investment company or from somebody at a cocktail party.

"You'd hear that Leon had a business and sold it, and invested in a couple of other ones successfully and has some money to invest," says Leon Rudanycz, a typical contributor to the largely unmeasured pool of informal investment capital that nurtures budding young companies.

Rudanycz, who has degrees in law and engineering, started up a computer distributing company in the mid-'80s. Now called Tech Data Canada Inc., it's one of the country's largest high-tech distributors. Rudanycz sold out, then became an angel by investing some of the proceeds in two other fledgling computer companies.

"Both were started out of people's homes, very lean and mean. I ended up selling my interest in both companies — one within four years, the other three. But they were both profitable from day one."

That's not always the case, and most venture capitalists make their money back when they take the company public, usually seeking an annual return of 30%-40%. In the crapshoot of angel investing, only a few ventures hit the big time, so the winners have to make up spectacularly for the many losers.

"Angel investing, by its nature, is less formal, involves smaller sums of money and usually does not involve a full-time position in the company," says Rudanycz. "It's generally more in the $100,000 range."

Carleton University has carried out the most extensive research into Canada's informal investment market, conducting a survey of 279 angels.

"The investors were found to be significantly more wealthy than most Canadians ... and occupy the top one percentile of wealth among Canadian households," says the Carleton report.

In plumbing the angel psychology, the research found that "investors tend to be men with an internal locus of control, very high needs for achievement and dominance."

Almost 90% expected to serve on a board of directors or advisers when investing. A third of them participate directly as an operating principle. And nearly two-thirds also stipulate some sort of operating covenants in the form of periodic reports, authorization of cash disbursements over a certain amount, and control of salaries and dividends.

Rudanycz fits the mould perfectly. "I demand a seat on the board, cheque-signing authority along with the owner, a good handle on the accounting and a hand in major decisions," he says.

His two subsequent high-tech investments were made in the form of a secured loan, and the shares were simply "the kicker, the bonus. I don't always do that, though." For example, Rudanycz says he's considering a straight equity investment in a clothing manufacture and design business. He'd get a piece of the action for a relatively measly $10,000.

"Projected sales in the first year are $100,000 and probably a million in the third, and for them this $10,000 is pivotal," says Rudanycz, describing a deal that's well beneath the threshold of the mainstream venture capital industry.

Excerpted from Gord MacLaughlin, "Divine Intervention," *The Financial Post*, May 6, 1995, p. 7.

Additional Sources of Financing

Personal Credit Cards

The credit limit extended by financial institutions on personal credit cards can provide you with ready access to a short-term loan but usually at interest rates that are considerably higher than more conventional financing (upwards of 18-22 percent). There may be occasions, however, where other sources of working capital are not available and drawing upon the personal line of credit associated with your cards may be the only source of funds available to sustain your business. This can be risky since you are personally liable for the expenditures on the card even though they may have been made for business purposes but it may be useful if you are expecting a major payment or other injection of cash into the business within a few days.

Suppliers Inventory Buying Plans

In some industries one way of obtaining working capital may be through supplier's financing. Suppliers may be prepared to extend payment terms to 60, 90, or even 120 days for some customers. Other suppliers may offer floor plan financing or factoring options to help their dealers finance inventory purchases, usually in advance of the peak selling season. In addition, many suppliers offer discounts off the face value of their invoice (typically 2 percent for payment within 10 days) or penalize slow paying customers with interest charges (often 1-1/2 percent a month). These programs can impact your financing requirements.

Leasing vs. Buying

In competitive equipment markets, specialized leasing and finance companies will arrange for the lease of such items as expensive pieces of equipment, vehicles, copiers, and computers. Leasing, often with an option to buy, rather than purchasing can free up your scarce capital for investment in other areas of your business. While the interest rates charged on the lease contract may be somewhat higher than you might pay through the bank, the lease expenses are usually fully deductible from your taxable income. A lease contract will fix your cost of having the equipment for a fixed term and may provide the flexibility to purchase the equipment at a later date at a predetermined price.

Leasehold Improvements

When locating your business in rented premises it is usually necessary to undertake a number of leasehold improvements in order to make the premises appropriate to your needs. Installing new electrical outlets, adding additional partitions and walls, laying carpet, painting, installing fixtures, and similar modifications can add considerably to the cost of launching your business. Sometimes it may be possible to get the landlord of your location to assist in making these improvements, particularly if there is a lot of other space available to rent. The landlord or property manager may agree to provide a portion (an allowance of a dollar amount per square foot of space) or cover all of your leasehold improvement in return for a longer-term lease (typically three to five years). Reducing your initial expenditures in this way can reduce the start-up cash and equity you require to launch your business, even though you will be paying for these improvements in your monthly rent over the course of the lease.

Advance Payment From Customers

It may be possible to negotiate a full or partial payment from some customers in advance to help finance the costs of taking on their business. In some industries, construction for example, it is customary to receive a partial payment at certain defined stages during the course of the project rather than waiting until completion. These payments can reduce the cash needs of running your business. Any work that involves special orders or custom designs for products specifically tailored to the requirements of one customer should require a significant deposit or full payment in advance.

EVALUATING YOUR ABILITY TO SECURE FINANCING

An important aspect of your financial condition is your ability to obtain financing. When seeking a loan, it is wise to shop around for the best available terms. In preparing to approach a banker regarding a loan, there are several suggestions you should keep in mind to increase your probability of getting the funds:

- Don't just drop in on your bank manager; make an appointment.
- Start your presentation briefly describing your business and the exact reason you require a loan.

- Be prepared to answer any questions your banker may have. He or she wants to determine how well you really understand your business. If you can't answer certain questions, explain why and say when you will be able to provide the information.
- Be prepared to discuss collateral and other security you may be required to provide.
- If your business is currently operating, invite the banker to stop by to see it first-hand.
- Ask when you can expect a reply to your request. If there is a delay, inquire whether there is additional information you need to provide.

A financial institution may turn down your loan application for any of a number of reasons, and it is important that you ask what they are. This knowledge may help you in future attempts to secure funding. Some of the most frequent reasons why a loan application can be rejected are as follows:

1. The business idea might be considered ill advised or just too risky.
2. You may not have offered sufficient collateral. Lenders want some assurance that they will be able to recover most or all of their money should you default on the payments.
3. The lender may feel there is insufficient financial commitment on your part.
4. You have not prepared a comprehensive and detailed business plan.
5. Your reason for requesting the loan is unclear or not acceptable to the lender. It is important that you specify the intended application of the requested funds and that this application be outlined in detail. This outline should also show your planned schedule for the repayment of the loan.
6. You do not appear confident, enthusiastic, well-informed, or realistic enough in your objectives. The lender's assessment of your character, personality, and stability are important considerations in their evaluation of your loan application.

The worksheet shown in Figure 9.1 will allow you to assess some of the critical factors that may affect your ability to secure external funding. It will also give you some indication of what aspects of your personal character, development of your business plans, or quality of the basic idea underlying your new venture could be improved. On the worksheet, indicate your assessment of your personal situation on each of the indicated factors as honestly as you can. How do you rate? Could some factors be improved on? What can you do to strengthen these areas, or how might you overcome this negative factor?

One question you should consider is, "How much can I possibly lose on my venture should it fail?" The losses in some types of businesses can wipe out virtually all of the funds you have invested or personally guaranteed. This tends to be true in situations like a financial planning and counselling business, a travel agency, or a hair salon, in which very little property or equipment is owned by the business. In other situations, such as manufacturing, construction, or real estate, there is usually an opportunity to sell the assets solely or partially owned by the business to recover at least part of your initial investment.

The way to explore this question is to consider alternative scenarios for different ways in which the business might fail and estimate the liquidation value of any residual assets. To the extent that this value falls short of the initial cost of those assets less any outstanding claims, you could lose that amount of money plus the opportunity cost of the time and effort you spent in trying to develop the business.

PROTECTING YOUR INVESTMENT

One way to reduce some of the financial risks associated with your new venture is to obtain a *comprehensive insurance package*, one specifically designed to meet your business' protection requirements.

FIGURE 9.1 LOAN APPLICATION ASSESSMENT WORKSHEET

	Poor		Good	Excellent	
Assessment Factor	**1**	**2**	**3**	**4**	**5**
Personal credit rating	___	___	___	___	___
Capacity to pay back loan from personal assets if business fails	___	___	___	___	___
Collateral to pay back loan from personal assets if business fails	___	___	___	___	___
Character (as perceived in the community)	___	___	___	___	___
Commitment (your personal investment of time, energy, and money)	___	___	___	___	___
Clarity and completeness of your business plan	___	___	___	___	___
Viability of business concept (e.g., moderate risk)	___	___	___	___	___
Personal experience in the proposed business	___	___	___	___	___
Successful experience in your own business	___	___	___	___	___
Balanced management team available	___	___	___	___	___
Suitability of your personality to the pressures and responsibilities of the business	___	___	___	___	___

What can you do to improve the weak areas (where you have rated yourself 1 or 2)?

_____

_____

_____

_____

From D. A. Gray, *The Entrepreneur's Complete Self-Assessment Guide* (Vancouver: International Self-Counsel Press Ltd., 1986), p. 123.

Doug Gray suggests asking your insurance agent about the following 21 types of insurance:

1. General liability
2. Home office
3. Fire
4. Theft
5. Automobile
6. Product liability
7. Disability
8. Business loan
9. Malpractice
10. Errors and omissions
11. Business interruption
12. Life
13. Surety and fidelity bonds
14. Employee
15. Workers' compensation
16. Property
17. Overhead expense
18. Group
19. Medical
20. Key person
21. Partner or shareholder

Adapted from D. A. Gray, "Business Insurance Checklist," *Home Inc. The Canadian Home-Based Business Guide,* second edition (Toronto: McGraw-Hill Ryerson Limited, 1994).

This kind of program won't protect you from *all* the risks associated with running your business, but it will provide you with some comfort against unpredictable occurrences in several areas that could threaten the survival of your venture.

STAGE
TEN

PREPARING YOUR BUSINESS PLAN

The final stage in building a dream for a new venture of your own is developing your business plan. A *business plan* is a written document that describes all aspects of your business venture — your basic product or service, your prospective customers, the competition, your production and marketing methods, your management team, how the business will be financed, and all the other things necessary to implement your idea. It might be called the "game plan" of your business.

BUSINESS PLANNING — THE "BIG PICTURE"

Why Consider the "Big Picture"?

When you start your business you will find that there are many things that happen that you didn't expect, or didn't work out the way you expected. Don't worry. Your experience in this regard won't be unique. This happens to almost everyone. What is important is for you to be prepared for this to happen and ready to make adjustments. In making these changes it is important that you don't lose sight of what it is that you are really trying to do. This means that you need to keep the "Big Picture" in mind. The "Big Picture" is brought together in the business planning process.

The Steps in the Business Planning Process

The business planning process focuses on the future. It enables you to relate what you wish to achieve to what your business concept or idea can deliver. It entails working your way through each of the following steps in a logical and sequential way:

1. Develop a Vision Statement

A Vision Statement focuses on the *what* of your business. Your Vision Statement should describe your idealized perception of what your business will look like under perfect conditions, if all your goals and objectives have been met. It lays out the "Super Goal" that you would like your business to achieve. The key components of your Vision Statement will be:

- The name of your planned business venture

- The product/service offering you plan to provide
- The target market(s) you intend to serve

Your Vision Statement should be short (a sentence or two). It should also be easy to understand and easy to remember.

For example, a typical Vision Statement might be: "The Hockey House plans to provide a wide range of hockey-related products and services to casual skaters, minor hockey players, community clubs and organizations, and competitive hockey teams and players."

2. Formulate a Mission Statement

A Mission Statement focuses on the *how* of your business. It defines the purpose of your venture. It outlines the reason for being for your business and provides some understanding of how your business will be operated. It is, in fact, the "Super Strategy" of your business. The key components of your Mission Statement will describe:

- What your business will do
- Its market focus, niche, or particular image
- Your planned location and the geographic market served
- How you plan to grow the business
- Your sustainable uniqueness or what will distinguish your business from others and will continue to do so on a long-term basis

Your Mission Statement should be a series of short phrases that addresses each of these elements. For example, a Mission Statement for The Hockey House might state: "The Hockey House will provide a broad range of skates, sticks, pads, sweaters, and other related hockey equipment and services intended to meet the requirements of ice and in-line hockey players at all levels of ability; from beginners to semi-professional and professionals. It will also sell related supplies and equipment such as goal nets and timers with a view to being the one-stop shop for hockey in Manitoba and northwestern Ontario. It will sell to individuals, teams, and community clubs through a retail outlet located adjacent to a major hockey complex in Winnipeg but will also produce a four-colour catalogue and call personally on groups in communities outside the city. Our principal competitive edge will be the breadth of selection we can offer and the quality of service we plan to provide."

3. Define the Fundamental Values By Which You Will Run Your Business

Many arguments, particularly in family businesses or partnerships, occur because the members do not share common values, even when they often assume that they do. For a new business to have a good chance of succeeding all principals should agree on a basic set of values by which they will operate. The process of discussing and trying to achieve agreement on these values is likely to identify points of difference that should be addressed before the business is started. This process can be conducted in two steps. Step 1 requires you and any other principals associated with the business to define their own personal values. Step 2 consolidates the common values by which the business will be operated.

An example of a statement of business values might look like the following:

"In conducting our business, we will implement our Vision by conducting our affairs so that our actions provide evidence of the high value we place on:

Integrity by dealing honestly with our customers, employees, suppliers, and the community

Responsibility by taking into account the environment in which we do business, community views, and the common good

Profitability by being conscious that an appropriate level of profit is necessary to sustain the business and allow our values to continue to be observed

Value by providing quality products that are recognized as delivering value for money

Employees by providing quality, equitable opportunities for development in a healthy workplace, with appropriate rewards"

4. Set Clear and Specific Objectives

Setting objectives for your business provides you with yardsticks with which to measure your ability to achieve your Vision. Objectives define measurable targets whose achievement can also contribute directly to the successful accomplishment of the mission of your business. Unlike "Goals," which provide a broad direction for your business, "Objectives" provide you with the means to measure directly the performance of your business.

Business objectives usually relate to such issues as:

- the return on investment the business should achieve
- a desired level of market position or market share
- projected stages of technological development
- specific levels of financial performance.

To be effective an objective should:

- refer to a specific outcome, not an activity
- be measurable
- be realistic and achievable based on the actual capabilities of the business
- contain a specific time deadline

For example, a reasonable set of objectives for The Hockey House might be:

1. To generate $XXXX in sales by the end of year one
2. To achieve $YYY in after tax profits in year one
3. To increase inventory turnover from X times to Y times during year one.

5. Making It Happen! Develop a Realistic Business Plan.

Your business plan is the most important business document you will ever prepare and it is also probably the most difficult. It takes a lot of time, research, self-discipline, and commitment to complete properly and is not a lot of fun. However, regardless of whether you intend to start a small, part-time business in the basement of your home or launch a sophisticated, high-growth venture, you still need a business plan.

Your business plan is the culmination of all your self-evaluation, ideas, research, analysis, assessment, round-table discussions, bull sessions, schemes, and daydreams. It lays out for everyone to see precisely where you are now, where you are going, and how you plan to get there. It presents everything about you and what you intend to do — your goals and objectives, opportunities and threats facing you, your business strengths and weaknesses, and so on. It is a comprehensive but concise disclosure of all aspects of your business venture.

How you define your business plan, however, affects your approach to writing it. If you view it as a very complex and boring task, your plan will come across that way to any reader. As a result, many business plans are dry, rambling, and highly technical because the entrepreneurs behind them see them largely as some sort of formal academic exercise.

Your business plan should be viewed as a selling document, not unlike a piece of sales literature you would distribute about your company. Except with your business plan, rather than just promoting a particular product or service you are selling the whole company as a package. If you are really excited about your company and the idea upon which it is based, it should come through in your business plan. Your plan should convey to readers the excitement and promise that you feel about your venture.

FIGURE 10.1 DEVELOPING THE "BIG PICTURE"

1. DEVELOP YOUR VISION STATEMENT

   a. Write short phrases to describe each of the three elements in your Vision Statement:
- the name of your planned venture
- your product/service offering
- the target market(s) you plan to serve

   b. Combine these phrases into a single sentence

_____

_____

_____

_____

_____

2. FORMULATE YOUR MISSION STATEMENT

   a. Write short phrases to describe each of the following elements of your business:
- what your business will do
- its market focus, niche, or particular image
- its planned location and geographic market served
- how growth of the business will be achieved
- your sustainable uniqueness or distinguishing characteristics

   b. Combine these phrases into short, linked sentences.

_____

_____

_____

_____

_____

_____

3. DEFINE THE FUNDAMENTAL VALUES BY WHICH YOUR BUSINESS WILL BE RUN

Step 1 Personal Values

Have each principal involved in the business complete the following framework for *five* values that they hold to be personally important.

   a. *Value:* Express as a single word _____

     What: A brief explanation of what the word means to you. _____

_____

_____

     Why? Outline why it is important that the business operate this way to you. _____

_____

_____

   b. *Value:* Express as a single word _____

What: A brief explanation of what the word means to you. _____

_____

_____

Why? Outline why it is important that the business operate this way to you. _____

_____

_____

c. *Value:* Express as a single word _____

   What: A brief explanation of what the word means to you. _____

_____

_____

   Why? Outline why it is important that the business operate this way to you. _____

_____

_____

d. *Value:* Express as a single word _____

   What: A brief explanation of what the word means to you. _____

_____

_____

   Why? Outline why it is important that the business operate this way to you. _____

_____

_____

e. *Value:* Express as a single word _____

   What: A brief explanation of what the word means to you. _____

_____

_____

   Why? Outline why it is important that the business operate this way to you. _____

_____

_____

Step 2   Values by Which the Business Will Be Managed

Complete Step 2 from the information provided by each of the principals in Step 1. Include only values that were *common to all principals*. Others should only be included after discussion, negotiation, and consensus among all individuals. Since some values will differ, it is necessary for all parties to agree which will be the common values used to guide the operations of the business. This list should contain five or six values at a maximum and it is important that they are compatible with each other. Each principal will then have to decide whether they will be able to work in a business where, perhaps, only some, or none of their personal values will be given expression.

a. *Value:* _____

   What: _____

_____

_____

_____

   Why? _____

_____

_____

_____

continued

Developing the "Big Picture" — continued

b. *Value:* _____

   What: _____

   _____

   _____

   _____

   Why? _____

   _____

   _____

   _____

c. *Value:* _____

   What: _____

   _____

   _____

   _____

   Why? _____

   _____

   _____

   _____

d. *Value:* _____

   What: _____

   _____

   _____

   _____

   Why? _____

   _____

   _____

   _____

e. *Value:* _____

   What: _____

   _____

   _____

   _____

   Why? _____

   _____

   _____

   _____

4. DEFINE YOUR OBJECTIVES

The business' Vision will be achieved when the following objectives have been attained:

a. Objective _____

b. Objective _____

c. Objective _____

d. Objective _____

e. Objective _____

Observe in Exhibit 10.1 the time and effort Kent Groves dedicated to the development of his business plan. He spent over a year researching the mail-order industry, studying the competition, and asking questions of people who were experts in the business. Then, with the assistance of an accountant, he wrote his "road map" to guide him through every aspect of the implementation of his business. With the plan, he was also able to win the confidence of a banker who provided him with the necessary line of credit to carry his seasonal business over its slow periods. His business plan has become a combined operations manual/corporate bible that can be continually referred to so that he knows if, in fact, the business is evolving as he had originally anticipated.

EXHIBIT 10.1

Some businesspeople call them "the lies we tell our bankers." In this economy, however, a company looking for credit must put a lot more than creative writing in its business plan.

Kent Groves, president of catalogue retailer Maritime Trading Co. of Falmouth, N.S. and a former Nutrilawn International manager who spent a lot of time approving franchises, knows the importance of business plans. "Some of the best plans I saw were put together by people who totally ignored them once the loan was approved. And their franchises were in trouble."

Groves took a year to research the mail-order industry, studying catalogues, trade magazines and reports, and asking questions of industry experts. Then, with an accountant, he spent six weeks writing what he calls a "road map to guide you through every aspect of your operations."

The result: a 68-page plan with 16 appendices. Groves' Rand-McNally approach to mapping business highways offers an executive summary, mission statement ("we are the leader in the direct marketing of the highest quality Maritime products in the world"), profile, industry overview, and bibliography. And he provided details on sales and marketing, operations, and financing. "It helped to have an accountant who would say, 'Those figures don't make sense'," says Groves. "She asked the hard questions."

Most of Groves' efforts were geared to winning a line of credit — essential for a firm that makes all its money at Christmas. But the effort proved frustrating: MTC's application was rejected by Scotiabank, CIBC, and Hongkong Bank. The setback soured Groves: "The banks advertise 'We support small business.' Yeah, until you need money. What a crock!"

After moving to Nova Scotia full-time in June, Groves approached the Royal Bank in Halifax. There he met account manager Earl Covin, who got excited by his plan. "It was a breath of fresh air," says Covin. "I didn't have to do a lot of background work. It had more detail than most bankers ever expect, and it was very realistic." Once past the collateral hurdle — Groves' father helped out — the bank approved a $75,000 credit line in a day.

Beyond winning financial support, MTC's business plan has become a combined operations manual/corporate bible. Says Groves, "We continually check our expenses and they're right on track. We know where we stand." So when he saw catalogue costs coming in 25% below projections, he knew he could boost marketing spending 20%.

More importantly, revenue projections are also on budget. Another catalogue company, using one of the same mailing lists as Groves, received a 1.5% response rate — "dead on" for MTC's projections. MTC forecast an operating deficit of $49,200 at the end of September; the actual amount was $45,000. With his catalogues just hitting the market in October, Groves still expects sales to reach $100,000 by Dec. 31.

Like most road maps, MTC's business plan allows for dirt roads and detours. "When we stray," says Groves, "we know it and at what capacity we're varying. What's important is flexibility that allows you to make changes."

Source: Allan Lynch writes for PROFIT magazine and is author of *Sweat Equity: Atlantic Canada's New Entrepreneurs.*

Why Develop a Business Plan?

Your business plan can accomplish many things for you and your proposed venture. These can largely be categorized into two basic areas:

1. **For the internal evaluation of your business**, both as a checklist to see that you have covered all the important bases and as a timetable for accomplishing your stated objectives

2. **For external use** in attracting resources and obtaining support for your venture

From an internal perspective, developing a plan forces you to seriously consider the important elements of your venture and the steps you feel are necessary to get it off the ground. Your plan can be used to inform employees about the goals and direction of your business. It lets everyone know how they fit into the organization and what you expect of them. Your plan can also help you develop as a manager. It requires you to deal with problems relating to competitive conditions, promotional opportunities, and other situations that will confront your business.

Externally, your business plan can serve as an effective sales document and is considered by many experts to be the heart of the capital-raising process. Any knowledgeable banker or prospective investor will expect you to be professional in your approach, fully prepared, and armed with a thoroughly researched, well-written business plan when seeking their support. Very little money has been raised for business ideas scribbled on the back of envelopes or on restaurant placemats despite considerable folklore to the contrary.

In the course of attracting external support for your venture a number of people may have occasion to read your plan. These include bankers, suppliers, prospective customers, and potential investors. Each of them will be viewing your business from a slightly different perspective. Bankers, for example, are primarily interested in the business' fixed assets and other available collateral. They want to know if you can pay back their loan at prevailing interest rates. Venture capitalists and other private investors, on the other hand, are more interested in their expected return on investment. They tend to like innovative products and services in growth industries that promise significant returns. These differing viewpoints should be taken into account in developing your plan.

How Long Should Your Business Plan Be?

Business plans can be broadly categorized into three types: the summary business plan, the full business plan, and the operational business plan.

The Summary Business Plan

Summary business plans commonly run about 10 pages or so; considerably shorter than the 40 or so pages traditional for business plans. Summary business plans have become increasingly popular and accepted for use by early-stage businesses in applying for a bank loan, or they may be all that is required for a small, lifestyle businesses such as a convenience store, home-based business, graphic design company, or consulting firm. A summary business plan may also be sufficient to whet the appetite of friends, relatives, and other private investors who might subsequently receive a copy of the full plan if sufficiently interested.

The Full Business Plan

A full business plan similar to the one you would develop by following the samples at the end of this Stage will likely run from 10 to 40 pages. This is the traditional plan. It covers all the key subjects in enough depth to permit a full exploration of the principal issues. The full business plan is most appropriate when you are trying to raise a substantial amount of external financing or if you are looking for a partner or other major private investors.

The Operational Business Plan

The operational business plan will usually exceed 40 pages in length but is used only infrequently, such as when a business is planning to grow very rapidly and must try to anticipate a wide variety of issues. Or it might be part of an annual process where it is necessary to get into great detail about distribution, production, advertising, and other areas where it is essential for everyone involved with the organization to understand clearly everything that is going on. Traditional business plans that grow to this length should be avoided as they reflect a lack of discipline and focus.

Who Should Write Your Business Plan

You should write your business plan. If someone else develops the business plan for you, it becomes *their* plan, not *yours*. If you are part of a management team, each individual should contribute his or her part to the overall project.

Do not under any circumstances hire someone else to write the plan for you. This doesn't mean that you shouldn't get help from others in compiling information, obtaining licences, permits, patents, and other legal considerations, or preparing your pro forma financial statements — only that the final plan should be written by you and your team.

The people who may be assessing your plan want to know that you see the big picture as it relates to your business and understand all the functional requirements of your company, not that you can hire a good consultant. It is very difficult to defend someone else's work. If you put it together yourself, you have a better understanding and feel for the business. Your business plan should be a personal expression written in your own unique style, though of course it should be professionally done.

How Long Does It Take?

Putting together a business plan does not happen overnight; the process can stretch over several months. Table 10.1 outlines the steps that should be taken to prepare a business plan, and the amount of time it may take to complete each step.

The flowchart in Figure 10.2 indicates how all these steps in developing a business plan interrelate. It shows how certain key steps cannot be undertaken until others have been completed. For example, you cannot effectively research the market (step 4) until you have selected a particular product or service idea (step 3). Similarly, until the market has been researched (step 4), a site chosen (step 6), and a revenue forecast prepared (step 5), you can't develop your detailed marketing plan (step 8).

The 16-week time span shown here is only for illustrative purposes — the actual time required to prepare your business plan will vary with the nature of your venture. A plan for a relatively simple, straightforward business might be completed within a few weeks, while a plan for a complex, high-growth new venture could take many months.

WHAT SHOULD YOUR PLAN CONTAIN?

Your business plan is the nuts and bolts of your proposed business venture put down on paper. You will have to decide exactly what information to include, how your plan can be best organized for maximum effectiveness, and what information should be given particular emphasis. All plans, however, require a formal, structured presentation so that they are easy to read and follow and tend to avoid confusion. A number of forms and sample outlines for a business plan are available but virtually all suggest that business plans contain the following components: (1) letter of

TABLE 10.1 SUGGESTED STEPS IN DEVELOPING YOUR BUSINESS PLAN

Step	Description	Completion Date
1	Decide to go into business for yourself.	
2	Analyze your strengths and weaknesses, paying special attention to your business experience, business education, and desires.	Third week
3	Choose the product or service that best fits your strengths and desires.	Fourth week
4	Research the market for your product or service.	Seventh week
5	Forecast your share of market if possible.	Eighth week
6	Choose a site for your business.	Eighth week
7	Develop your production plan.	Tenth week
8	Develop your marketing plan.	Tenth week
9	Develop your personnel plan.	Twelfth week
10	Decide whether to form a sole proprietorship, a partnership, or a corporation.	Twelfth week
11	Explain the kinds of records and reports you plan to have.	Twelfth week
12	Develop your insurance plan.	Twelfth week
13	Develop your financial plan.	Fifteenth week
14	Write a summary overview of your business plan, stressing its purpose and promise.	Sixteenth week

FIGURE 10.2 FLOWCHART OF THE STEPS IN DEVELOPING A BUSINESS PLAN

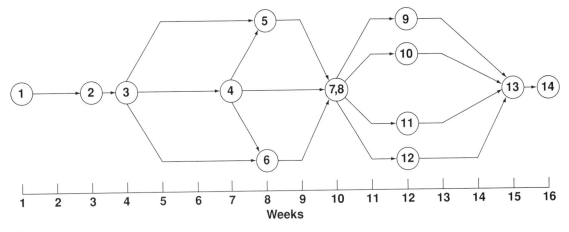

KEY

1. Decide to go into business.
2. Analyze yourself.
3. Pick product or service.
4. Research market.
5. Forecast sales revenues.
6. Pick site.
7. Develop production plan.
8. Develop marketing plan.
9. Develop personnel plan.
10. Decide whether to incorporate.
11. Explain need for records.
12. Develop insurance plan.
13. Develop financial plan.
14. Write summary overview.

Adapted from Nicholas C. Siropolis, *Small Business Management: A Guide to Entrepreneurship*, 2nd ed. (Boston: Houghton Mifflin Co., 1982), pp. 138–141.

transmittal, (2) title page, (3) table of contents, (4) executive summary and fact sheet, (5) body, and (6) appendixes.

1. Letter of Transmittal

The letter of transmittal officially introduces your business plan to the reader. It explains your reason for writing the plan, gives the title of the plan or the name of your business, and outlines the major features of your plan that may be of interest.

2. Title Page

The title page, or "cover page," of your plan provides identifying information about you and your proposed business. It should include the name, address, and telephone number of the business as well as similar information about yourself. The date the plan was finalized or submitted to the recipient should also be included on the title page.

3. Table of Contents

The table of contents is a list of the major headings and subheadings contained in your plan. It provides the reader with a quick overview of the contents of your plan and allows them to quickly access the particular sections that may be of primary interest to them.

4. Executive Summary and Fact Sheet

The executive summary may be the most important part of your business plan. It must capture the attention of the reader, stimulate interest, and get the reader to keep on reading the rest of your plan. In two or three pages this summary should concisely explain your business' current status; describe its products or services and their benefits to your customers; provide an overview of your venture's objectives, market prospects, and financial forecasts; and, if you are using the plan to raise external financing, indicate the amount of financing needed, how the money is to be used, and the benefits to the prospective lender or investor.

This summary should give the essence of your plan and highlight its really significant points. In many instances the summary will either sell the reader on continuing to read the rest of the document or convince them to forget the whole thing; the game may be won or lost on the basis of the executive summary.

The fact sheet should appear as a separate page at the back of the executive summary. It summarizes the basic information that relates to your venture:

1. Company name
2. Location and telephone
3. Type of business and industry
4. Form of business organization (proprietorship, partnership, or corporation)
5. Principal product or service line
6. Registered patents or trademarks
7. Number and name of founders/partners/shareholders
8. Length of time in business
9. Current and/or projected market share
10. Funds invested in the business to date and their source
11. Additional financing required

12. Proposed terms and payback period
13. Total value or net worth of the business
14. Name of business advisors (legal counsel, accountant, others)

5. Body of the Plan

The body of your business plan is by far the longest component, because it presents the detailed story of your business proposition. It should be broken down into major divisions using headings, and each major division divided into sections using subheadings. It is probably better to have too many rather than not enough headings and subheadings.

What follows is a typical overview of the kind of material that should be included in the body of your plan.

Your Company and the Industry

Describe the start-up and background of your business and provide the reader with some context within which to fit all the information you will be providing later in your plan.

Familiarize the reader with your company; the industry within which you will be competing, your understanding of it, and where it is headed; and what opportunities you see for your business.

YOUR COMPANY

Background Give the date your business was started, its present form of organization, its location, and pertinent historical information on the firm. Name the founders and other key people, how your key products or services were chosen and developed, and what success the business has achieved to date.

Current Situation Discuss such issues as how you have identified your market opportunity, assessed the competition, and developed some unique factor or distinctive competence that will make your business stand out from the rest.

Future Plans Discuss your goals and ambitions for the business and your strategy for achieving them.

THE INDUSTRY

Principal Characteristics Describe the current status and prospects for the industry in which your business will operate. How big is the industry? What are its total sales in dollars? In units? What are typical industry standards, gross margins, seasonal patterns, and similar factors?

Major Participants Identify the major industry participants and describe their role, market share, and other performance measures. What are their principal strengths and weaknesses and how do you feel you will be able to successfully compete in this situation?

Industry Trends Discuss how you feel the industry will evolve in the future. Is it growing or stable? What do you feel industry sales will be five and ten years from now? What general trends are evident and how is the industry likely to be affected by economic, social, technological, environmental, and regulatory trends?

Your Product/Service Offering

Description Describe the product or service you plan to sell in detail explaining any unique characteristics or particular advantages. How will features of your product or service give you some advantage over competitors?

Indicate the stage of development your product is at and whether prototypes, working models, or finished production units are available. Include photographs if possible.

Proprietary Position Describe any patents or trademarks you may hold or have applied for, or any licensing agreements or other legal contracts that may provide some protection for your product or service. Are there any regulatory or government-approved standards or requirements your product must meet? How and when do you plan to obtain this certification?

Potential Outline your market opportunity as you see it and explain how you plan to take advantage of it. What are the key success factors in this business and how do you plan to exploit them to your advantage?

Market Analysis

This section of your plan should convince the reader that you thoroughly understand the market for your product or service, that you can deal with the competition and achieve sufficient sales to develop a viable and growing business. You should describe the total market and how you feel it can be broken down into segments. You can then indicate the segment or niche you plan to concentrate on and what share of this business you will be able to obtain.

Your analysis of the market may be based on:

1. Market studies available from private research firms and government departments and agencies

2. Statistics Canada or U.S. Bureau of the Census data

3. Information from trade associations and trade publications

4. Surveys or informal discussions with dealers, distributors, sales representatives, customers, or competitors

This is often one of the most difficult parts of the business plan to prepare, but it is also one of the most important. Almost all other sections of your business plan depend on the sales estimates developed from your market analysis. The outline described in Stage Seven can help you in this process.

Target Market and Customers Identify who constitute your primary target markets — individual consumers, companies, health care or educational institutions, government departments, or other groups.

Examine beforehand if these target markets can be segmented or broken down into relatively homogeneous groups having common, identifiable characteristics such as geographic location, age, size, type of industry, or some other factor. Present these facts in the most logical or appropriate format.

Describe the profile of your principal target customers. Who and where are they? What are the principal bases for their purchase decisions? What are their major applications for your product? What principal benefit will they obtain from using your product rather than one of your competitors'?

Identify, if possible, some major buyers who may be prepared to make purchase commitments. If possible, get a purchase order.

Market Size and Trends Estimate the size of the current total market for your product or service in both units and dollars. How are sales distributed among the various segments you identified? Are there any strong weekly, monthly, or seasonal patterns? Ensure you include answers to these questions.

Describe how the market size for each of these segments has changed over the past three to four years in units and dollars. Outline how it is expected to change over the next three to four years.

Include the major factors that have affected past market growth, i.e., socioeconomic trends, industry trends, regulatory changes, government policy, population shifts, etc. What is likely to happen in these areas in the future?

Competition   Identify each of your principal competitors. Make a realistic assessment of each of these firms and their product or service offering. Compare these competing products or services on the basis of price, quality, performance, service support, warranties, and other important features.

Present your evaluation of the market share of each segment by each competitor, their relative profitability, and their sales, marketing, distribution, and production capabilities. How do you see these factors changing in the future?

Estimated Sales and Market Share   Estimate the share of each segment of the market and the sales in units and dollars that you feel you will acquire for each of the next three to five years. This should be developed by month for the next year and annually for each year thereafter. This information can best be presented in tabular form. Indicate on what assumptions you have based these projections.

Your Marketing Plan

Your marketing plan outlines how your sales projections will be achieved. It details the marketing strategy you plan to use to establish your product or service in the marketplace and obtain a profitable share of the overall market. Your marketing plan should describe *what* is to be done, *when* it is to be done, *how* it is to be done, and *who* will do it insofar as your sales strategy, advertising and promotion plans, pricing policy, and channels of distribution are concerned.

Pricing   Summarize the general financial characteristics of your business and the industry at large. What will be typical gross and net margins for each of the products or services you plan to sell? How do these compare with those of other firms in the industry? Provide a detailed breakdown of your estimated fixed, variable, and semivariable costs for each of your various products or services.

Discuss the prices you plan to charge for your product. How do they compare with your major competitors'? Is your gross margin sufficient to cover your transportation costs, selling costs, advertising and promotion costs, rent, depreciation, and similar expenses — and still provide some margin of profit?

Detail the markups your product will provide to the various members of your channel of distribution. How do these compare with those they receive on comparable products? Does your markup provide them with sufficient incentive to handle your product?

Indicate your normal terms of sale. Do these conform to industry norms? Do you plan to offer cash, quantity, or other discounts?

Indicate how long it will take you to break even, basing your opinion on your anticipated cost structure and planned price.

Sales and Distribution   Indicate the methods you will use to sell and distribute your product or service. Do you plan to use your own salaried or commissioned salespeople, rely on manufacturer's agents or other wholesalers and distributors, or utilize a more non-traditional means of distributing your product such as export trading companies, direct mail selling, mail order houses, party plan selling, or other means of selling direct to the final consumer?

If you plan to use your own sales force, describe how large it will be and how it will be structured. Indicate how salespeople will be distributed, who they will call on, how many calls you estimate it will take to get an order, the size of a typical order, how much you estimate a typical salesperson will sell each year, how he or she will be paid, how much he or she is likely to make in a year, and how this compares with the average for the industry.

If you plan to use distributors or wholesalers, indicate how they have been or will be selected, who they are if possible, what areas or territory they will cover, how they will be compensated, credit and collection policies, and any special policies such as exclusive rights, discounts, and cooperative advertising programs.

Indicate any plans for export sales or international marketing arrangements.

Advertising and Promotion Describe the program you plan to use to make consumers aware of your product or service. What consumers are you trying to reach? Do you plan to use the services of an advertising agency? What media do you plan to use — radio, television, newspapers, magazines, billboards, direct mail, coupons, brochures, trade shows, etc. How much do you plan to spend on each medium? When? Which specific vehicles?

Outline any plans to obtain free publicity for your product or company.

Service and Warranty Program Indicate your service arrangements, warranty terms, and method of handling service problems. Describe how you will handle customer complaints and other problems. Will service be handled by the company, dealers and distributors, or independent service centres? How do these arrangements compare with those of your competitors?

Your Development Plan

If your product or service involves some further technical development, the planned extent of this work should be discussed in your business plan. Prospective investors, bankers, and others will want to know the nature and extent of any additional development required, how much it will cost, and how long it will take before your business has a finished, marketable product.

Development Status Describe the current status of your product and outline what still remains to be done in order to make it marketable. Do you presently have only a concept, detailed drawings, a laboratory prototype, a production prototype, or a finished product? Is further engineering work required? Has the necessary tooling to produce the product been adequately developed? Are the services of an industrial designer or other specialist required to refine the product into marketable form?

Costs Indicate how much money has been spent on product development to date and where it has been spent. Present a development budget indicating the additional funds required, how they will be spent, and the timing involved in completing the project.

Proprietary Issues Indicate any patents or trademarks that you own, have, or for which you plan to apply. Are there any regulatory requirements to produce or market the product? Has the product undergone standardized testing through Underwriter's Laboratory, the Canadian Standards Association (CSA), or some other agency? If not, what are your plans? Have you tested the product at all in the marketplace? What was the result?

Your Production/Operations Plan

Your production/operations plan outlines the operating side of your business. It should describe your plant location, the kind of facilities needed, space requirements, capital equipment needed, and your labour requirements.

If your plan is for a manufacturing business, you should also discuss such areas as your purchasing policy, quality control program, inventory control system, production cost breakdown, and whether you plan to manufacture all subcomponents of the product yourself or have some of them produced for you by someone else.

Location Describe the planned location of your business and discuss any advantages or disadvantages of this location in terms of the cost and availability of labour, proximity to customers, access to transportation, energy supplies or other natural resources, and zoning and other legal requirements.

Discuss the characteristics of your location in relation to market size, traffic flows, local and regional growth rates, income levels, and similar market-related factors.

Facilities and Equipment Describe the property and facilities currently used or that will be required to operate your business. This should include factory and office space, selling space, storage space, property size and location, etc. Will these facilities be leased or purchased? What is the cost and timing of their acquisition?

Detail the machinery and equipment that is required for your manufacturing process. Is this highly specialized or general-purpose equipment? Is it leased or purchased? New or used? What is the cost? What will it cost for equipment setup and facility layout? What is its expected life? Will it have any residual or scrap value?

If possible, provide a drawing of the physical layout of the plant and other facilities.

Manufacturing Plans and Costs   Develop a manufacturing cost outline that shows standard production costs at various levels of operation. Break total costs down into raw material, component parts, labour, and overhead. Indicate your raw material, work-in-process, and finished goods inventory requirements at various sales levels. How will seasonal variations in demand be handled?

Indicate your key suppliers or subcontractors for various raw materials and components. What are the lead times for these materials? Are backup suppliers or other alternatives available?

Outline the quality control procedures you will use to minimize service problems. Do you need any other production control measures?

On the basis of this configuration of facilities and equipment, indicate your production capacity. Where can this be expanded? Do you have any plans to modify existing plant space? What is the timing and cost?

Labour   Describe the number of employees you have or need and their qualifications. Will they be full-time or part-time? Have you developed a job description for each position? What in-house training will be required? How much will each employee be paid? What kinds of pension plan, health insurance plan, profit-sharing plan, and other fringe benefits will be required? Have you registered with the necessary government departments?

Indicate whether your employees will be union or non-union. If employees will be members of a union, describe the principal terms of their contract and when it expires.

Environmental and Other Issues   Indicate any approvals that it may be necessary for you to obtain related to zoning requirements, permits, licences, health and safety requirements, environmental approvals, etc. Are there any laws or regulatory requirements unique to your business? Are there any other legal or contractual matters that should be considered?

Your Management Team

Your management team and your directors are the key to success. You should identify: who your key people are; their qualifications; what they are being paid; who has overall authority; who is responsible for the various functional areas of the business such as sales, marketing, production, research and development, and financial management; and so forth.

In most small businesses there are no more than two or three really key players — including yourself. Concentrate on these individuals, indicating their education, qualifications, and past business achievements. Indicate how they will contribute to the success of the present venture. Don't hire friends, relatives, or other people for key positions who do not have the proper qualifications.

Many external investors are more concerned about the management of the business than the business itself. They invest in the people rather than the project. They will conduct a thorough and exhaustive investigation of each of your key players to determine whether they are the kind of people in which they wish to invest. This portion of your plan should instill confidence in the management of your business in the mind of the reader.

Description of Management Team   Outline the exact duties and responsibilities of each key member of your management team. Prepare a brief résumé of each individual indicating age, marital status, education, professional qualifications, employment experience, and other personal achievements. (You will include a complete, more detailed résumé for each of these individuals in an appendix to your plan.)

Directors   Indicate the size and composition of your board of directors. Identify any individuals you are planning to invite to sit on your board. Include a brief statement on each member's background indicating what he or she will bring to the company.

Management and Directors' Compensation   List the names of all members of your management team and board of directors and the compensation they will receive in fees or salary. Initially, at least, you and your management team should be prepared to accept modest salaries, perhaps well below what you received in your previous job, if you hope to attract external investors to your business.

Shareholders   Indicate the name of each of the individual shareholders (or partners) in your business, the number of shares each owns, the percentage of ownership, and the price paid.

Describe any investors in your business other than your management team and members of your board. How many shares do they have? When were they acquired? What price did they pay?

Summarize any incentive stock option or bonus plans that you have in effect or plan to institute. Also indicate any employment contracts or agreements you may have made with members of your management team.

Professional Advisors   Indicate the name and complete address of each of your professional advisors, for example your lawyer, accountant, banker, and management or technical consultants. Disclose any fees or retainers that may have been paid to any of these people.

Implementation Schedule and Risks Associated with the Venture

It is necessary to present an overall schedule indicating the interrelationship among the various events necessary to launch your business and the timing required to bring it about. This is similar to the type of framework in Figure 10.1. A well-prepared schedule demonstrates to external investors that you have given proper thought to where you are going and have the ability to plan. This schedule can be a very effective sales tool.

Your plan should also discuss the major problems and risks you feel you will have to deal with in developing your business.

Milestones   Summarize the significant goals that you and your business have already reached and still hope to accomplish in the future. What still needs to be done in order for the business to succeed? Who is going to do these things? When will they be completed?

Schedule   Develop a schedule of significant events and their priority for completion. What kind of strategic planning has been done in order to see that things occur as necessary? Have you developed a fallback or contingency position in case things don't come off as you have planned?

Risks and Problems   You might start by summarizing the major problems you have already had to deal with and how they were resolved. Were any particularly innovative or creative approaches used in addressing these issues?

Identify the risks your business may be faced with in the future. What are you attempting to do to avoid these? How will you deal with them if they arise? How can their impact on your business be minimized?

Summarize the downside risk. What would happen in the "worst case" scenario? What, if anything, could be salvaged from the business for your investors?

Your Financial Plan

Your financial plan is basic in order to enable a prospective investor or banker to evaluate the investment opportunity you are presenting. The plan should illustrate the current financial status of your business and represent your best estimate of its future operations. The results presented should be both realistic and attainable.

Your financial plan should also describe the type of financing you are seeking, the amount of money you are looking for, how you plan to use these funds in the business, the terms of repayment and desired interest rate, or the dividends, voting rights, and redemption considerations related to the offering of any common or preferred stock.

Funding Requested   Indicate the amount and type (debt or equity) of funding you are looking for. For what do you intend to use the money? How will it be applied in your business — to acquire property, fixtures, equipment, or inventory, or to provide working capital?

Give an overview of the current financial structure of your business. Indicate the level of investment already made in the business and where the funds came from. What effect will the additional capital have on your business in terms of ownership structure, future growth, and profitability?

Outline your proposed terms of investment. What is the payback period and potential return on investment for the lender or investor? What collateral, tax benefit, or other security is being offered?

Current Financial Statements   If your venture is already in operation, you should provide copies of financial statements (profit and loss statement and a balance sheet) for the current year and the previous two years.

Financial Projections   In developing your financial plan, a number of basic projections must be prepared. These should be based on realistic expectations and reflect the effect of the proposed financing. The projections should be developed on a monthly basis for the first year of operation and a quarterly or annual basis for another two to four years. These projections should include the following statements:

1. **Profit and loss forecasts** These pro forma income statements indicate your profit expectations for the next few years of operation of your business. They should be based on realistic estimates of sales and operating costs and represent your best estimate of actual operating results.

2. **Pro forma balance sheets** Your pro forma balance sheet indicates the assets you feel will be required to support your projected level of operations and how you plan to finance these assets.

3. **Projected cash flow statements** Your cash flow forecasts are probably your most important statements, because they indicate the amount and timing of your expected cash inflows and outflows. Typically the operating profits during the start-up of a new venture are not sufficient to finance the business' operating needs. This often means that the inflow of cash will not meet your business' cash requirements, at least on a short-term basis. These conditions must be anticipated in advance so that you can predict cash needs and avoid insolvency.

4. **Breakeven analysis** A breakeven analysis indicates the level of sales and production you will require to cover all your fixed and variable costs. It is useful for you and prospective lenders and investors to know what your breakeven point is and how easy or difficult it will likely be to attain.

An example of each of these statements and a discussion on how to determine the breakeven point for your venture is presented in Stage Eight of this book.

6. Appendixes

The appendixes are intended to explain, support, and supplement the material in the body of your business plan. In most cases this material is attached to the back of your plan. Examples of the kind of material that might be included in an appendix are:

1. Product specifications and photographs
2. Detailed résumés of the management team
3. Lists of prospective customers
4. Names of possible suppliers
5. Job descriptions for the management team
6. Consulting reports and market surveys
7. Copies of legal documents such as leases, franchise and licensing agreements, contracts, licences, patent or trademark registrations, and articles of incorporation
8. Letters of reference
9. Relevant magazine, trade journal, and newspaper articles

CONCLUSION

It is important that your plan make a good first impression. It should demonstrate that you have done a significant amount of thinking and work on your venture. You should ensure your material is presented to prospective investors, lenders, and others in an attractive, readable, and understandable fashion.

To assist you in completing your business plan, sample business plan forms are provided in Figures 10.3 and 10.4. The forms shown are intended for use as a rough draft only, from which you will prepare a formal, *typewritten* business plan. Figure 10.5 provides a checklist that should be used to check your plan for completeness, clarity, and persuasiveness.

The length of your business plan should not exceed 40 double-spaced, typewritten pages, not including appendixes. Each section should be broken down into appropriate and clearly identifiable headings and subheadings. Make sure your plan contains no errors in spelling, punctuation, or grammar.

Prepare a number of copies of your plan and number each one individually. Make sure each copy is appropriately bound with a good-quality cover on which the name of your business has been printed or embossed.

FIGURE 10.3 SAMPLE BUSINESS PLAN FOR A RETAIL OR SERVICE FIRM

A. LETTER OF TRANSMITTAL

B. TITLE PAGE

C. TABLE OF CONTENTS

D. EXECUTIVE SUMMARY

1. Fact Sheet

Company name _____

Location and telephone _____

_____

_____

_____

Type of business and industry _____

_____

_____

Form of business organization _____

_____

Principal product or service line _____

_____

_____

Registered patents or trademarks (if any) _____

_____

_____

Names of founders/partners/shareholders _____

_____

_____

Length of time in business (if appropriate) _____

_____

Current and/or projected market share _____

_____

Funds invested in the business to date and their source _____

_____

_____

_____

_____

Additional financing required _____

_____

_____

Proposed terms and payback period _____

_____

_____

_____

Total value or net worth of the business _____

_____

_____

_____

_____

NAMES OF BUSINESS ADVISORS

Legal counsel _____

_____

Accountant _____

_____

Banker _____

_____

Other _____

_____

E. BODY

1. Your Company and the Industry

THE COMPANY

Date business started _____

Location _____

_____

Form of business organization _____

_____

Founders and other key individuals _____

_____

_____

Principal products and services _____

_____

_____

Success the Business Has Achieved to Date

	Estimated Total Annual Market (year)	Company Sales (year)	Market Share (%)
Product/service 1	$_____	$_____	_____
	_____ units	_____ units	_____
Product/service 2	$_____	$_____	_____
(etc.)	_____ units	_____ units	_____

continued

Sample Business Plan (Retail or Service) — continued

Future Goals and Plans

_____

_____

_____

_____

_____

_____

Principal strategy for achieving these goals _____

_____

_____

_____

_____

_____

_____

THE INDUSTRY

Prospects for the Industry

Total Estimated Industry Sales ($)

Product/ Service	Three Years Ago	Two Years Ago	Last Year	This Year	Next Year	In Two Years	In Three Years
1. _____	$_____	$_____	$_____	$_____	$_____	$_____	$_____
2. _____	$_____	$_____	$_____	$_____	$_____	$_____	$_____
3. _____	$_____	$_____	$_____	$_____	$_____	$_____	$_____

(etc.)

General industry standards and performance requirements _____

_____

_____

General trends within the industry and factors likely to affect these trends _____

_____

_____

Major Industry Participants

Name and Location of Competitor	Estimated Sales	Estimated Market Share (%)	Principal Strengths and Weaknesses
_____	$_____	_____	_____
_____			_____
_____	$_____	_____	_____
_____			_____
_____	$_____	_____	_____
_____			_____

Sample Business Plan (Retail or Service) — continued

2. Product/Service Offering

DESCRIPTION OF PRINCIPAL PRODUCTS/SERVICES

Product/Service	Description	Unique Features	Stage Of Development

Patents or trademarks held or applied for _____
_____
_____

Franchise or licensing agreements and regulatory, certification, or other requirements
_____
_____

Discuss key success factors in your business and how you plan to exploit them _____
_____
_____
_____
_____
_____

Outline your time frame and schedule for the implementation of your program _____
_____
_____

3. Market Analysis (repeat for each product/service offered)

TARGET MARKET AND CUSTOMERS

Describe your target market and prospective customers in terms of geography and/or customer type or profile _____
_____
_____

Describe the principal factors these consumers consider in the purchase of products like yours
_____
_____
_____

Outline the principal benefit they will receive from patronizing your firm rather than one of your competitors_____
_____
_____

continued

Sample Business Plan (Retail or Service) — continued

Describe how your target market might be broken down into segments, and outline how these segments have changed over time and how they might be expected to change in the future

_____
_____
_____

Describe any weekly, monthly, seasonal, or other sales patterns _____

_____
_____
_____
_____

COMPARISON WITH COMPETITORS

	Name of Competitor		
Factor	1. _____	2. _____	3. _____
Price	_____	_____	_____
Convenience of location	_____	_____	_____
Availability of parking	_____	_____	_____
Image	_____	_____	_____
Breadth of product/service line	_____	_____	_____
Depth of product/service line	_____	_____	_____
Credit policy	_____	_____	_____
Display and fixtures	_____	_____	_____
Sales training and effectiveness	_____	_____	_____
Sales support	_____	_____	_____
Availability of delivery	_____	_____	_____
Other:	_____	_____	_____
_____	_____	_____	_____
_____	_____	_____	_____

Indicate what, if anything, is really unique about your product/service offering or firm situation

_____
_____
_____
_____
_____
_____
_____
_____

Sample Business Plan (Retail or Service) — continued

SUMMARY OF ESTIMATED SALES BY PRODUCT/SERVICE LINE AND MARKET SEGMENT

Market Segment Description I _____

Product/Service Line	1	2	3	4	5	6	7	8	9	10	11	12	Total
_____													
_____													
_____													
_____													___
											Total		

Estimated Sales by Month ($ or units)

Market Segment Description II _____

Product/Service Line	1	2	3	4	5	6	7	8	9	10	11	12	Total
_____													
_____													
_____													
_____													___
											Total		

Estimated Sales by Month ($ or units)

Market Segment Description III _____

Product/Service Line	1	2	3	4	5	6	7	8	9	10	11	12	Total
_____													
_____													
_____													
_____													___
											Total		

Estimated Sales by Month ($ or units)

(etc.)

4. Marketing Plan

PRICING

Principal Direct-Cost Elements of Your Operation

Material and supplies costs _____

_____

Labour costs _____

_____

Operating expenses and overhead _____

_____

continued

Sample Business Plan (Retail or Service) — continued

Discuss the prices you plan to charge, and typical gross and net margins for each of your product/ service lines and how they compare with those of other firms _____

_____

_____

Describe your credit arrangements, returns policy, and other terms of sale _____

_____

_____

_____

PERSONAL SELLING PROGRAM

Outline your personal selling requirements — the number and type of people in your sales force and how they will be paid _____

_____

_____

ADVERTISING AND PROMOTION PROGRAMS

Media	Audience Size	Schedule	Frequency of use	x	Cost of a Single Occasion	=	Estimated Cost
_____	_____	_____	_____		$_____		$_____
_____	_____	_____	_____		$_____		$_____
_____	_____	_____	_____		$_____		$_____
_____	_____	_____	_____		$_____		$_____
_____	_____	_____	_____		$_____		$_____
_____	_____	_____	_____		$_____		$_____

Total Estimated Cost $_____

Describe any plan to obtain free publicity or other sales promotion activity _____

_____

_____

Other services you plan to provide and their anticipated costs:

Service	Estimated Cost
_____	$_____
_____	_____
_____	_____
_____	_____

5. Operations Plan

Describe your location and its pros and cons:

Location _____

_____

Advantages _____

_____

Sample Business Plan (Retail or Service) — continued

Disadvantages _____

_____

Traffic flows and patterns _____

_____

Zoning requirements _____

_____

Access _____

_____

Parking _____

_____

Visibility _____

_____

Cost _____

_____

Condition _____

_____

Other _____

_____

_____

_____

_____

Indicate the major fixtures and equipment you will require:

Type of Fixture or Equipment	Buy or Lease	Number Required	x	Unit Cost	=	Total Cost
_____	_____	_____		$_____		$_____
_____	_____	_____		_____		_____
_____	_____	_____		_____		_____
_____	_____	_____		_____		_____
_____	_____	_____		_____		_____
_____	_____	_____		_____		_____
_____	_____	_____		_____		_____

Total Cost $_____

Develop a drawing or floor plan of the physical layout of your store or other facilities.

Where do you plan to buy your floor stock for resale?

Name of Item	Name of Supplier	Price	Order Policy	Discounts Offered	Delivery Time	Freight Costs	Back Order Policy
_____	_____	$_____	_____	_____	_____	$_____	_____
_____	_____	_____	_____	_____	_____	_____	_____
_____	_____	_____	_____	_____	_____	_____	_____
_____	_____	_____	_____	_____	_____	_____	_____
_____	_____	_____	_____	_____	_____	_____	_____
_____	_____	_____	_____	_____	_____	_____	_____

continued

Sample Business Plan (Retail or Service) — continued

Where do you plan to buy your operating supplies and materials?

Name of Item	Name of Supplier	Price	Order Policy	Discounts Offered	Delivery Time	Freight Costs	Back Order Policy
_____	_____	$_____	_____	_____	_____	$_____	_____
_____	_____	_____	_____	_____	_____	_____	_____
_____	_____	_____	_____	_____	_____	_____	_____
_____	_____	_____	_____	_____	_____	_____	_____
_____	_____	_____	_____	_____	_____	_____	_____
_____	_____	_____	_____	_____	_____	_____	_____

Outline your inventory control procedures

OPENING INVENTORY REQUIREMENTS

Item	Number Required	x	Cost per Unit	=	Total Cost
_____	_____		$_____		$_____
_____	_____		_____		_____
_____	_____		_____		_____
_____	_____		_____		_____
_____	_____		_____		_____
_____	_____		_____		_____

Total Initial Inventory $_____

OUTLINE OF EMPLOYEE REQUIREMENTS

Job	Qualification Required	Full-or Part-time	Job Description (yes or no)	Compensation	Benefits
_____	_____	_____	_____	$_____	_____
_____	_____	_____	_____	_____	_____
_____	_____	_____	_____	_____	_____
_____	_____	_____	_____	_____	_____

PERMITS OR LICENCES REQUIRED AND NECESSARY INSPECTIONS

Permit, Licences, or Necessary Inspection	Date Received or Completed
_____	_____
_____	_____
_____	_____
_____	_____

Sample Business Plan (Retail or Service) — continued

6. Management Team

Develop an organization chart indicating who is responsible for each of the major areas of activity in your business; list each function and indicate the name of the individual who will perform that function and to whom he or she will be responsible:

Function	Performed by:	Responsible to:
Sales	_____	_____
Marketing	_____	_____
Operations management	_____	_____
Bookkeeping and accounting	_____	_____
Personnel management	_____	_____
_____	_____	_____

Present a brief résumé of each of these individuals _____

_____

_____

_____

Outline the size and composition of your board of directors _____

_____

_____

_____

Present a brief résumé of each individual on your board who is not part of your management team

_____

_____

_____

Indicate the compensation received by each member of your management team and board of directors:

Individual	Salary	Fees or Bonuses	Total Compensation
_____	$_____	$_____	$_____
_____	_____	_____	_____
_____	_____	_____	_____
_____	_____	_____	_____
_____	_____	_____	_____
_____	_____	_____	_____

Describe the ownership structure of your business:

Individual	Types of Shares Held	Percentage of Total Issued	Number of Shares Held	x	Price Paid per Share	=	Total
_____	_____	_____	_____		$_____		$_____
_____	_____	_____	_____		_____		_____
_____	_____	_____	_____		_____		_____
_____	_____	_____	_____		_____		_____
_____	_____	_____	_____		_____		_____

Total Capitalization $_____

continued

Sample Business Plan (Retail or Service) — continued

Indicate any options to acquire additional stock that may be held or could be earned by your management team or others _____

_____

_____

Provide complete information regarding your professional advisors:

Advisor	Name	Address	Telephone	Fees or Retainers Paid
Lawyer	_____	_____	_____	$_____
		_____		
Accountant	_____	_____	_____	$_____
		_____		
Banker	_____	_____	_____	$_____
		_____		
Other	_____	_____	_____	$_____
		_____		

7. Implementation Schedule

Lay out a schedule of milestones or significant events for the implementation of your business and a timetable for completion; indicate who will be responsible for the completion of each task:

Milestone	Tasks Required to Accomplish	Who is Responsible	Scheduled Completion
_____	_____	_____	_____
	_____	_____	_____
	_____	_____	_____
	_____	_____	_____
_____	_____	_____	_____
	_____	_____	_____
	_____	_____	_____
	_____	_____	_____
_____	_____	_____	_____
	_____	_____	_____
	_____	_____	_____
	_____	_____	_____

Describe the risks your business may be faced with in implementing your plan, and the risk for any prospective investor _____

_____

_____

_____

Sample Business Plan (Retail or Service) — continued

8. Financial Plan

START-UP COSTS

If yours is a new venture, indicate your estimate of the start-up financial requirements of your business:

Estimated One-Time Financial Requirements

Item	Total Cost	Cash Required	Balance	How Financed
Land	$_____	$_____	$_____	_____
Building	_____	_____	_____	_____
Improvements:				
Mechanical	_____	_____	_____	_____
Electrical	_____	_____	_____	_____
Construction	_____	_____	_____	_____
Machinery and equipment	_____	_____	_____	_____
Installation of equipment	_____	_____	_____	_____
Shop tools and supplies	_____	_____	_____	_____
Office equipment and supplies	_____	_____	_____	_____
Vehicles	_____	_____	_____	_____
Starting inventory	_____	_____	_____	_____
Utility hookup and installation fees	_____	_____	_____	_____
Licences and permits	_____	_____	_____	_____
Pre-opening advertising and promotion	_____	_____	_____	_____
Accounts payable	_____	_____	_____	_____
Cash for Unexpected Expenses		$_____		
Other cash requirements		$_____		
Total Estimated One-Time Cash Requirements		$_____		

continued

Sample Business Plan (Retail or Service) — continued

Estimated Start-Up Operating Expenses

Item	Estimate of Monthly Expense	x	Number of Months* Before Breakeven	=	Total Cash Required
Owners' salaries	$_____		_____		$_____
Employees' salaries, wages, and benefits	_____		_____		_____
Rent	_____		_____		_____
Promotion expenses	_____		_____		_____
Supplies and postage	_____		_____		_____
Vehicle expense	_____		_____		_____
Telephone	_____		_____		_____
Other utilities	_____		_____		_____
Insurance	_____		_____		_____
Travel	_____		_____		_____
Legal and other professional fees	_____		_____		_____
Interest	_____		_____		_____
Maintenance	_____		_____		_____
Other expenses	_____		_____		_____

Total Cash Required to Cover Operating Expenses $_____

Plus: Total One-Time Cash Requirements (from previous table) $_____

Total Cash or Operating Line of Credit Required for Start-Up $_____

* Two to three months *minimum* are typical here.

PRESENT FINANCIAL STRUCTURE

Provide an overview of the current financial structure of your business and the proportion of your total start-up requirements obtained to date:

Source of Funds	Amount	Debt or Equity	Repayment Schedule
Self	$_____	_____	_____
Friends, neighbours, relatives	_____	_____	_____
Other private investors	_____	_____	_____
Banks, savings and loans, credit unions, and other financial institutions	_____	_____	_____
Mortgage and insurance companies	_____	_____	_____
Credit from suppliers	_____	_____	_____
Government grants and loans	_____	_____	_____
Other sources:	_____	_____	_____
_____	_____	_____	_____
_____	_____	_____	_____
_____	_____	_____	_____
_____	_____	_____	_____

Sample Business Plan (Retail or Service) — continued

_____ _____ _____ _____

_____ _____ _____ _____

Additional Funds Required

Indicate the additional funds required and the shares, return on investment, collateral, or other security you are prepared to provide to the prospective lender or investor

_____

_____

_____

_____

_____

_____

_____

_____

_____

_____

_____

_____

_____

continued

Sample Business Plan (Retail or Service) — continued

Current Financial Statements

If your business is already in operation, provide an income statement and a balance sheet for the current year to date and the previous two years; the following forms will serve as guidelines indicating the basic information to provide for each year:

**INCOME STATEMENT
for the period ending [date]**

Gross sales	$_____		
Less: Cash discounts	_____		
Net Sales		$_____	**(A)**
Less: Cost of goods sold:			
Beginning inventory	$_____		
Plus: Net purchases	_____		
Total goods available for sale	_____		
Less: Ending inventory	_____		
Cost of Goods Sold		_____	**(B)**
Gross Margin (or Profit) (C = A – B)		$_____	**(C)**
Less: Operating expenses:			
Owners' salaries	$_____		
Employees' wages and salaries	_____		
Employee benefits	_____		
Rent	_____		
Utilities (heat, light, water, power)	_____		
Telephone	_____		
Supplies and postage	_____		
Repairs and maintenance	_____		
Advertising and promotion	_____		
Vehicle expense	_____		
Delivery expense	_____		
Taxes and licences	_____		
Depreciation or Capital Cost Allowance	_____		
Bad debt allowance	_____		
Interest	_____		
Travel	_____		
Insurance	_____		
Legal and accounting fees	_____		
Other expenses	_____		
Total Operating Expenses		_____	**(D)**
Net Operating Profit (Loss) (E = C – D)		_____	**(E)**
Income Tax (estimated)		_____	**(F)**
Net Profit (Loss) After Income Tax (G = E – F)		_____	**(G)**

Sample Business Plan (Retail or Service) — continued

**BALANCE SHEET FOR
[NAME OF COMPANY]
as of [date]**

ASSETS

    Current Assets

Cash	\$_____	
Accounts receivable	_____	
Inventory	_____	
Other current assets	_____	
Total current assets		_____ **(A)**

    Fixed Assets

Land and buildings	\$_____	
Furniture and fixtures	_____	
Equipment	_____	
Trucks and automobiles	_____	
Other fixed assets	_____	
Total fixed assets		_____ **(B)**

    Total Assets (C = A + B)   \$_____ **(C)**

LIABILITIES

    Current Liabilities (debt due within 12 months)

Accounts payable	\$_____	
Bank loans/other loans	_____	
Taxes owed	_____	
Total current liabilities		_____ **(D)**

    Long-Term Liabilities

Notes payable (due after 1 year)	_____	
Total long-term liabilities		_____ **(E)**

    Total Liabilities (F = D + E)   \$_____ **(F)**

NET WORTH (CAPITAL)

    Total Net Worth (G = C - F)   _____ **(G)**

    Total Liabilities and Net Worth (H = F + G)   \$_____ **(H)**

FINANCIAL PROJECTIONS

Develop profit and loss forecast, projected cash flow statements, and pro forma balance sheets for your business. Each of these statements should be presented for the following time frames:

- **Pro forma profit and loss statements** Monthly for the next year of operation and quarterly or annually for another two to four years
- **Cash flow forecasts** Monthly for the next year of operation and annually for another two years
- **Pro forma balance sheets** Annually for each of the next three to five years

The following forms will serve as guidelines to be followed in developing and presenting this information.

continued

Sample Business Plan (Retail or Service) — continued

PRO FORMA INCOME STATEMENT
For the period ending [date]

		Month												
		1	2	3	4	5	6	7	8	9	10	11	12	Total
Gross sales															
Less Cash discounts															
Net Sales (A)															
Cost of goods sold:															
Beginning inventory															
Plus: Net purchases															
Total goods available for sale															
Less: Ending inventory															
Cost of Goods Sold (B)															
Gross Margin (C = A – B) (C)															
Less: Variable expenses															
Owner's salary															
Employees' wages and salaries															
Supplies and postage															
Advertising and promotion															
Delivery expense															
Bad debt expense															
Travel															
Legal and accounting fees															
Vehicle Expenses															
Miscellaneous expenses															
Total Variable Expenses (D)															
Less: Fixed expenses															
Rent															
Utilities (heat, light, water, power)															
Telephone															
Taxes and licences															
Depreciation or Capital Cost Allowance															
Interest															
Insurance															
Other Fixed Expenses															
Total Fixed Expenses (E)															
Total Operating Expenses (F = D + E) (F)															
Net Operating Profit (Loss) (G = C – F) (G)															
Income Taxes (estimated) (H)															
Net Profit (Loss) After Income Tax (I = G – H) (I)															

ESTIMATED CASH FLOW FORECAST

	Month 1	Month 2	Month 3	Month 4	Month 5	Month 6	Month 7	Month 8	Month 9	Month 10	Month 11	Month 12	Year 1 TOTAL	Year 2 TOTAL	Year 3 TOTAL
Cash Flow From Operations (during month)															
1. Cash Sales															
2. Payments for Credit Sales															
3. Investment Income															
4. Other Cash Income															
A. TOTAL CASH FLOW ON HAND	$	$	$	$	$	$	$	$	$	$	$	$	$	$	$
Less Expenses Paid (during month)															
5. Inventory or New Material															
6. Owners' Salaries															
7. Employees' Wages and Salaries															
8. Supplies and Postage															
9. Advertising and Promotion															
10. Delivery Expense															
11. Travel															
12. Legal and Accounting Fees															
13. Vehicle Expense															
14. Maintenance Expense															
15. Rent															
16. Utilities															
17. Telephone															
18. Taxes and Licences															
19. Interest Payments															
20. Insurance															
21. Other Cash Expenses															
B. TOTAL EXPENDITURES	$	$	$	$	$	$	$	$	$	$	$	$	$	$	$
Capital															
Purchase of Fixed Assets															
Sale of Fixed Assets															
C. CHANGE IN CASH FROM PURCHASE OR SALE OF ASSETS	$	$	$	$	$	$	$	$	$	$	$	$	$	$	$
Financing															
Payment of Principal of Loan															
Inflow of Cash From Bank Loan															
Issuance of Equity Positions															
Repurchase of Outstanding Equity															
D. CHANGE IN CASH FROM FINANCING	$	$	$	$	$	$	$	$	$	$	$	$	$	$	$
E. INCREASE (DECREASE) IN CASH	$	$	$	$	$	$	$	$	$	$	$	$	$	$	$
F. CASH AT BEGINNING OF PERIOD	$	$	$	$	$	$	$	$	$	$	$	$	$*	$**	$**
G. CASH AT END OF PERIOD	$	$	$	$	$	$	$	$	$	$	$	$	$	$	$
MEET MINIMUM CASH BALANCE	Acceptable	Acceptable	Acceptable	Acceptable	Acceptable	Acceptable	Acceptable	Acceptable	Acceptable	Acceptable	Acceptable	Acceptable	Acceptable	Acceptable	Acceptable

* This entry should be the same amount as for month 1 at the beginning of the year. All other rows will be the total for the entire year.

** These entries should be the same as the ending cash balance from the previous period.

Sample Business Plan (Retail or Service) — continued

PRO FORMA BALANCE SHEET
[NAME OF COMPANY]
as of [date]

ASSETS

   Current Assets

      Cash $_____

      Accounts receivable   _____

      Inventory   _____

      Other current assets   _____

      Total current assets   _____ **(A)**

   Fixed Assets

      Land and Buildings $_____

      Furniture and fixtures   _____

      Equipment   _____

      Trucks and automobiles   _____

      Other fixed assets   _____

      Total fixed assets   _____ **(B)**

   Total Assets (C = A + B) $_____ **(C)**

LIABILITIES

   Current Liabilities (debt due within 12 months)

      Accounts payable $_____

      Bank loans/other loans   _____

      Taxes owed   _____

      Total current liabilities   _____ **(D)**

   Long-Term Liabilities

      Mortgages payable $_____

      Notes payable (due after 1 year)   _____

      Loans from partners or shareholders   _____

      Total long-term liabilities   _____ **(E)**

   Total Liabilities (F = D + E) $_____ **(F)**

NET WORTH (CAPITAL)

   Total Net Worth (G = C – F)   _____ **(G)**

   Total Liabilities and Net Worth (H = F + G) $_____ **(H)**

Indicate the minimum level of sales you will require to cover all your fixed and variable costs and to break even:

$$\text{Breakeven Point (in Sales Dollars)} = \frac{\text{Total Estimated Operating Expenses}}{1 - \dfrac{\text{Gross Margin Percentage}}{100}}$$

(F in Pro Forma Profit and Loss Statement)

F. APPENDIXES

FIGURE 10.4   SAMPLE BUSINESS PLAN FOR A MANUFACTURING COMPANY

A. LETTER OF TRANSMITTAL

B. TITLE PAGE

C. TABLE OF CONTENTS

D. EXECUTIVE SUMMARY

1. Fact Sheet

Company name _____

Location and telephone _____

_____

_____

Type of business and industry _____

_____

_____

Form of business organization _____

_____

_____

Principal product or service line _____

_____

_____

Registered patents or trademarks (if any) _____

_____

_____

Names of founders/partners/shareholders _____

_____

_____

_____

Length of time in business (if appropriate) _____

_____

Current and/or projected market share _____

_____

Funds invested in the business to date and their source _____

_____

_____

_____

Additional financing required _____

_____

_____

_____

continued

Sample Business Plan (Manufacturing Company) — continued

Proposed terms and payback period _____

_____

_____

Total value or net worth of the business _____

_____

_____

NAMES OF BUSINESS ADVISORS

Legal counsel _____

_____

Accountant _____

_____

Banker _____

_____

Other _____

_____

E. BODY

1. Your Company and the Industry

THE COMPANY

Date business started _____

Location _____

_____

Form of business organization _____

_____

Founders and other key individuals _____

_____

_____

Principal products and related services _____

_____

_____

Success the Business Has Achieved to Date

	Estimated Total Annual Market (year)	Company Sales (year)	Market Share (%)
Product 1	$_____ _____ units	$_____ _____ units	_____ _____
Product 2	$_____ _____ units	$_____ _____ units	_____ _____
(etc.)			

Sample Business Plan (Manufacturing Company) — continued

Future Goals and Plans

_____

_____

_____

_____

_____

Principal strategy for achieving these goals _____

_____

_____

_____

_____

_____

_____

THE INDUSTRY

Prospects for the Industry

Total Estimated Industry Sales ($)

Product/ Service	Three Years Ago	Two Years Ago	Last Year	This Year	Next Year	In Two Years	In Three Years
1. _____	$_____	$_____	$_____	$_____	$_____	$_____	$_____
2. _____	$_____	$_____	$_____	$_____	$_____	$_____	$_____
3. _____	$_____	$_____	$_____	$_____	$_____	$_____	$_____
(etc.)							

Describe general trends within the industry and factors likely to affect these trends _____

_____

_____

Describe general industry standards and performance requirements _____

_____

_____

Major Industry Participants

Name and Location of Competitor	Estimated Sales	Estimated Market Share (%)	Principal Strengths and Weaknesses
_____	$_____	_____	_____
_____			_____
_____	$_____	_____	_____
_____			_____
_____	$_____	_____	_____
_____			_____

continued

Sample Business Plan (Manufacturing Company) — continued

2. Product Offering

DESCRIPTION OF PRINCIPAL PRODUCTS

Product	Description	Unique Features	Stage Of Development

Describe patents or trademarks held or applied for _____

_____

Describe franchise or licensing agreements, and regulatory, certification, or other requirements

_____

_____

Discuss key success factors in your business and how you plan to exploit them _____

_____

Outline your time frame and schedule for the implementation of your program _____

_____

3. Market Analysis (repeat for each product or product line offered)

TARGET MARKET AND CUSTOMERS

Describe your target market and prospective customers in terms of geography and/or customer type or profile _____

_____

_____

Describe the principal factors these consumers consider in the purchase of products like yours

_____

_____

Outline the principal benefit they will receive from patronizing your firm rather than one of your competitors_____

_____

Sample Business Plan (Manufacturing Company) — continued

Describe how your target market might be broken down into segments, and outline how these segments have changed over time and how they might be expected to change in the future

_____

_____

_____

_____

Describe any weekly, monthly, seasonal, or other sales patterns _____

_____

_____

COMPARISON WITH COMPETITORS

	Name of Competitor		
Factor	*1.* _____	*2.* _____	*3.* _____
Price	_____	_____	_____
Breadth of product line	_____	_____	_____
Depth of product line	_____	_____	_____
Performance	_____	_____	_____
Speed and accuracy	_____	_____	_____
Durability	_____	_____	_____
Versatility	_____	_____	_____
Ease of operation or use	_____	_____	_____
Ease of maintenance or repair	_____	_____	_____
Ease or cost of installation	_____	_____	_____
Size or weight	_____	_____	_____
Design or appearance	_____	_____	_____
Other characteristics:	_____	_____	_____
_____	_____	_____	_____
_____	_____	_____	_____

Indicate what, if anything, is really unique about your product offering or firm situation

_____

_____

_____

_____

_____

_____

_____

_____

_____

continued

Sample Business Plan (Manufacturing Company) — continued

SUMMARY OF ESTIMATED SALES BY PRODUCT LINE AND MARKET SEGMENT

Market Segment Description I _____

Product Line	Estimated Sales by Month ($ or units)												
	1	2	3	4	5	6	7	8	9	10	11	12	Total
_____													
_____													
_____													
_____													___
											Total		___

Market Segment Description II _____

Product Line	Estimated Sales by Month ($ or units)												
	1	2	3	4	5	6	7	8	9	10	11	12	Total
_____													
_____													
_____													
_____													___
											Total		___

Market Segment Description III _____

Product Line	Estimated Sales by Month ($ or units)												
	1	2	3	4	5	6	7	8	9	10	11	12	Total
_____													
_____													
_____													
_____													___
											Total		___

(etc.)

4. Marketing Plan

PRICING

Bill of Material List for Principal Products or Product Lines

Raw Material or Component Part	Description	Supplier	Direct Material Costs			
			Landed Cost	x No./or Quantity Reqd. per Unit	=	Cost per Unit Prod.
_____	_____	_____	$_____	_____		$_____
_____	_____	_____	_____	_____		_____
_____	_____	_____	_____	_____		_____
_____	_____	_____	_____	_____		_____

Total Material Costs per Unit $_____ **(A)**

Sample Business Plan (Manufacturing Company) — continued

Direct Labour Costs

Assembly or Manufacturing Process	Estimated Labour Time per Unit	x	Hourly Rate	=	Labour Cost per Unit
_____	_____	$_____			$_____
_____	_____	_____			_____
_____	_____	_____			_____

Total Labour Cost per Unit	$_____	**(B)**
Total Direct Manufacturing Cost per Unit (C = A + B)	$_____	**(C)**
Total Estimated Packaging and Shipping Cost per Unit	_____	**(D)**
Total Direct Cost per Unit (E = C + D)	$_____	**(E)**

Discuss the prices you plan to charge distributors and customers for your product, typical gross and net margins for each of your product lines, and how they compare with those of other firms

_____

_____

_____

Describe your schedule for quantity, cash, functional and other discounts, credit arrangements, returns policy, and other terms of sale _____

_____

_____

_____

_____

DISTRIBUTION

Describe the channels of distribution you will use to get your product to the ultimate consumer

_____

_____

_____

_____

Outline your personal selling requirements — the number and type of people and how they will be paid

_____

_____

_____

continued

Sample Business Plan (Manufacturing Company) — continued

List your principal distributors by name and their expected sales:

Distributor	Address	Territory	Terms of Sale	Exclusive or Non-Exclusive	Total Expected Sales ($ or units)
_____	_____	_____	_____	_____	_____
	_____				
_____	_____	_____	_____	_____	_____
	_____				
_____	_____	_____	_____	_____	_____
	_____				

List your principal customers by name and the total amount they are expected to buy from you:

Customer	Product	Total Expected Purchases ($ or units)	Share of Your Sales (%)
_____	1. _____	_____	_____
	2. _____	_____	_____
	3. _____	_____	_____
_____	1. _____	_____	_____
	2. _____	_____	_____
	3. _____	_____	_____
_____	1. _____	_____	_____
	2. _____	_____	_____
	3. _____	_____	_____

ADVERTISING AND PROMOTION PROGRAM

Describe product packaging requirements and estimated costs for development and use

_____

_____

Outline requirements for product brochures and similar descriptive material indicating development costs and expected cost of production _____

_____

_____

Indicate the trade shows you plan to attend to exhibit your product:

Trade Show	Location	Timing	Estimated Cost
_____	_____	_____	$ _____
_____	_____	_____	_____
_____	_____	_____	_____

Total Estimated Cost $ _____

Sample Business Plan (Manufacturing Company) — continued

Advertising Program

Media	Audience Size	Schedule	Frequency of use	x	Cost of a Single Occasion	=	Estimated Cost
_____	_____	_____	_____		$_____		$_____
_____	_____	_____	_____		$_____		$_____
_____	_____	_____	_____		$_____		$_____
_____	_____	_____	_____		$_____		$_____
_____	_____	_____	_____		$_____		$_____
_____	_____	_____	_____		$_____		$_____

Total Estimated Cost $_____

Describe any plan to obtain free publicity or other sales promotion activity _____

_____

_____

Describe any repair, informational, or other support services you plan to provide and their anticipated costs:

Service	Estimated Cost
_____	$_____
_____	_____
_____	_____
_____	_____

5. Production/Operating Plan

Describe your location and its pros and cons:

Location _____

_____

Description_____

_____

Advantages _____

_____

Disadvantages _____

_____

Accessibility to suppliers _____

_____

Availability of transport services _____

_____

Zoning situation _____

_____

Cost_____

_____

continued

Sample Business Plan (Manufacturing Company) — continued

Condition_____

_____

Other factors _____

_____

Describe your basic manufacturing processes and list the basic operations your facility will have to perform_____

_____

_____

Indicate the space required or allocated to each of the following activities:

Activity	Space Required or Allocated (sq. ft.)
Manufacturing:	
Fabrication	_____
Machining	_____
Assembly	_____
Finishing	_____
Inspection	_____
Other_____	_____
_____	_____
Storage	_____
Shipping	_____
Receiving	_____
Office area	_____
Restrooms and employee facilities	_____
Other activities _____	_____
_____	_____
_____	_____

Total Space Required or Allocated (sq. ft.)　_____

Develop a scale drawing or floor plan of the physical layout of your facility.

List the machinery and equipment you will need to perform your manufacturing and other operations:

Type of Machinery or Equipment	Buy or Lease	Number Required	x	Unit Cost	=	Total Cost
_____	_____	_____		$_____		$_____
_____	_____	_____		_____		_____
_____	_____	_____		_____		_____
_____	_____	_____		_____		_____
_____	_____	_____		_____		_____
_____	_____	_____		_____		_____
				Total Cost		$_____

Sample Business Plan (Manufacturing Company) — continued

Indicate where you plan to buy your raw materials and component parts:

Raw Material/ Component	Supplier	Price	Order Policy	Discount Offered	Delivery Time	Freight Costs	Back Order Policy
———	———	$———	———	———	———	$———	———
———	———	———	———	———	———	———	———
———	———	———	———	———	———	———	———
———	———	———	———	———	———	———	———
———	———	———	———	———	———	———	———
———	———	———	———	———	———	———	———

Indicate where you plan to buy your consumable tools and shop supplies:

Tools or Supplies	Supplier	Price	Order Policy	Discounts Offered	Delivery	Freight Costs	Back Order Policy
———	———	$———	———	———	———	$———	———
———	———	———	———	———	———	———	———
———	———	———	———	———	———	———	———
———	———	———	———	———	———	———	———
———	———	———	———	———	———	———	———
———	———	———	———	———	———	———	———

Outline your inventory control procedures _____

_____

_____

_____

OPENING INVENTORY REQUIREMENTS

Raw Materials and Component Parts

Item	Quantity Required	x	Cost per unit	=	Total Cost
———	———		$———		$———
———	———		———		———
———	———		———		———
———	———		———		———
———	———		———		———
———	———		———		———

Total Raw Material Inventory $_____ (A)

continued

Sample Business Plan (Manufacturing Company) — continued

Consumable Tools and Supplies

Item	Quantity Required	x	Cost per unit	=	Total Cost
_____	_____		$_____		$_____
_____	_____		_____		_____
_____	_____		_____		_____
_____	_____		_____		_____
_____	_____		_____		_____
_____	_____		_____		_____

Total Tools and Supplies $_____ **(B)**

Total Opening Inventory Requirements (C = A + B) $_____ **(C)**

OUTLINE OF EMPLOYEE REQUIREMENTS

Job	Qualifications Required	Full-or Part-time	Job Description (yes or no)	Compensation	Benefits
_____	_____	_____	_____	$_____	_____
_____	_____	_____	_____	_____	_____
_____	_____	_____	_____	_____	_____
_____	_____	_____	_____	_____	_____

Describe permits or licences required and necessary inspections:

Permit, Licences, or Necessary Inspection	Date Received or Completed
_____	_____
_____	_____
_____	_____

6. Management Team

Develop an organization chart indicating who is responsible for each of the major areas of activity in your business; list each function and indicate the name of the individual who will perform that function and to whom they will be responsible:

Function	Performed by:	Responsible to:
Sales	_____	_____
Marketing	_____	_____
Operations management	_____	_____
Bookkeeping and accounting	_____	_____
Personnel management	_____	_____
Research and development	_____	_____

Present a brief résumé of each of these individuals.

Outline the size and composition of your board of directors _____

_____

_____

_____

Sample Business Plan (Manufacturing Company) — continued

Present a brief résumé of each individual on your board who is not part of your management team.

Indicate the compensation received by each member of your management team and board of directors:

Individual	Salary	Fees or Bonuses	Total Compensation
_____	$_____	$_____	$_____
_____	_____	_____	_____
_____	_____	_____	_____
_____	_____	_____	_____
_____	_____	_____	_____
_____	_____	_____	_____

Describe the ownership structure of your business:

Individual	Types of Shares Held	Percentage of Total Issued	Number of Shares Held	x	Price Paid per Share	=	Total
_____	_____	_____	_____		$_____		$_____
_____	_____	_____	_____		_____		_____
_____	_____	_____	_____		_____		_____
_____	_____	_____	_____		_____		_____
_____	_____	_____	_____		_____		_____

Total Capitalization $_____

Indicate any options to acquire additional stock that may be held or could be earned by your management team or others _____
_____
_____

Provide complete information regarding your professional advisors:

Advisor	Name	Address	Telephone	Fees or Retainers Paid
Lawyer	_____	_____ _____	_____	$_____
Accountant	_____	_____ _____	_____	$_____
Banker	_____	_____ _____	_____	$_____
Other	_____	_____ _____	_____	$_____

continued

Sample Business Plan (Manufacturing Company) — continued

7. Implementation Schedule

Lay out a schedule of milestones or significant events for the implementation of your business and a timetable for completion; indicate who will be responsible for the completion of each task:

Milestone	Tasks Required to Accomplish	Who is Responsible	Scheduled Completion
_____	_____	_____	_____
	_____	_____	_____
	_____	_____	_____
	_____	_____	_____
_____	_____	_____	_____
	_____	_____	_____
	_____	_____	_____
	_____	_____	_____
_____	_____	_____	_____
	_____	_____	_____
	_____	_____	_____
	_____	_____	_____

Describe the risks your business may be faced with in implementing your plan, and the risk for any prospective investor _____

_____

_____

_____

_____

8. Financial Plan

START-UP COSTS

If yours is a new venture, indicate your estimate of the start-up financial requirements of your business:

Estimated One-Time Financial Requirements

Item	Total Cost	Cash Required	Balance	How Financed
Land	$_____	$_____	$_____	_____
Building	_____	_____	_____	_____
Improvements:				
Mechanical	_____	_____	_____	_____
Electrical	_____	_____	_____	_____
Construction	_____	_____	_____	_____
Machinery and equipment	_____	_____	_____	_____
Installation of equipment	_____	_____	_____	_____

Sample Business Plan (Manufacturing Company) — *continued*

Shop tools and supplies	_____	_____	_____	_____
Office equipment and supplies	_____	_____	_____	_____
Vehicles	_____	_____	_____	_____
Starting inventory	_____	_____	_____	_____
Utility hookup and installation fees	_____	_____	_____	_____
Licences and permits	_____	_____	_____	_____
Pre-opening advertising and promotion	_____	_____	_____	_____
Accounts payable	_____	_____	_____	_____
Cash for Unexpected Expenses	$_____			
Other cash requirements	$_____			
Total Estimated One-Time Cash Requirements	$_____			

Estimated Start-Up Operating Expenses

Item	Estimate of Monthly Expense	x	Number of Months* Before Breakeven	=	Total Cash Required
Owners' salaries	$_____		_____		$_____
Manufacturing salaries, wages, and benefits	_____		_____		_____
Office salaries, wages, and benefits	_____		_____		_____
Rent	_____		_____		_____
Promotion expenses	_____		_____		_____
Supplies and postage	_____		_____		_____
Vehicle expense	_____		_____		_____
Telephone	_____		_____		_____
Other utilities	_____		_____		_____
Insurance	_____		_____		_____
Travel	_____		_____		_____
Legal and other professional fees	_____		_____		_____
Interest	_____		_____		_____
Maintenance	_____		_____		_____
Other expenses	_____		_____		_____

Total Cash Required to Cover Operating Expenses $_____

Plus: Total One-Time Cash Requirements (from previous table) $_____

Total Cash or Operating Line of Credit Required for Start-Up $_____

* Two to three months *minimum* are typical here.

continued

Sample Business Plan (Manufacturing Company) — continued

PRESENT FINANCIAL STRUCTURE

Provide an overview of the current financial structure of your business and the proportion of your total start-up requirements obtained to date:

Source of Funds	Amount	Debt or Equity	Repayment Schedule
Self	$_____	_____	_____
Friends, neighbours, relatives	_____	_____	_____
Other private investors	_____	_____	_____
Banks, savings and loans, credit unions, and other financial institutions	_____	_____	_____
Mortgage and insurance companies	_____	_____	_____
Credit from suppliers	_____	_____	_____
Government grants and loans	_____	_____	_____
Other:			
_____	_____	_____	_____
_____	_____	_____	_____
_____	_____	_____	_____
_____	_____	_____	_____
_____	_____	_____	_____

Additional Funds Required

Indicate the additional funds required and the shares, return on investment, collateral, or other security you are prepared to provide to the prospective lender or investor

_____
_____
_____
_____
_____
_____
_____
_____
_____
_____
_____
_____
_____

Current Financial Statements

If your business is already in operation, provide an income statement and a balance sheet for the current year to date and the previous two years. The following forms will serve as guidelines indicating the basic information to provide for each year.

Sample Business Plan (Manufacturing Company) — continued

INCOME STATEMENT
for the period ending [date]

Gross sales $_____

Less: Cash discounts   _____

Net Sales $_____   **(A)**

Less: Cost of goods sold:

    Beginning inventory $_____

    Plus: Net purchases   _____

    Total goods available for sale   _____

    Less: Ending inventory   _____

    Cost of Goods Sold   _____   **(B)**

Gross Margin (or Profit) (C = A − B) $_____   **(C)**

Less: Operating expenses:

    Owner's salary $_____

    Employees' wages and salaries   _____

    Employee benefits   _____

    Rent   _____

    Utilities (heat, light, water, power)   _____

    Telephone   _____

    Supplies and postage   _____

    Repairs and maintenance   _____

    Advertising and promotion   _____

    Vehicle expense   _____

    Delivery expense   _____

    Taxes and licences   _____

    Depreciation or Capital Cost Allowance   _____

    Bad debt allowance   _____

    Interest   _____

    Travel   _____

    Insurance   _____

    Legal and accounting fees   _____

    Other expenses   _____

    Total Operating Expenses   _____   **(D)**

Net Operating Profit (Loss) (E = C − D)   _____   **(E)**

Income Tax (estimated)   _____   **(F)**

Net Profit (Loss) After Income Tax (G = E − F) $_____   **(G)**

continued

Sample Business Plan (Manufacturing Company) — continued

**BALANCE SHEET FOR
[NAME OF COMPANY]
as of [date]**

ASSETS

   Current Assets

      Cash $_____

      Accounts receivable   _____

      Inventory   _____

      Other current assets   _____

      Total current assets   _____ **(A)**

   Fixed Assets

      Land and buildings $_____

      Furniture and fixtures   _____

      Equipment   _____

      Trucks and automobiles   _____

      Other fixed assets   _____

      Total fixed assets   _____ **(B)**

   Total Assets (C = A + B) $_____ **(C)**

LIABILITIES

   Current Liabilities (debt due within 12 months)

      Accounts payable $_____

      Bank loans/other loans   _____

      Taxes owed   _____

      Total current liabilities   _____ **(D)**

   Long-Term Liabilities

      Notes payable (due after 1 year)   _____

      Total long-term liabilities   _____ **(E)**

   Total Liabilities (F = D + E) $_____ **(F)**

NET WORTH (CAPITAL)

   Total Net Worth (G = C - F)   _____ **(G)**

   Total Liabilities and Net Worth (H = F + G) $_____ **(H)**

FINANCIAL PROJECTIONS

Develop profit and loss forecast, projected cash flow statements, and pro forma balance sheets for your business. Each of these statements should be presented for the following time frames:

- **Pro forma profit and loss statements** Monthly for the next year of operation and quarterly or annually for another two to four years
- **Cash flow forecasts** Monthly for the next year of operation and annually for another two years
- **Pro forma balance sheets** Annually for each of the next three to five years

The following forms will serve as guidelines to be followed in developing and presenting this information.

Sample Business Plan (Manufacturing Company) — continued

PRO FORMA INCOME STATEMENT
For the period ending [date]

		Month												
		1	2	3	4	5	6	7	8	9	10	11	12	Total
Gross sales															
Less Cash discounts															
Net Sales	**(A)**														
Cost of goods sold:															
Beginning inventory															
Plus: Net purchases															
Total goods available for sale															
Less: Ending inventory															
Cost of Goods Sold	**(B)**														
Gross Margin (C = A – B)	**(C)**														
Less: Variable expenses															
Owner's salary															
Employees' wages and salaries															
Supplies and postage															
Advertising and promotion															
Delivery expense															
Bad debt allowance															
Travel															
Legal and accounting fees															
Vehicle Expenses															
Miscellaneous expenses															
Total Variable Expenses	**(D)**														
Less: Fixed expenses															
Rent															
Utilities (heat, light, water, power)															
Telephone															
Taxes and licences															
Depreciation or Capital Cost Allowance															
Interest															
Insurance															
Other Fixed Expenses															
Total Fixed Expenses	**(E)**														
Total Operating Expenses (F = D + E)	**(F)**														
Net Operating Profit (Loss) (G = C – F)	**(G)**														
Income Taxes (estimated)	**(H)**														
Net Profit (Loss) After Income Tax (I = G – H)	**(I)**														

continued

ESTIMATED CASH FLOW FORECAST

	Month 1	Month 2	Month 3	Month 4	Month 5	Month 6	Month 7	Month 8	Month 9	Month 10	Month 11	Month 12	Year 1 TOTAL	Year 2 TOTAL	Year 3 TOTAL
Cash Flow From Operations (during month)															
1. Cash Sales															
2. Payments for Credit Sales															
3. Investment Income															
4. Other Cash Income															
A. TOTAL CASH FLOW ON HAND	$	$	$	$	$	$	$	$	$	$	$	$	$	$	$
Less Expenses Paid (during month)															
5. Inventory or New Material															
6. Owners' Salaries															
7. Employees' Wages and Salaries															
8. Supplies and Postage															
9. Advertising and Promotion															
10. Delivery Expense															
11. Travel															
12. Legal and Accounting Fees															
13. Vehicle Expense															
14. Maintenance Expense															
15. Rent															
16. Utilities															
17. Telephone															
18. Taxes and Licences															
19. Interest Payments															
20. Insurance															
21. Other Cash Expenses															
B. TOTAL EXPENDITURES	$	$	$	$	$	$	$	$	$	$	$	$	$	$	$
Capital															
Purchase of Fixed Assets															
Sale of Fixed Assets															
C. CHANGE IN CASH FROM PURCHASE OR SALE OF ASSETS	$	$	$	$	$	$	$	$	$	$	$	$	$	$	$
Financing															
Payment of Principal of Loan															
Inflow of Cash From Bank Loan															
Issuance of Equity Positions															
Repurchase of Outstanding Equity															
D. CHANGE IN CASH FROM FINANCING	$	$	$	$	$	$	$	$	$	$	$	$	$	$	$
E. INCREASE (DECREASE) IN CASH	$	$	$	$	$	$	$	$	$	$	$	$	$	$	$
F. CASH AT BEGINNING OF PERIOD	$	$	$	$	$	$	$	$	$	$	$	$	$*	$**	$**
G. CASH AT END OF PERIOD	$	$	$	$	$	$	$	$	$	$	$	$	$	$	$
MEET MINIMUM CASH BALANCE	Acceptable	Acceptable	Acceptable	Acceptable	Acceptable	Acceptable	Acceptable	Acceptable	Acceptable	Acceptable	Acceptable	Acceptable	Acceptable	Acceptable	Acceptable

* This entry should be the same amount as for month 1 at the beginning of the year. All other rows will be the total for the entire year.

** These entries should be the same as the ending cash balance from the previous period.

Sample Business Plan (Manufacturing Company) — continued

PRO FORMA BALANCE SHEET
[NAME OF COMPANY]
as of [date]

ASSETS

Current Assets

Cash $_____

Accounts receivable   _____

Inventory   _____

Other current assets   _____

Total current assets   _____ **(A)**

Fixed Assets

Land and buildings $_____

Furniture and fixtures   _____

Equipment   _____

Trucks and automobiles   _____

Other fixed assets   _____

Total fixed assets   _____ **(B)**

Total Assets (C = A + B) $_____ **(C)**

LIABILITIES

Current Liabilities (debt due within 12 months)

Accounts payable $_____

Bank loans/other loans   _____

Taxes owed   _____

Total current liabilities   _____ **(D)**

Long-Term Liabilities

Mortgages payable $_____

Notes payable (due after 1 year)   _____

Loans from partners or shareholders   _____

Total long-term liabilities   _____ **(E)**

Total Liabilities (F = D + E) $_____ **(F)**

NET WORTH (CAPITAL)

Total Net Worth (G = C – F)   _____ **(G)**

Total Liabilities and Net Worth (H = F + G) $_____ **(H)**

continued

Sample Business Plan (Manufacturing Company) — continued

Indicate the minimum level of sales you will require to cover all your fixed and variable costs and to break even:

$$\text{Breakeven Point (in Units)} = \frac{\text{Total Operating Expenses (F in Pro Forma Profit and Loss Statement)}}{\text{Your Average Selling Price per Unit} - \text{Total Direct Cost per Unit}}$$

$$\text{Breakeven Point (in Sales Dollars)} = \frac{\text{Total Operating Expenses (F in Pro Forma Profit and Loss Statement)}}{1 - \frac{(\text{Average Selling Price per Unit} - \text{Total Direct Cost per Unit})}{100}}$$

F. APPENDIXES

FIGURE 10.5 BUSINESS PLAN CHECKLIST

After completion of your business plan, you should thoroughly review it. This checklist will help you to do so. Decide whether or not you think the answers you have provided are clear and complete. Evaluate the information from the standpoint of a prospective investor or lending agency and ask yourself whether you are satisfied with your responses.

	Answer is Included (X)	Answer is Clear (Yes or No)	Answer is Complete (Yes or No)
1. YOUR COMPANY AND THE INDUSTRY			
a. Type of business you are planning	_____	_____	_____
b. Products or services you will sell	_____	_____	_____
c. History of the company	_____	_____	_____
d. Why does business promise to be successful?	_____	_____	_____
e. Your future goals and objectives	_____	_____	_____
f. Description of the industry	_____	_____	_____
g. Major participants and significant trends	_____	_____	_____

General Comments

_____

_____

_____

_____

_____

2. PRODUCT/SERVICE OFFERING			
a. Description of your product/service	_____	_____	_____
b. Present stage of development	_____	_____	_____
c. Patent/trademark position	_____	_____	_____
d. Other formal requirements	_____	_____	_____
e. Growth opportunities and key factors for success	_____	_____	_____

General Comments

_____

_____

_____

_____

_____

continued

Business Plan Checklist — continued

	Answer is Included (X)	Answer is Clear (Yes or No)	Answer is Complete (Yes or No)
3. MARKETING ANALYSIS AND PLAN			
a. Who are your target customers?	_____	_____	_____
b. What are their characteristics?	_____	_____	_____
c. How do they buy?	_____	_____	_____
d. How large is the market and its various segments?	_____	_____	_____
e. Factors affecting the market	_____	_____	_____
f. Who are your competitors? How are they doing?	_____	_____	_____
g. How much of the market will you be able to attract?	_____	_____	_____
h. What will your principal marketing strategy be?	_____	_____	_____
i. Have you detailed all aspects of your marketing plan? i.e.:	*Yes*	*No*	
a. Pricing	_____	_____	
b. Sales and distribution	_____	_____	
c. Advertising and promotion	_____	_____	

General Comments

_____

_____

_____

_____

	Answer is Included (X)	Answer is Clear (Yes or No)	Answer is Complete (Yes or No)
4. PRODUCTION/OPERATIONS PLAN			
a. Where will your business be located?	_____	_____	_____
b. What are the characteristics of your location?	_____	_____	_____
c. Description of machinery and equipment you will require	_____	_____	_____
d. What are your costs to produce your product?	_____	_____	_____
e. What are your inventory requirements?	_____	_____	_____
f. Who will be your principal suppliers or subcontractors?	_____	_____	_____
g. Description of your quality control procedures	_____	_____	_____
h. How many employees will you require? What type? How will they be paid?	_____	_____	_____
i. Will you require any licences, permits, or other authorizations?	_____	_____	_____

Business Plan Checklist — continued

General Comments

_____

_____

_____

_____

	Answer is Included (X)	Answer is Clear (Yes or No)	Answer is Complete (Yes or No)
5. MANAGEMENT TEAM			
a. Who will manage your business?	_____	_____	_____
b. What are their qualifications?	_____	_____	_____
c. What is the size and composition of your board of directors?	_____	_____	_____
d. What are your managers and directors being paid?	_____	_____	_____
e. What is the ownership structure of the business?	_____	_____	_____
f. Who are your advisors and consultants?	_____	_____	_____

General Comments

_____

_____

_____

_____

	Answer is Included (X)	Answer is Clear (Yes or No)	Answer is Complete (Yes or No)
6. FINANCIAL PLAN			
a. How much money will you need to start the business and sustain it for the first few months?	_____	_____	_____
b. How much money do you have now?	_____	_____	_____
c. How much more do you need?	_____	_____	_____
d. How will this additional money be used?	_____	_____	_____
e. What kind of collateral or security will be provided?	_____	_____	_____
f. How will this money be repaid?	_____	_____	_____
g. Provided financial statements:			
For the current year	_____	_____	_____
For the past two years	_____	_____	_____
h. Total estimated net income:			
Monthly for the first year	_____	_____	_____
Quarterly or annually for the next two to four years	_____	_____	_____
i. Estimated cash flow situation:			
Monthly for the first year	_____	_____	_____
Annually for the next two years	_____	_____	_____
j. What is your estimated financial position at the end of each of the next three to five years?	_____	_____	_____
k. What sales volume will you need to break even?	_____	_____	_____

continued

Business Plan Checklist — continued

General Comments

_____

_____

_____

_____

7. APPENDIXES

Do you need to include the following appendixes?	Yes	No
a. Product photographs and specifications	_____	_____
b. Résumés of your management team	_____	_____
c. List of prospective customers	_____	_____
d. List of possible suppliers	_____	_____
e. Job descriptions for management team	_____	_____
f. Consulting reports	_____	_____
g. Market surveys	_____	_____
h. Legal agreements and contracts	_____	_____
i. Publicity articles and promotional pieces	_____	_____
j. Other supporting material	_____	_____

CAPITAL COST ALLOWANCE RATES

Capital Cost Allowance (CCA) for a number of the more common types of business assets are listed below. These are only a few examples of the classes of asset to which CCA applies for tax purposes. For a more comprehensive listing of CCA classes, consult Chapter IV of the 1995 *Canadian Master Tax Guide*, published by CCH Canadian Ltd., or contact your local office of Revenue Canada.

ALPHABETICAL TABLE OF RATES

Item	Rate	Class
Aircraft	25%	9
Automobiles	30%	10
Buildings:		
Brick, stone, cement, etc.	4%	1
Frame, log, stucco on frame, galvanized, or corrugated iron	10%	6
Computer hardware and systems	30%	10
Computer software	100%	12
Contractors' movable equipment:		
Normal	30%	10
Heavy	30%	38
Display fixtures (window)	20%	8
Electrical advertising signs	20%	8
Furniture	20%	8
Manufacturing and processing machinery and equipment	25%	39
Parking area	8%	17
Tools (under $200)	100%	12

Note: If using CCA rates, only 1/2 may be claimed in the first year.

FURTHER READING

For further information on many of the subjects discussed in this book you may wish to refer to the following materials. Most are available free of charge or for a very nominal cost from the indicated sources. They can help you flesh out much of the material that should be incorporated into your business plan and inform you of the particular requirements of the municipality or province in which your business will be located.

Banks

Royal Bank of Canada

Starting Out Right
The Source Book
Borrowing Money
Managing Your Cash Flow
Disk: The Big Idea

Bank of Montreal

Small Business Problem Solver Series
The Cycles of Your Business
Using Other People's Help
Sources of Capital
Developing Your Business Plan
Making Sense of Terms and Jargon
Cash Flow Planning
Measuring Performance
Managing Your Cash Flow
The Financial Proposal
Dealing With Your Banker
Are You an Entrepreneur
Marketing Your Business
Becoming a People Manager
Computers for Your Business
Doing Business Internationally

Other Publications
*Business: Export Financing. New Financing Options for Small and Medium Sized Canadian
        Exporters.*
Financing Your Business: Small Business Loan Application Guide
Planning Your Success: Outline for a Business Plan

Canadian Imperial Bank of Commerce

Gateway to Canada
Franchise Financing

Cash Management Services
Financing an Independent Business
A Guide for the Franchisor
Franchising in Canada
Professional Loans Program
Capital at Work: Selected Corporate Ratios
Your Guide to Business Planning

Toronto Dominion Bank

Business Banking Services
Small Business Loans
Commercial Installment Loans
Commercial Installment Lease
Commercial Lease
Commercial Mortgage
Cash Flow Budgeting Brochure
Case-Retailing
Case-Rental
Case-Manufacturing

Business Development Bank of Canada

Analyzing Financial Statements
Arranging Financing
Credit and Collection Tips
Evaluating the Purchase of a Small Business
Forecasting and Cash Flow Budgeting

Accounting Firms

Dunwoody & Company

Going Public
Business Plan: 10 Steps to Success
Financing Today's Business
Doing Business in Canada
Free Trade Strategies

Coopers & Lybrand

Starting Out in Business
Three Keys to Obtaining Venture Capital
Financial Statement Services for the Entrepreneur
Tax Planning Checklist
Raising Equity on the Vancouver Stock Exchange

Ernst & Young

The Enterprisers – Quarterly Newsletter for Entrepreneurs
Managing Your Personal Taxes

Federal Government

Industry Canada

A Guide to Patents, Trademarks, Copyright and Industrial Designs
Federal Incorporation
Bankruptcy
Consumer Protection
Market Intelligence Reports

Foreign Affairs and International Trade Canada

Export Information Kit
Directory of Canadian Foreign Trade Representatives and Canadian Consulates Abroad
Guide for Canadian Exporters Series

Revenue Canada — Customs and Excise

Thinking About Importing? What You Should Know.

Statistics Canada

Catalogue of Available Publications

Public Works and Government Services Canada

Information Kit
Supplier's Guide

Provincial Governments

Newfoundland Department of Industry, Trade, and Technology

Investing in Newfoundland and Labrador (updated yearly)

Prince Edward Island Economic Development and Tourism

Small Business Planning Guide
How to Start a Small Business on Prince Edward Island (not printed any more, copies circulating)

New Brunswick Department of Economic Development and Tourism

Marketing a Small Business
Key Steps to Business Improvement
Corporate Directories
Going Public

Québec ministre de l'Industrie, du Commerce, de la Science et de la Technologie

L'entrepreneurship féminin: en tête de nos affaires
Corporate Directories
PME: entrepreneurship et croissance
Starting Up Right
Partnership Guide

Ontario Ministry of Economic Development and Trade

Business Plan Preparation Series:
- *Manufacturing*
- *Service*
- *Retail*
- *Professional Service*

Co-Operative Accounting Guide with KPMG.

Manitoba Department of Industry, Trade, and Tourism

Information Pamphlets
Starting a Small Business in Manitoba
Monter une petite enterprise au Manitoba

Small Business Management Systems
Retail Business Plan
Service Business Plan
Construction Business Plan
Manufacturing Business Plan
Small Business Finance Plan
Marketing
Bookkeeping
Manitoba Franchise Guide

Entrepreneur's Handbooks
Importing
Forms of Business Organization
Starting a Retail Clothing Outlet
Starting a Bookstore
Starting a Convenience Food Store
Starting a Sporting Goods Store
Starting a Service Station
Starting a Mail Order Business
Starting a Hardware Store
Starting a Restaurant

Self-Evaluation Guides to Starting a Business of Your Own
Stage 1: Assessing Your Potential for an Entrepreneurial Career
Stage 2: Finding and Evaluating a Product or Service idea
Stage 3: Should You Start a New Business or Buy an Existing One?

Saskatchewan Department of Economic Development

Financial Management Series
- *The ABC's of Borrowing*
- *Budgeting in a Small Business Service Firm*
- *Basic Budgets for Profit Planning*
- *Cash Flow in a Small Plant*
- *Credit and Collections*
- *Attacking Business Decision Problems with Break-even Analysis*
- *Accounting Services for Small Service Firms*
- *Simple Break-even for Small Stores*

- *Analyze Your Records to Reduce Costs*
- *Profit by Your Wholesaler's Services*
- *Sound Cash Management and Borrowing*
- *Keeping Records in Small Business*
- *Checklist for Profit Watching*
- *Profit Pricing and Costing Services*

General Management and Administration Series
- *Delegating Work and Responsibility*
- *Preventing Retail Theft (out of print, still in circulation)*
- *Preventing Burglary and Robbery Loss*
- *Preventing Embezzlement*

Planning Series
- *Problems in Managing a Family-Owned Business*
- *Succession Problems in Family Business*
- *Business Plan for Small Manufacturers*
- *Business Plan for Service Firms*
- *Can You Make Money With Your Idea or Invention?*
- *Computer Orientation and Basic Software Ideas*
- *Checklists for Going into Business*
- *Feasibility Checklist for Starting a Small Business*
- *Business Plan for Retailers*

Marketing Series
- *Creative Selling: The Competitive Edge*
- *Measuring Salesforce Performance*
- *Selling Products on Consignment*
- *Tips on Getting More for Your Marketing Dollar*
- *Developing New Accounts*
- *Marketing Checklist for Small Retailers*
- *A Pricing Checklist for Small Retailers*
- *Improving Personal Selling in Small Service Firms*
- *Learning About Your Business*
- *Plan Your Budget*

Alberta Economic Development and Trade

Financing a Small Business
Marketing for a Small Business
Starting a Small Service Firm
Buying a Franchise
Franchising Checklist
Buying a Business
Accounting and Bookkeeping in a Small Business

British Columbia Ministry of Small Business, Tourism, and Culture

Your Business Options
Exporting in Canada
B.C. Directory of Corporations
B.C. Business Planner and Guide
Market Assessment of New Ventures
Protecting Your Idea

Preparing a Business Plan
Preparing Financial Statements
Glossary of Import Export Terms (put out by Federal Government)
Overview of Government Financial Incentives (both Provincial and Federal)
Licensing an Innovation
The Business of Innovation
Operating an Independent Service Business
Operating an Independent Retail Business

Associations and Other Organizations

Canadian Franchise Association

Franchising in Canada
Franchising Statistics (Canada)
CFA Membership Directory
How to Franchise your Business

The CFA Information Kit

CFA Code of Ethics
Franchise Evaluation Checklist
Affiliate Member List
Investigate Before Investing

Dun and Bradstreet

Canadian Business Ratios on Disk
Canadian Business Failure Record
Guide to Canadian Manufacturers
Business Directory (Canada)

SOME USEFUL CONTACTS

Federal Government

Industry Canada
235 Queen St.
Ottawa, Ontario
K1A 0H5
Tel.: (613) 995-8900

Foreign Affairs and International Trade Canada
125 Sussex Drive
Ottawa, Ontario
K1A 0G2
Tel.: (613) 996-9134
Toll free: 1-800-267-8376

Statistics Canada
Customer Inquiries
Tunney's Pasture
Ottawa, Ontario
K1A 0T6
Tel.: (613) 951-8116

Canadian Intellectual Property Office

Industry Canada
50 Victoria Street
Place du Portage, Phase 1
Hull, Quebec
K1A 0C9
Tel.: (819) 997-1936

Canada Business Service Centres (CBSCs)

- Canada/British Columbia Business Service Centre
  601 West Cordova Street
  Vancouver, British Columbia
  V6B 1G1
  Tel.: (604) 775-5525
  Toll Free: 1-800-667-2272
  Fax: (604) 775-5520
  FaxBack: (604) 775-5515

- Canada Business Service Centre
  9700 Jasper Avenue, Suite 122
  Edmonton, Alberta
  T5J 4H7
  Tel.: (403) 495-6800
  Toll Free: 1-800-272-9675
  Fax: (403) 495-7725

- Canada/Saskatchewan Business Service Centre
  122 – 3rd Avenue, North
  Saskatoon, Saskatchewan
  S7K 2H6
  Tel.: (306) 956-2323
  Toll Free: 1-800-667-4374
  Fax: (306) 956-2328
  FaxBack: (306) 956-2310
  FaxBack: 1-800-667-9433

- Canada Business Service Centre
  330 Portage Avenue, 8th Floor
  P.O. Box 981
  Winnipeg, Manitoba
  R3C 2V2
  Tel.: (204) 984-2272
  Toll Free: 1-800-665-2019
  Fax: (204) 983-2187
  FaxBack: (204) 984-5527
  FaxBack: 1-800-665-9386

- Canada/Nova Scotia Business Service Centre
  1575 Brunswick Street
  Halifax, Nova Scotia
  B3J 2G1
  Tel.: (902) 426-8604
  Toll Free: 1-800-668-1010
  Fax: (902) 426-6530

FaxBack: (902) 426-3201
FaxBack: 1-800-401-3201

- Canada Business Service Centre
90 O'Leary Avenue
P.O. Box 8687
St. John's, Newfoundland
A1B 3T1
Tel.: (709) 772-6022
Toll Free: 1-800-668-1010
Fax: (709) 772-6090
FaxBack: (709) 772-6030

- Canada Business Service Centre
Toronto, Ontario
M5V 3E5
Tel: (416) 954-INFO (4636)
Toll Free: 1-800-567-2345
Fax: (416) 954-8597
FaxBack: (416) 954-8555
FaxBack: 1-800-240-4192

- Info entrepreneurs
5 Place Ville Marie
Plaza Level, Suite 12500
Montreal, Quebec
H3B 4Y2
Tel.: (514) 496-INFO (4636)
Toll Free: 1-800-322-INFO (4636)
Fax: (514) 496-5934
Info-Fax: (514) 496-4010
Info-Fax: 1-800-322-4010

- Canada/New Brunswick Business Service Centre
570 Queen Street
Fredericton, New Brunswick
E3B 6Z6
Tel.: (506) 444-6140
Toll Free: 1-800-668-1010
Fax: (506) 444-6172
FaxBack: (506) 444-6169

- Canada/Prince Edward Island Business Service Centre
232 Queen Street
P.O. Box 40
Charlottetown, Prince Edward Island
C1A 7K2
Tel.: (902) 368-0771
Toll Free: 1-800-668-1010
Fax: (902) 566-7098
FaxBack: (902) 368-0776
FaxBack: 1-800-401-3201

Provincial Governments

British Columbia

Ministry of Small Business, Tourism, and Culture
1117 Wharf Street
Victoria, B.C.
V8W 2Z2
Tel.: (604) 356-6363
Fax: (604) 356-8248

Alberta

Alberta Economic Development and Trade
Small Business and Tourism Division
Sterling Place
9940 – 106th Street
6th Floor
Edmonton, Alberta
T5K 2P6
Tel.: (403) 297-6284
Fax: (403) 297-6168

999 – 8th Street
5th Floor
Calgary, Alberta
T2P 1J5

Saskatchewan

Department of Economic Development
1919 Saskatchewan Drive
Regina, Saskatchewan
S4P 3V7
Tel.: (306) 787-2232

Manitoba

Manitoba Industry, Trade, and Tourism
Business Resource Centre
155 Carlton Street
5th Floor
Winnipeg, Manitoba
R3C 3H8
Tel.: (204) 945-1354
Fax: (204) 945-1354

Ontario

Ministry of Economic Development and Trade
900 Bay Street
Toronto, Ontario
M7A 2E1
Tel.: (416) 325-6666
Fax: (416) 325-6688

Quebec

Ministère de l'Industrie du Commerce, de la Science et de la Technologie
710 Place d'Youville
9th Floor
Quebec City, Quebec
G1H 4Y4
Tel.: (418) 691-5950
Fax: (418) 644-0118

Place Mercantile
10th Floor
770 Sherbrooke Street West
Montreal, Quebec
H3A 1G1
Tel.: (514) 982-3000
Fax: (514) 873-9913

New Brunswick

Department of Economic Development and Tourism
670 King Street
5th Floor
P.O. Box 6000
Fredericton, New Brunswick
E3B 5H1
Tel.: (506) 453-2850
Fax: (506) 444-4586

Nova Scotia

Economic Renewal Agency
World Trade and Convention Centre
1800 Argyle Street
7th Floor
P.O. Box 955
Halifax, Nova Scotia
B3J 2V9
Tel.: (902) 421-8686
Fax: (902) 422-2922

Prince Edward Island

Department of Economic Development and Tourism
Shaw Building
P.O. Box 2000
Charlottetown, Prince Edward Island
C1A 7N8
Tel.: (902) 368-4240
Fax: (902) 368-4224

Newfoundland

Department of Industry, Trade, and Technology
Confederation Annex
4th Floor
P.O. Box 8700
St. John's, Newfoundland
A1B 4J6
Tel.: (709) 729-5600
Fax: (709) 729-5936

Northwest Territories

Department of Economic Development and Tourism
Corporate and Technical Services
P.O. Box 1320
Yellowknife, N.W.T.
X1A 2L9
Tel.: (403) 920-4182
Fax: (403) 873-0101

Yukon Territory

Yukon Economic Development
211 Main Street
Suite 400
P.O. Box 2703
Whitehorse, Y.T.
Y1A 2C6
Tel.: (403) 667-5466
Fax: (403) 668-8601

Others

Canadian Franchise Association
5045 Orbitor Drive, Unit 201, Building 12
Mississauga, Ontario
L4W 4Y4
Tel.: (905) 625-2896
Fax: (905) 625-9076
Toll free: 1-800-665-4232

International Franchise Association
#900 – 1350 New York Ave., N.W.
Washington, D.C.
20005
Tel.: (202) 628-8000

Association of Canadian Venture Capital Companies
1000-120 Eglinton Avenue East
Toronto, Ontario
M4P 1E2
Tel.: (416) 487-0519

GLOSSARY OF FINANCIAL TERMS

Accounts payable Money owed by a firm to its suppliers for goods and services purchased for the operation of the business. A current liability.

Accounts receivable Money owed to a firm by its customers for goods or services they have purchased from it. A current asset.

Amortization To pay off a debt over a stated time, setting aside fixed sums for interest and principal at regular intervals, like a mortgage.

Assets The resources or property rights owned by an individual or business enterprise. Tangible assets include cash, inventory, land and buildings, and intangible assets including patents and goodwill.

Bad debts Money owed to you that you no longer expect to collect.

Balance sheet An itemized statement which lists the total assets and total liabilities of a given business, to portray its net worth at a given moment in time.

Bankruptcy The financial and legal position of a person or corporation unable to pay debts.

Capital asset A possession, such as a machine, which can be used to make money and has a reasonably long life, usually more than a year.

Capital costs The cost involved in the acquisition of capital assets. They are "capitalized," showing up on the balance sheet and depreciated (expensed) over their useful life.

Capital requirement The amount of money needed to establish a business.

Capital stock The money invested in a business through founders' equity and shares bought by stockholders.

Cash discount An incentive provided by vendors of merchandise and services to speed up the collection of accounts receivable.

Cash flow The movement of cash in and out of a company. Its timing is usually projected month by month to show the net cash requirement during each period.

Cash flow forecast A schedule of expected cash receipts and disbursements (payments) highlighting expected shortages and surpluses.

Collateral Assets placed by a borrower as security on a loan.

Cost of goods sold The direct costs of acquiring and/or producing an item for sale. Usually excludes any overhead or other indirect expenses.

Current assets Cash or other items that will normally be turned into cash within one year (accounts receivable, inventory and short-term notes), and assets that will be used up in the operation of a firm within one year.

Current liabilities Amounts owed that will ordinarily be paid by a firm within one year. Such items include accounts payable, wages payable, taxes payable, the current portion of a long-term debt and interest, and dividends payable.

Current ratio Current assets divided by current liabilities. Used as an indication of liquidity showing how easily a business can meet its current debts.

Debt Money that must be paid back to someone else, usually with interest.

Debt capital Capital invested in a company which does not belong to the company's owners. Usually consists of long-term loans and preferred shares.

Debt-to-equity ratio The ratio of long-term debt to owner's equity. Measures overall profitability.

Depreciation A method of writing off the costs to a firm of using a fixed asset, such as machinery, buildings, trucks, and equipment over time.

Equity The difference between the assets and liabilities of a company, often referred to as net worth.

Equity capital The capital invested in a firm by its owners. The owners of the equity share capital in the firm are entitled to all the assets and income of the firm after all the claims of creditors have been paid.

Financial statements Documents that show your financial situation.

Fiscal year An accounting cycle of 12 months that could start at any point during a calendar year.

Fixed assets Those things that a firm owns and uses in its business and that it keeps for more than one year (including machinery, land, buildings, vehicles, etc.).

Fixed costs or expenses Those costs that don't vary from one period to the next and usually are not affected by the volume of business (e.g., rent, salaries, telephone, etc.).

Goodwill The value of customer lists, trade reputation, etc., which is assumed to go with a company and its name, particularly when trying to arrive at the sale price for the company. In accounting terms it is the amount a purchaser pays over the book value.

Income statement The financial statement that looks at a business' revenue, less expenses, to determine net income for a certain period of time. Also called profit-and-loss statement.

Industry ratios Financial ratios established by many companies in an industry, in an attempt to establish a norm against which to measure and compare the effectiveness of a company's management.

Intangible asset Assets such as trade names or patent rights which are not physical objects or sums of money.

Inventory The supply of goods, whether materials, parts, or finished products, owned by a firm at any one time, and its total value.

Inventory turnover The number of times the value of inventory at cost divides into the cost of goods sold in a year.

Investment capital The money set aside for starting a business. Usually this would cover such costs as inventory, equipment, pre-opening expenses, and leasehold improvements.

Liabilities All the debts of a business. Liabilities include short-term or current liabilities such as accounts payable, income taxes due, the amount of long-term debt that must be paid within 12 months; and long-term liabilities such as long-term debts and deferred income taxes. On a balance sheet, liabilities are subtracted from assets; what remains is the shareholder's equity.

Liquid assets Cash on hand and anything that can easily and quickly be turned into cash.

Liquidation value The estimated value of a business after its operations are stopped and the assets sold and the liabilities paid off.

Liquidity A term that describes how readily a firm's assets can be converted into cash.

Long-term liabilities Debts that will not be paid off within one year.

Markup The amount a vendor adds to the purchase price of a product to take into account their expenses plus profit.

Net worth The value of a business represented by the excess of the total assets over the total amounts owing to outside creditors (total liabilities) at a given moment in time. Also referred to as book value.

Operating costs Expenditures arising out of current business activities. What it costs to do business — the salaries, electricity, rental, deliveries, etc., that are involved in performing the operations of a business.

Overhead Expenses such as rent, heat, property tax, etc. (e.g., monthly, fixed, or variable) incurred to keep a business open.

Pro forma A projection or estimate. A pro forma financial statement is one that shows how the actual operations of the business will turn out if certain assumptions are realized.

Profit The excess of the selling price over all costs and expenses incurred in making the sale. Gross profit is the profit before corporate income taxes. Net profit is the final profit of the firm after all deductions have been made.

Profit-and-loss statement A financial statement listing revenue and expenses and showing the profit (or loss) for a certain period of time. Also called an income statement.

Profit margin The ratio of profits (generally pre-tax) to sales.

Quick ratio Current cash and "near" cash assets (e.g., government bonds, current receivables, but excluding inventory) compared to current liabilities (bank loans, accounts payable). The quick ratio shows how much and how quickly cash can be found if a company gets into trouble. Sometimes called acid test ratio.

Retained earnings The profits that are not spent or divided among the owners but kept in the business.

Return on investment (ROI) The determination of the profit to be accrued from a capital investment.

Terms of sale The conditions concerning payment for a purchase.

Trade credit The credit terms offered by a manufacturer or supplier to other businesses.

Turnover The number of times a year that a product is sold and reordered.

Working capital The funds available for carrying on the day-to-day operation of a business. Working capital is the excess after deduction of the current liabilities from the current assets of a firm, and indicates a company's ability to pay its short-term debts.